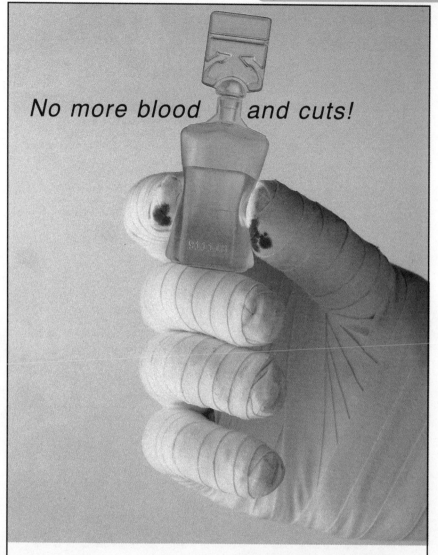

No more blood and cuts!

UNBREAKABLE **MARCAIN**®
bupivacaine hydrochloride
POLYAMP®

Marcain for regional anaesthesia-in an unbreakable polypropylene Polyamp.

Further information is available on request from
ASTRA Astra Pharmaceuticals Ltd., Home Park, Kings Langley, Herts, WD4 8DH.

MAR 0758   POM Date of preparation October 1995

THE NEW APPROACH TO SERVICE DELIVERY

The Need to Improve Services

In a recent survey of Service Delivery conducted by SDI, Trust managers identified the following needs to help improve the quality and efficiency of services:

• The need for Quality Bench Marks to make informed judgements on performance levels.

• The need for service audit to establish where problems exist and where performance is satisfactory.

• The need to address cultural and attitudinal issues with management and staff.

• The need for independent external support to provide necessary back up when required.

The Solution

Salomons Centre and International Hospitals Group believe that by combining forces they can offer a new consultancy service which will assist Trusts to adopt an **integrated** approach to service delivery. The service will have a number of components aimed at meeting the differing needs outlined above. This new approach, entitled SERVICE DEVELOPMENT INITIATIVE (SDI) was launched in April 1995 and is already enjoying considerable success.

Aims of the Service Development Initiative

SDI aims to:

• *Provide an Independent Bench Marking Service* driven by the needs of Trust members

• *Provide on Site Service Audit* to follow up any problems which might be highlighted by bench marks or for other reasons.

• *Provide Retained Consultancy Teams* to operate on a term contract basis. This concept should avoid the perennial problem of briefing new consultants every time they are used for separate assignments.

• *Provide Executive Consultants* as required for short periods of time to manage on site operations to assist Trust to resolve particular problems.

SDI believes that this holistic approach to Service Delivery is to the ultimate benefit of NHS Trusts ensuring a tailored consultancy suitable to most Trust needs

Further Information

To find out more about this new service and how it can help you make substantial improvements in Service Delivery, call David Decker on: 01892 515152 ext. 3020.

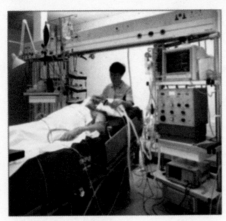

Genesis from MEDÆS

The Genesis medical care system supplied by MEDÆS Ltd is designed to help improve the layout of the increasing amount of services and medical equipment typically used to diagnose and monitor patients in intensive care and neonatal units. The Genesis system helps to maximise the space and floor area around the bed, thus helping to ease working conditions and the potential risk of hazard to both patient and staff.

MEDÆS can customise the Genesis system to meet the specific demands of each application in terms of the positioning of gas outlets, electrical sockets, nurse call systems and monitoring equipment. The system is pre-piped and pre-wired, and then tested to ensure it arrives ready for rapid installation.

A vast array of medical equipment can be mounted on shelf units, or if a ventilator is trolley mounted, underneath a shelf.

Low voltage equipment is located within the upper section of the main body of the system. Electrical sockets can be sited at both high and low levels of the system for complete flexibility.

The medical gases are situated below the electrical services, with a vertical cover plate in use here. A fluorescent uplighter, situated between the front and rear sections provides general room illumination. Other lighting can be incorporated if required.

To discuss the unrivalled flexibility of the Genesis medical care system, contact MEDÆS Ltd on 01246 474242.

The HEALTHCARE MANAGEMENT HANDBOOK

Consultant Editor
Keith Holdaway

Foreword from
Philip Hunt

Published in association with

NATIONAL ASSOCIATION OF HEALTH AUTHORITIES AND TRUSTS

KOGAN PAGE

First published in 1995

Kogan Page Ltd
120 Pentonville Road
London N1 9JN

© Kogan Page 1995 (except Chapter 3.3, © Coopers & Lybrand)

British Library Cataloguing in Publication Data

ISBN 0 7494 1477 4

Typeset by BookEns Ltd, Royston, Herts.
Printed and bound in Great Britain by Clays Ltd, St Ives plc

Contents

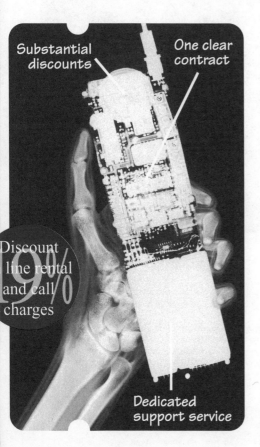

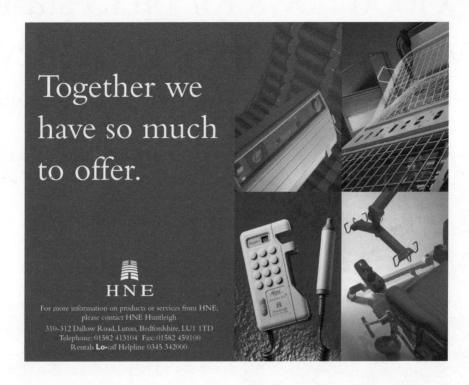

Together we
have so much
to offer.

HNE

HNE offers one of the most comprehensive ranges of medical equipment available to the hospital, community and nursing home markets.

The HNE portfolio includes equipment for Pressure Area Management, day surgery, physiotherapy, sports medicine, mobility, occupational therapy, elderly care, rehabilitation and general nursing.

In November 1993, Huntleigh Technology plc acquired the Nesbit Evans Group. The acquisition brought together two highly respected British companies to form HNE one of the largest healthcare equipment and service groups in the UK.

To retain the names of market leaders such as Huntleigh, Nesbit Evans and Akron, each division adopted HNE alongside its own identity. HNE comprises:-

HNE Huntleigh – one of the worlds leading manufacturers of mattress and seating systems for the care of patients assessed to be at risk of developing pressure sores and manufacturers of the Nimbus®II Dynamic Flotation System.

HNE Rentals – a specialist rental service for healthcare equipment operating 14 regional centres and a 24 hour a day, personally answered rentals helpline.

HNE Nesbit Evans – the principal suppliers of the King's fund bed to UK hospitals and manufacturers of hospital and community beds, day surgery equipment, patient trolleys and specialist ITU/CCU beds.

HNE Diagnostics - manufacturers of an extensive range of Dopplex® pocket Dopplers for vascular and obstetric medicine.

HNE Mobility – one of the leading manufacturers of powered wheelchairs in the UK.

HNE Community Care – suppliers of rehabilitation equipment for the elderly and disabled and manufacturers of bath lifters and patient hoists.

HNE National Care – a home loan distribution and facilities management service.

HNE Akron – providers of physiotherapy, patient positioning and sports medicine products and manufacturers of a wide range of plinths and couches for out-patient departments.

HNE David Baker – manufacturers of high quality, functional, storage furniture for healthcare environments.

HNE David Baker Laboratories – specialist manufacturers of laboratory furniture for educational, research and commercial establishments.

Foreword

For some time NAHAT has been seeking an opportunity to provide NHS managers, who day-by-day make practical decisions about the implementation of its many services, with up-to-date and accurate information about the numerous new developments now emerging. As far as we are concerned, *The Healthcare Management Handbook* came along at exactly the right time and we are very pleased to be associated with its publication.

The many changes taking place in the NHS pose enormous challenges for managers. And very often they are faced with competing choices. Their dilemma is what to buy, who to deal with, and how to maintain the high standards we all expect.

New drugs and medical advances are changing the face of the service so that in a few years the NHS may be unrecognisable from what it is today. People are living longer and more people expect a wider range of services.

Services have to be provided within an ever tightening financial framework. Year on year, efficiency savings have to be made right through the NHS to fund some of these increased demands and to meet pay awards. All this lands at the feet of healthcare managers, putting them under increasing pressure.

But time and time again that pressure produces innovation and visionary ideas. There is no getting away from it, some of our managers are the best in the world. Their ideas are captured in the new *Handbook* for the benefit of everyone. Practical help and advice about a wide range of issues from market testing to risk management and from reducing unit labour costs to casemix management − it's all there.

The Healthcare Management Handbook is a perfect complement to NAHAT's well established *NHS Handbook*. It fills in the practical detail that managers cannot do without and will be invaluable to them as well as to all those who have to supply the NHS with its myriad services.

I commend it to you

Philip Hunt
Director, NAHAT

Making it work more effectively

Key Principles

Information is person-based

Information comes from operational principles

Information needs to be shared

Information supports management

Information enables business objectives

Information focuses on health

Information is our business

Can we talk?
Just pick up the phone!

Information is vital to the NHS

The NHS is an increasingly complex and diverse organisation. The separation of the purchaser and provider functions with the establishment of the 419 NHS trusts and over 2000 GP fund-holding practices has created a whole new set of relationships and information needs.

If we are all to maximise the benefits of these developments we need to take advantage of modern information technology to gather information from many and often remote sources; to assemble and present information where and when we want it; and to make it accessible to all those who need it.

That's where we come in. IMG is charged with providing an NHS wide strategy for delivering effective healthcare, through better use of IT resources. We understand the management and implementation issues of IM&T, can suggest ways of presenting the concept of IM&T to management and then help draw up a nationwide strategy of clearly focused delivery.

And, because we've worked on every type of project across the NHS, our unrivalled experience means you can enjoy the best systems and help drive efficiency through the NHS. In other words, make plans and take action to implement the IM&T strategy and its infrastructure.

After all, information is more than a resource, it's a shared strategy.

IMG Information Point/NHS Register of Computer Applications
c/o Cambridge and Huntingdon Health Commission
Primrose Lane, Huntingdon, Cambs PE18 6SE
Tel: 01480 415118 Fax: 01480 415160

Information
Management
Group

Executive

Introduction

Managers in the Health Service are extremely busy. Our jobs have become more difficult as we get caught between demands for severe efficiency savings on the one hand and changes in the pattern of healthcare delivery on other.

One of the adverse consequences of the creation of Trusts has been the increased isolation of managers within them. An old district health authority would contain an acute hospital unit or two, a mental health, learning disabilities, community or priority services unit as well as an overall district management team looking at issues of strategic provision. These functions are now usually separated physically, financially and socially in a way which has drastically reduced the levels of interchange which were the norm only three or four years ago. But managers in fast changing environments need to concentrate on their main responsibilities, leaving time to scan little more than the healthcare journals to keep in touch with developments. Why then should you take the trouble to read this book?

The contributors to this book have been asked either to comment on trends and developments in national initiatives or to give first hand experience of how they have sought to implement changes and improvements to their services.

The lessons learned from the early simulations of the workings of the internal market such as Numberside and The Rubber Windmill showed how easy it was for financial questions to dominate those of service quality in the minds of the managers (and clinicians) involved. Amanda Stokes-Roberts gives hard-headed analysis of the impact of **quality league tables** on public perception of NHS quality as well as their implications for managers; from news management to quality improvement. In his chapter on **medical audit** Dr Robin Stott gives a sideways look at the changes clinicians need to make, not only in their

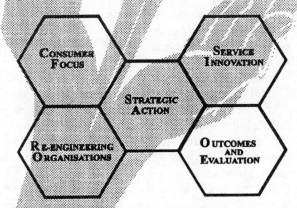

practice of audit but in their perceptions of what constitutes a good service and the involvement of patients in the process. He asks the question: Whose outcome is it, the doctor's or the patient's?

The haste with which contracting for healthcare was introduced resulted in a rash of simple block contracts rolling over established service activity. Dr Barbara Ghodse identifies **trends in contracting** involving differing contract types as well as new and diversifying 'currencies' to identify activity volumes and qualities. Her comments on overambitious contracts with intrusive or excessive monitoring arrangements will ring true with many. Another angle is presented by Jean Roberts-Jones in her chapter on **GP Multifunds** and the influence such arrangements can have on the practices involved. The difficulties of bringing together a group of people who, from habit or preference, treasure their independence are described together with the actions required by the Multifund manager in co-ordination and team building. **Changes in business planning** and increased levels of joint working and future projection are predicted by Nick Owens in his outline of the necessary alternatives to current working arrangements.

Whatever happened to casemix and RMI? High profile failures in the commissioning of computer systems are not restricted to the NHS. The Stock Exchange lost an able and determined chief executive following delays and overspending in their dealing system. What chance do NHS managers stand in the face of these risks? There have been indications that many of the casemix systems procured during RMI projects and afterwards are proving a disappointment to their owners; Alistair Lord assesses the truth of the position and details the lessons to be learned in getting the most from your casemix system and future procurements. The other system that we wonder about is **HISS** – the solution to hospital information problems. Do managers still believe that large and complex computerised systems can deliver the benefits required to cover their capital costs? Matthew Robins reviews the position.

So much of the literature on information technology assumes a level of understanding which many staff do not possess. For those who are not technically minded or familiar with personal computing Philip Burnard comes to the rescue with his introductory **review of computer software** which is aimed unashamedly at the almost computer illiterate.

An important part of the RMI project which often became submerged beneath the computers was the requirement to involve doctors more closely in the management of healthcare services, typically by the creation of clinical directorates. Cultural change takes many years to achieve in well-established organisations and Jenny Simpson discusses the **doctor/manager relationship** in the light of recent history.

Ron Steed discusses the practical aspects of developing a **risk management strategy**. Steve Goodchild expands on how to respond to the **Health and Safety legislation** which is creating problems for many managers who are seeking to do what they can within the resources available. A nightmare scenario following the poor **management of medical records** is presented by Dr John Hickey. He follows this up with sound and inexpensive advice on how to reduce risks by getting the simple things right rather than looking at high-tech solutions to the problems posed. Recent, highly publicised, but mercifully still rare breaches of **security** and more common thefts and assaults have meant increased attention in this area. Jean Trainor describes the range of managerial and personal actions needed to make healthcare premises and staff more secure.

The NHS is concerned with people – people as patients and people as staff caring for them. The efficiency savings alluded to in the opening paragraph are creating pressures to reduce labour costs by employing fewer staff and altering skill mix. But how do you know whether you are employing too many or too few staff for a particular service? In his chapter on **unit labour costs**, David Cochrane explains the methodology behind identifying the costs of labour for different activities and shows how to convert these figures into indices which can be used for comparative purposes. An alternative method of analysing and changing skill mix, in this case in response to **the introduction of automation in pathology lab**, is given by Alan Thorne. His pragmatic approach takes what is available and seeks to improve it by small, iterative steps. Alternatively, you may decide upon a more radical view of the changes needed and redesign a service as if from scratch. Peter Homa and Helen Bevan give practical examples of **process re-engineering** of healthcare services from Leicester, describing one-stop clinics in which patients complete in a couple of hours treatment which previously took several days.

One of the greatest process re-engineering schemes in the NHS is the Care in the Community Act. Many concerns have been raised about its impact on **discharge practice** and the necessary working relationships with social services. Mary Burton describes the results of her research in this field and provides advice on helping it to work well.

Another common solution to the problem of providing services more efficiently is **outsourcing**. Iain Herbertson illustrates how agencies can assist with far more than just temporary staff, either by undertaking specific projects or particular aspects of work. The experience of the Lister Hospital in **contracting out a pathology service** is described by Alan Howard, while the mechanisms of **market testing** are explained by Andy Evans. There has been some criticism of the **Private Finance Initiative** as a brake on development rather than an aid. Paul Nash looks at some of the problems it has created and describes how NHS organisations and the private sector are coming to terms with its requirements to build fruitful relationships. Major changes in services and staffing result in the need to redeploy staff or to make posts redundant. This process of **right sizing** is described by Lew Swift with his usual mix of experience and concern for the individuals involved. Like John Hickey, he emphasises the need to get the simple things right, even when under the considerable stress these exercise can create.

Absence control has become a highly topical issue. Karen Baker analyses the reasons for this recent upsurge in interest and offers a review of the different approaches taken by healthcare organisations. Since many organisations tend to increase the responsibilities of line managers to control absence she goes on to describe productive actions open to us all.

National Vocational Qualifications are now established and are expanding further into areas of professional qualifications. Chris McMahon, Kate Arter and Isabelle Cook describe how **NVQs** and their Scottish equivalents are influencing nursing. Further changes are affecting the ways in which management qualifications are delivered, structured and assessed. The association of NVQs with non-professional groups in the Health Service has created a view among some managers that they are inferior qualifications. Dr Christine Townsend strongly disabuses this notion in describing some of the innovative and exciting developments in the field of management qualifications.

In his chapter on **clinical audit** Robin Stott emphasises that the condition of the estate and buildings in which healthcare is delivered is extremely important to patients. This is an area which has been sadly neglected in many parts of the Health Service. The approach to **facilities management** described by Andrew Collingwood stresses the customer/client relationship which the core healthcare services have with 'hotel services' in particular, and seeks to improve quality and cost effectiveness by concentrating on what is needed. Gordon Massey demonstrates how estates may be made **better by design** to fulfil their role.

The Handbook concludes by investigating **relationships with purchasers** and **relationships between Trusts** in chapters by Barry Fisher and Louise Adams. Both authors draw on their personal experiences and work histories to suggest ways to reduce some of the increasing isolation.

As a result of reading the various contributions, or of dipping into them as the need arises, we anticipate that you will gain a better sense of how you and your organisation match up with others in the Health Service facing similar challenges and restrictions Reviewing the work has reinforced my belief that, despite the clichés and occasional cynicism, NHS managers throughout the service are devising and implementing truly imaginative and effective improvements to healthcare in the UK.

Keith Holdaway

The Radiation Safety Service at the Royal Sussex County Hospital has been providing personal dosimetry services to the NHS for over forty years. It is a high quality and cost effective service which currently monitors over four thousand personnel. Film badges are used for whole body dosimetry while thermoluminescent dosemeters are used for superficial measurements primarily for finger doses.

The service is flexible and tailored to the needs of our customers as far as possible. Particular emphasis is placed on our being available to our customers for any queries – specifically, a member of the Service, who has direct access to the dosemeter and result that causes concern, can be contacted and can directly answer your queries.

Recent developments in the Service include the provision of results on computer disc, connection to the Internet email system for result distribution, the labelling of film dosemeters with the wearer's name and issue period and the provision of a record keeping service.

For further information contact John Davis or Sue Donbroski by phone on 01273 664698, fax 01273 664503, or email: rss@rsch.org.uk.

List of Contributors

Louise Adams is Trust Group Manager at NAHAT.

Kate Arter is the former Secretary to the Royal College of Nursing Vocational Qualifications Forum.

Karen Baker until recently was Director of Personnel at North Middlesex NHS Trust.

Helen Bevan is Re-engineering Programme Leader at The Leicester Royal Infirmary NHS Trust.

Mary Burton is Ward Sister at Mayday Healthcare.

Philip Burnard is Director of Postgraduate Nursing Studies at the University of Wales College of Medicine, Cardiff.

David Cochrane is a Healthcare Management Consultant and founder of Cochrane Consulting.

Andrew Collingwood is Director of Estates at the South Tees Hospital NHS Trust.

Isabelle Cook is Secretary to the Royal College of Nursing Vocational Qualifications Forum.

G A Evans is Director of Corporate Management at St Mary's Trust, Paddington, London.

Barrie Fisher is Chief Executive of North Yorkshire Health Authority.

Dr Barbara Ghodse is Service Contracts Manager at St George's Healthcare Trust.

Steve Goodchild is Estates Manager at East Gloucestershire NHS Trust.

Iain Herbertson is Marketing Director of Manpower Plc.

Dr John Hickey is Commercial Director of the Medical Protection Society.

Keith Holdaway is Assistant Director of Human Resources (Training and Development) at Mayday Healthcare.

Peter Homa is Chief Executive of The Leicester Royal Infirmary NHS Trust.

Alan Howard is Deputy Managing Director of Unilabs UK.

Alistair Lord is Managing Consultant at Pareto Consulting.

Chris McMahon is former Chair of the Royal College of Nursing Vocational Qualifications Forum.

Gordon Massey is Head of Estate Policy at NHS Estates, Leeds.

Nick Owens is Director of Healthcare Consultancy for Coopers & Lybrand's Management Consultancy Services.

Paul Nash is Management Consultant at Newchurch & Co.

Jean Roberts-Jones is Project Manager for Southampton East Multifund.

Matthew Robins is Managing Consultant at Pareto Consulting.

Dr Brian Salter is a Reader in Public Policy at the Centre for Health Service Studies, University of Canterbury.

Dr Jenny Simpson is Chief Executive of The British Association of Medical Managers.

Ron Steed is Back Care Adviser, Manual Handling Training at the Lewisham Hospital NHS Trust, London.

Amanda Stokes-Roberts is Director of Quality at St George's Healthcare NHS Trust, London.

Dr Robin Stott is Medical Director of Lewisham Hospital NHS Trust.

Lew Swift is Head of Human Resources at Aintree Hospital NHS Trust.

Alan Thorne is Head of Medical Laboratory Scientific/Business Manager, Public Health Laboratory, West Dorset Hospital, Dorchester, Dorset.

Dr Christine Townsend is Chief Executive of Business & Technology Education Council (BTEC), London.

Jean Trainor is Deputy Director of NAHAT.

PART ONE

OVERVIEW

1.1

The Politics of Management in the NHS

Brian Salter

Introduction

The NHS is a £36-billion public industry with over half a million employees producing in excess of 10 million finished consultant episodes each year. Today's management of this industry finds itself subject to two contradictory pressures. On the one hand, the ever expanding demand for health care requires an increasingly skilful management of the finite resources available. On the other, national politicians choose to scapegoat the management function as an easy target for popular discontent. So management is simultaneously objectively necessary and politically vulnerable. Such is life.

The politics of management in the NHS are the product of this paradox and, regardless of government, are unlikely to change, because both sets of pressures are rooted in enduring characteristics of the NHS. It is as well that those using this book should be aware of this context. Management in the NHS is not just a technical activity within an organisation. It is at the political cutting edge of the NHS.

Managing demand

Popular discontent with the NHS, to which politicians as true democrats naturally respond, exists because people are not getting what they have been taught to expect as of right: free health care when they want it. Ironically it is the politicians who, while lamenting the widening gap between the demands on the NHS and its ability to meet them, do their best to make it bigger. Hence, the *Patients Charter* and the *Health of the Nation* initiatives, among others, set new and

3

higher standards for healthcare delivery which, as official government policy, people have every right to expect will be met. The growing industry of Charter monitoring and league tables then actively encourages patients to be less tolerant of their unmet demands while the mandatory new complaints procedures ensure that this new intolerance is appropriately channelled to maximise its impact.

In such a climate of openness, transparency and, some would say, exposure, the traditional method of bridging the demand-supply gap — ie covert rationing by clinicians using waiting lists — becomes virtually impossible. There is no hiding place. Waiting times are constantly being ratcheted down by Department of Health (DoH) fiat. Yet purchasing agencies that have tried explicit rationing find themselves with no central support and if they move beyond taboos into, say In-Vitro Fertilisation (IVF), risk the legitimate fury of those denied. The tendency, therefore, is to pass the management of demand buck to the providers — which in effect means increased cost pressures on the management of supply.

Managing supply

Purchasing agencies cannot explicitly manage demand because, in the present political climate, it is not regarded as legitimate to limit the right to free health care in anything other than the most minor of conditions. Traditionally, the management of the supply of health care was the province of the clinicians. From the very foundation of the Health Service it was assumed that the disposal of NHS resources should occur under the guidance of doctors who, after all, knew best. Serendipity rather than efficiency was the guiding motif, but so long as the NHS remained a non-issue and the public quiescent, which was the case up to the early 1980s, this was not a problem.

Griffiths and general management had only a limited impact on the belief that the management of scarce NHS resources was simply a matter of money following clinical decisions uninformed by any wider consideration. To suggest otherwise was, and is, to challenge medicine's dominance of the system. However, the devolution of budgetary responsibility and control to approximately 430 individual Trusts, coupled with the political failure to control demand, has meant that positive management at Trust level is required to meet targets, avoid contractual sanctions and ration the available supply of healthcare. Such an activity is bound to involve more than purely clinical decisions and is an inevitable target for the frustrations of public, politicians and doctors alike. No-one likes to be disappointed.

Managing change

Managers do not operate in a static environment, and must become accustomed to negotiating numerous uncertainties. The changes initiated by the 1990 NHS Act continue to develop momentum. In 1996, the eight Regional Health Authorities (RHAs) will formally become offices of the NHS Executive (NHSE) and the mergers of District Health Authorities (DHAs) and Family Health Service Authorities (FHSAs), creating 90–100 new health authorities, will take statutory form with unknown consequences for their operation and their relationship with GP fundholders. The numbers of GP fundholders will continue to expand and the budgets of health authorities to reduce, a process probably accelerated by a move to total purchasing of secondary care by GP fundholders. Cost and volume contracts will become more the norm. Private-sector linkage will become more common, both in terms of buying and selling and, the Private Finance Initiative permitting, in terms of joint ventures.

Meanwhile the rigidities of the occupational structure of the NHS, preserved for generations in the aspic of medical power and by the inertia of bureaucracy, are, if not crumbling, certainly flaking at the edges. The New Deal on junior doctor hours and the Calman proposals on postgraduate medical training are creating unprecedented stresses for the delivery of both medical service and training, and raising questions about the boundaries between medicine and nursing. At the same time the nursing profession, having elevated its training status through Project 2000, is uncertain as to what it should do about its relationship with medicine and, equally important, with the burgeoning area of NVQ-accredited support/generic workers. With changes in medical technology combining with the shift to day patients to produce higher levels of in-patient dependency, reviews of skill mix must lead to a re-negotiation of occupational territories.

Managing the bureaucratic web

The uncertainties facing managers are matched by the certainty that the bureaucratic web of the Health Service will continue to constrain, if not actually enmesh, the management activity. Health authorities will continue to be driven by their corporate contracts with the NHSE and will find ways of translating the imperatives therein into pressures on Trusts. As at present, Trusts will remain directly accountable to the Secretary of State, will be financially monitored by the regional NHSE office, will receive the customary deluge of official guidance and circulars, and their chairmen will oblige the Minister's more immediate political needs as expressed either directly or via the regional chairman. Outside of this web, so far, stands the 'wild card' of the GP fundholders, unremittingly hostile to the planning systems inherent in the rest of the NHS structure and to the overtures of the newly merged DHAs/FHSAs; bureaucracy and non-bureaucracy side-by-side.

The politics of management

The pivotal position of the NHS in the public psyche, the understandable reluctance of politicians to alienate those who elect them, yet the dawning reality that tax ceilings mean having to say 'No', have combined to politicise the Health Service. As the new boys, managers offer themselves as the target for a quick political fix for short-term political gain. While management is seen as a common-sense activity with esoteric pretensions and not much political clout (a not uncommon view) it will remain vulnerable to attack from every angle. Yet, while the demand for health care continues to rise unchecked at the same time as the responsibility for supply is operationally devolved, management of scarce resources will remain a priority. Add to this the unknowns of the changes at work in the system vying with the controlling instincts of the bureaucracy, and it could be said that the NHS cannot do without its managers. Don't bank on it!

PART TWO

MANAGING SERVICE DELIVERY

Discharge from Hospital: the Transfer of Care from Hospital to Community

Mary Burton

To the patient, discharge from hospital usually indicates recovery from the acute episode of illness or treatment. To the hospital staff it often means that the care and treatment has been successful and that the patient may now return to be cared for in the community. The successful transfer to health professionals in the community is an important part of the care given to patients in hospital. Although hospital care and treatment of the acute illness is often excellent, well managed and co-ordinated, discharge planning and co-ordination may be hurried and accorded less importance. Timely discharge of patients (that is where discharge is not unnecessarily delayed) satisfies the patient's wish to return home as soon as possible, and the hospital's need to provide beds for new patients. However, poor co-ordination of effort, communication and planning may lead to avoidable delays.

Many studies have identified problems associated with the discharge of patients from hospital. The findings have been consistent, showing poor communication and lack of co-ordination between healthcare professionals, poor communication with patients and relatives, and tensions between different agencies responsible for the patient's care. The result is that patients are discharged with little preparation or information about what to expect or the services arranged on their behalf; delays to discharge resulting in poor use of resources; and sometimes readmission to hospital.

Increasingly, patients are treated in hospital during an acute episode of illness, and discharged back to the community for 'convalescence'. This has meant that the problems already identified assume even greater importance. There is now less time to identify a patient's

The CIPFA Advanced Diploma in Business and Financial Management

WHAT IS THE CIPFA ADVANCED DIPLOMA?
The CIPFA Advanced Diploma is a unique programme developed for middle and senior level public service managers who do not want or need to have a professional accountancy qualification.

HOW COULD YOU BENEFIT FROM THE PROGRAMME?
The highly practical course offers managers the opportunity to learn theory and techniques that are necessary to perform effectively within the context of their own working environment.

WOULD MY EMPLOYERS GAIN IF I PARTICIPATE?
Undoubtedly yes. In addition to the advantages for you personally, there are distinct benefits for your employers, your colleagues and your organisation as a whole, in terms of:

- Immediate work enhancing skills and knowledge
- Increased performance
- Links with managers from other organisations
- Access to CIPFA's library and information systems

HOW IS THE TRAINING CONDUCTED AND WHAT WILL I LEARN?
The flexible post-graduate programme taught at Masters level is studied part-time normally over an 18 month period and comprises finance, resource management and Information Technology which is incorporated throughout.

The dynamic and effective programme with the emphasis very much on active participation uses a broad variety of learning methods, including, tutor led instruction, case studies, group discussion, workshops, role playing, CCTV, management games and seminars. There are no formal examinations, but each of the eight modules carries a mandatory work based assignment. Each module feeds into the final element of the course, an extended work based project.

WHAT REWARDS ARE TO BE GAINED?
These are many and various. As well as the development of new skills, other benefits include; An advanced qualification from a recognised and respected Accountancy Body; Exemptions from many MBA programmes; Membership of the CIPFA Business & Financial Management Network.

TO FIND OUT MORE
To obtain an Advanced Diploma information pack containing all the necessary documents and application details, please contact Stephen Smith on 0171 895 8823 ext 251.

Racal Network Services

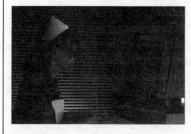

Racal Network Services Ltd provides managed telecommunications services (including voice, data and mobile networks). These services are provided to Government organisations under the Government Data Network (GDN) framework agreement which runs until 2004. The Healthlink contract forms an access agreement to GDN.

Healthlink is a data networking and messaging service dedicated to Health professionals and is based on the NHS strategy of following international standards – eg: X.400 (84 and 88). There are currently in excess of 10,000 users connected to Healthlink including all 98 FHSAs, 5,000 GP practices, 350 hospitals and 3,500 dentists. Typical messaging applications include:–

- pathology requests/results
- radiology requests/results
- Discharge/referral letters
- non emergency ambulance bookings
- patient registrations
- GP items of service claims.

A number of networking protocols are supported eg: X.25, LAN Interconnect and dial-in connections. These electronic links can improve the speed of communication between NHS organisations, avoid rekeying of data therefore reducing costs and allowing improvements to patient care.

Racal also provide managed mobile voice and data networks including Private Mobile Radio (PMR), cordless telephony, paging services (both local and wide area), interactive voicemail services and cellular services. An example of mobile data services usage is telemedicine services to ambulance vehicles whilst a patient is being transported to hospital.

For further information on these services please contact the Healthlink customer service desk on 01256 700262.

needs, communicate with the members of the hospital and community team responsible for discharge and with patients and relatives. The patient will often return home with the expectation that he or she is now 'fully recovered', and may be anxious and concerned to find that the twenty-four hour care and advice available while in hospital is often not easily available in the community. Elderly patients, and those with complex needs, are more often cared for in the community than previously. This means that the arrangements made for their care after discharge often involve many members of the community multidisciplinary team and difficulties in communication and co-ordination are exacerbated.

Most studies identify poor communication as a major cause for concern. Bowling and Betts (1984) report that 'despite much research into the subject ... there is still a lack of effective communication in the management of the discharge of patients. The problem is compounded by the fact that the arrangements for discharge may be made by any one of a number of professionals'. The *Discharge Workbook* issued in March 1994 by the Department of Health recommends that a 'key worker' is identified, who will be responsible for co-ordinating the different agencies. Discharge arrangements made on behalf of a patient with complex needs may involve ten or more healthcare professionals, all of whom must be involved in the assessment of the patient's needs, planning of care, and communication with their colleagues in the community.

Another problem often identified is the lack of information and advice given to the patient and carers; Skeet (1970) reports that 'In this study the patient needed information and advice about his illness and convalescence and staff needed information about the patient's home conditions and home care needs. Most of the maternity patients had this two way communication; the majority of patients in other specialities did not'. Where patients and carers have insufficient information about what to expect in terms of recovery, they may return to the general practitioner or to the accident and emergency department with anxieties and concerns about whether their experience is 'normal', or whether it indicates that 'something has gone wrong'.

An audit of discharge planning

An audit of discharge planning and arrangements carried out at Mayday Healthcare Trust in 1994 identified many of the problems mentioned above. The audit involved examination of the records of 3674 patients discharged from hospital over a period of one year. This represented a randomly chosen sample of 1:10 of the patients discharged during this period. The records were examined for evidence of assessment of a patient's needs, planning for discharge, and effective communication between the members of the multidisciplinary team. Delays to discharge due to late referral to members of the team and poor co-ordination and planning were also identified, where appropriate.

In addition, questionnaires were sent to each patient whose record had been examined, to 154 general practitioners working in the area, and to 255 nurses working on the wards from which the patients had been discharged. The questionnaires aimed to identify problems associated with discharge from the point of view of the patient, general practitioner, and nurses. A summary of the results of the audit of records and responses to patient questionnaires was prepared quarterly; this allowed for communication of the results to those involved in discharge planning, as well as action to be taken to address the problems identified.

Initial examination of the records identified problems in documentation of the arrangements made for discharge. Often these would be documented by each member of the multidisciplinary team in separate parts of the patient record. This resulted in confusion, duplication of effort and poor communication. In addition, it was apparent that much of the planning for discharge took place in the final twenty-four hours before discharge. This resulted in hurriedly made, last-minute arrangements.

A programme of staff education for those involved in discharge planning was undertaken by the discharge co-ordinator, a senior nurse already in post. This aimed to highlight the importance of accurate and complete documentation of arrangements made, and to encourage staff to start planning for discharge from the time of admission. This programme was highly successful, resulting in a sixfold improvement in the standard of documentation over the period of the audit. Quarterly results identified areas where documentation and planning were well carried out and those where it might be improved, as well as making suggestions as to how this improvement might be carried out.

Response to the patient questionnaire was 49 per cent. Most patients were satisfied with the arrangements made for their discharge home, but many would have liked more information and advice about what to expect in terms of recovery. Many patients reported that they had little notice of discharge home and would have liked more time to prepare themselves. Conversely, another cause for concern was delay in discharge. Patients reported delays while waiting for arrangements to be made, for instance in dispensing of drugs to take home. These findings often suggested late planning for discharge, with little time to discuss treatment and convalescence with the patient, and to make the necessary arrangements.

A quarterly report of the results of the patient questionnaires was also presented to staff involved in discharge planning. Anecdotal evidence illustrating problems reported by patients after leaving hospital was used to guide practice development. It was felt to be important that staff not only received information about problems, but also were informed of the many comments expressing thanks and satisfaction. These reports resulted in only a slight change in the level of overall satisfaction expressed by patients, which had been high (92 per cent on average); it was noticeable, however, that the comments made by patients in relation to lack of information showed a reduction over the period of the audit.

Response to the questionnaire sent to general practitioners was 71 per cent. GPs reported that patients often returned to their surgeries after discharge with questions about their treatment and recovery. They also reported delayed communication of information relating to their patient's stay in hospital, often resulting in difficulties in treating the patient in the community.

Nurses working on the wards from which the patients were discharged reported that they had little time in which to make arrangements and that communication with other members of the multidisciplinary team was often difficult. This was felt to be due to the number of professionals involved in complex discharge arrangements.

In summary, the main problems identified were that assessment of a patient's needs was often not carried out until immediately prior to discharge. Arrangements were then made hurriedly, and communication between healthcare professionals and patients and carers did not include advice and information about what to expect after discharge. Delays were often caused by late planning. These problems were addressed by a programme of staff education, which used anecdotal evidence provided by the responses to patient questionnaires, together with the results of measurement of the quality of documentation and discharge planning, in order to guide improvements.

Suggested solutions

Many of the problems identified during the audit of discharge planning reflected those described in earlier studies. Although most patients expressed satisfaction relating to their treatment and discharge from hospital (patients tended not to separate the two) it was nevertheless obvious that improvements could be made.

Waters (1987) reported, 'The first step (towards effective discharge planning) is a thorough assessment as near to admission as possible.' Assessment of probable needs on discharge as early as possible in the patient's stay, or even prior to admission for those patients admitted electively, would allow more time for communication within the complex multidisciplinary team and for discussion with the patient and carers. The aim should be to involve the patient and carer in the assessment and decisions relating to care after discharge, and to provide them with information about what to expect in terms of recovery and convalescence. However, discussion should be approached with tact. Patients and carers may feel that such discussion threatens early discharge, creating anxieties about their ability to cope. It is therefore necessary to explain that the reason for early assessment is to allow careful and timely planning, rather than to discharge the patient from hospital before he or she is ready.

A single document should be used to record the assessment of needs and arrangements made. This should be available to all members of the team and to the patient and carers. Where possible, a copy of this documentation should be sent home with the patient on discharge. This will provide the community carers with information relating to the patient's needs and named staff involved in the planning for discharge. Making the document available to the patient and carer while in hospital allows them to follow the progress of planning for discharge and to raise any anxieties before discharge.

Written information about the treatment given in hospital, medication prescribed to take home and a contact telephone number for advice should be given to the patient prior to discharge. The written information should not take the place of a discussion with the patient. The large percentage of general practitioners who reported a patient's return to their surgery with questions about their treatment and medication would indicate that this is an area of particular concern to patients.

A single 'key worker' should be appointed to be responsible for co-ordination of all the arrangements made on behalf of the patient and carers, and for communication between the different agencies within the hospital and community.

At Mayday Healthcare Trust action to improve the quality of discharge from hospital has resulted in identification of problems associated with discharge and responses to address these problems. Communication of the findings to all members of staff involved in discharge planning, and especially the use of the patient's 'own words' to illustrate the problems he or she has experienced, has resulted in an increased awareness among staff of the importance of discharge planning. Suggestions for improvements put forward by patients have been implemented. For instance, many patients suggested that written information about their treatment and medication would be useful. This is now provided. An ongoing quality assurance programme will ensure that the quality of discharge planning continues to be monitored and improvements made.

The two most important factors which will ensure successful transfer of patient care from hospital to community are early planning for discharge and effective communication between the patient, carer and healthcare professionals.

References

Bowling, A and Betts G (1984) 'From hospital to home', *Nursing Times*, 8 August, pp 31–3.

Department of Health (1989) *Discharge of Patients from Hospital*, February, Health Circular HC (89)5.

Department of Health (1992) *The Patient's Charter*, Department of Health, London.

Department of Health (1994) *Hospital Discharge Workbook – A Manual on Hospital Discharge Practice*, Department of Health, London.

Skeet, M (1970) *Home from Hospital - A Study of the Health Care Needs of Recently Discharged Hospital Patients*, The Dan Mason Nursing Research Committee, Macmillan, London.

Waters, K R (1987) 'Discharge planning – an exploratory study of the process of discharge planning on geriatric wards', *Journal of Advanced Nursing* 12, pp 71–83.

2.2

Contracting Out Pathology Services: the Lister Experience

Alan Howard

Introduction

A 'Partnership in Pathology' whereby an independent pathology company operates the laboratories of an NHS Trust began in December 1994. At the time the deal provoked much controversy, but now many NHS Trusts are considering similar ventures.

Considerable financial savings, investment in facilities, information technology (IT) and analytical equipment have given the Trust concerned substantial benefits. There were and will always be, obstacles to deal with, but as the concept of partnership between the NHS and independent sector becomes more clearly understood then those obstacles are gradually being reduced or overcome.

The obvious financial benefits combined with guaranteed service levels make such deals very attractive, not only to NHS managers but increasingly to pathologists and laboratory staff. The latter face a very uncertain time in an increasingly competitive environment as fund-holding GPs shop around for their pathology. Also, Trusts have many other demands on limited resources, and those related to direct patient care are likely to be given priority.

Background

In December 1994 a seven-year agreement commenced between Unilabs UK and the North Herts NHS Trust for the provision of pathology laboratory services at the Lister Hospital, Stevenage.

This agreement, the first of its kind within the NHS, prompted a wide debate and attracted considerable professional and media

attention. Much of what was said by commentators was based on inadequate or inaccurate information. Hospital managers and, indeed, anyone else with an interest in the development of NHS pathology, may wish to know more about how the agreement came into being, what obstacles arose, what lessons were learned and perhaps most importantly, what subsequent benefits were achieved.

In late 1991 the Trust's Chief Executive initiated an option appraisal of pathology services at the Lister Hospital. The laboratories had many of the features prevalent in the NHS – the building fabric was poor, the IT system required updating or replacing, new analysers were required. This was at a time when the Trust faced financial constraints and there were other priorities for spending limited funds. Perhaps not surprisingly, the option appraisal showed that a financial partner offered the most benefits and the framework for a joint venture was drawn up. A suitable partner was sought, initially via a corporate finance company, which would have an understanding of and track record in pathology. This was a difficult task since most UK independent laboratories are relatively small. The Trust had insisted that comprehensive services be retained on site and therefore a partner willing to invest in and develop the service was needed. In the end a European company, Unilabs, expressed an interest and direct negotiations for a joint venture ensued. By late 1992 joint venture proposals were submitted to the Trust board. Although accepting the merits of the proposals, a decision was made to go to tender. Meanwhile, Unilabs announced the acquisition of JS Pathology plc, the largest independent laboratory organisation in the UK, which previously had been reticent about investment at the Lister.

The tender

The tendering process took place in early 1993. Seven organisations responded: there was an in-house bid, three from other NHS Trusts and three independent companies. Of these, three were shortlisted: the in-house bid, Unilabs/JS Pathology and a neighbouring Trust.

An assessment panel comprising Trust board members, clinicians and external advisors heard presentations from the three bidders. Unilabs/JS Pathology was awarded the contract, subject to post-tender negotiations and clarification on a number of professional and operational issues.

Post-tender negotiations

Unilabs had given an indication in its tender of the investment it was prepared to make along with the likely level of savings which the Trust would enjoy. To quantify these aspects of the tender required agreement between the parties on the current true cost of pathology. A major part of the post-tender negotiations therefore involved a project team from each party scrutinising statistical data and defining total costs, including all overheads and capital charges. Against this figure a discount was applied.

The investment profile was also firmed up and guaranteed levels of investment were determined. Agreement was reached with regard to the existing assets. To protect the Trust against early termination of the contract, it was decided that Unilabs would lease the assets, but pay the lease costs up-front, thus giving the Trust a sizeable cash windfall. Budget sums for training, research and development were also negotiated along with a share in new business for the Trust.

The contracting process

With all the main points of principle agreed, lawyers were instructed. This did not mean that negotiations were over, indeed the contracting process revealed the need for more negotiation as anomalies and inequities were revealed. Since TUPE Regulations applied, the company managed to establish a pension scheme which was later certified by the Government Actuary's Department as broadly comparable to the NHS Superannuation Scheme.

A pricing structure had to be designed that enabled each party to minimise risks of erratic workload patterns. A block contract scheme was arrived at which met this objective. The 'block' was essentially a number of workload units or 'points' based on the Trust's data for the preceding year and their estimates for the current year. The points were weighted by test so that variations in particular types of test would accurately reflect the cost of providing the service. The price per point was set and this will only change through an agreed form of indexation.

The retention of services on site was another key factor for the Trust. The contract therefore incorporates a schedule of all tests, categorising them A, B or C.

- Category A – tests to be referred off site.
- Category B – tests which may be referred off site, (subject to certain quality, economic and service level criteria).
- Category C – tests which will remain on site.

The result of this categorisation is that all histology and cytology remain on site; 85 per cent of tests from other departments fall into Category C; 10 per cent in Category B and only 5 per cent in Category A.

Since Unilabs was investing heavily in a new computer system contractual commitments to compatibility and ongoing support were required.

Service Level Agreements, including turnaround times and quality monitoring mechanisms, were appended to the main contract. Other areas included:

- termination clauses;
- equipment lease;
- premises lease;
- insurance;
- warranties.

In August 1994 the contract was completed and signed with the commencement date scheduled for December 1994.

Implementation

The period from signing contracts and commencing operations was one of consultation and planning. New working relationships between consultant pathologists (who remained Trust employees), Unilabs and the Trust needed to be defined. The key issue here related to the service remaining consultant-led. A working model has now been established that enables Unilabs to manage its resources and investment in line with the professional leadership of the consultant pathologists. A Professional Advisory Committee was formed comprising pathologists, clinicians, Trust management and Unilabs personnel to give guidance and to oversee ethical matters.

Consultation with the Trade Unions began in accordance with TUPE Regulations. Architects were appointed and the design for a new laboratory reconfiguration and refurbishment programme initiated. An IT implementation project also began and an assessment of the current assets undertaken.

At time of writing the refurbishment is well under way and the new laboratory became operational in June 1995. The new working relationships are developing well. Hospital clinicians and GPs are continuing to receive a good service, which will be enhanced as the investment programme continues. No doubt many managers and pathologists will look to the Lister experience and see if they can benefit from a partnership in pathology.

Managing Laboratory Services
How to Identify and Deal with the Effects of Automation on Skill Mix

Alan Thorne

Introduction

For the hospital manager looking at 'skill mix' in the Medical Laboratory Service it is essential to have a full understanding of the cultures which exist within a pathology department, the associated staff groups and the undoubted fear which the term induces.

The NHS pathology laboratory has evolved into four distinctive disciplines, each with its own peculiarities, but more importantly with a differing utilisation of automation. Biochemistry and haematology have by far the highest degree of automation. This is clearly demonstrated by data from the Audit Commission Report (1993) indicating that of the total annual capital charge of £14.5 million associated with the 466 departments surveyed, £6 million and £5.3 million were attributed to biochemistry and haematology departments respectively. Opportunities for automation in microbiology have increased recently due to advances in technology, but histopathology remains primarily a 'hands-on' discipline.

Apart from medical staff, there are two principal staff groups involved in investigative laboratory work.

1. Medical Laboratory Scientific Officers (MLSO) or Biomedical Scientists – generally graduate entry with clear requirements for training and education to attain state registration.
2. Medical Laboratory Assistants (MLA) for whom there are no specific qualifications or training programmes. However, the Institute of Biomedical Sciences has issued draft guidelines for

the use of this grade of staff and a system of competence assessment is being developed.

A third group, the Clinical Scientists, also exists. The role of this staff group should be primarily in Research and Development (R&D). Any involvement in routine analytical procedure would suggest an inappropriate use of expertise.

Fear of skill mix

The fear of skill mix that is held by MLSOs can easily be gauged by the response to articles advocating change (Mobey, 1992, 1994) and the antipathy demonstrated towards the views of Professor Roger Dyson (1991). This resistance is based essentially on the attitude that skill-mix adjustments within pathology always involve down-grading of jobs and a movement towards MLA from MLSOs. While the astute manager considers the process of reprofiling a pathology workforce to include all grades which contribute to the provision of service (not just those directly associated with specimen processing), the introduction of automation clearly affects the MLSO and MLA groups most strongly. It is essential that the fears of these groups are understood, but they should not be allowed to form an insuperable barrier to implementing necessary changes. The remainder of this chapter explores the nature of these fears and how they can be addressed.

Automation – opening the door for change

In his paper 'Reprofiling the Labour Force' Robin Gourlay (1992) suggested that to achieve successful alterations to staffing structures, a department or organisation should be in a state of 'crisis' or 'committed to continuous improvement'. Crisis implies that the future of the organisation is in doubt and, given that most pathology departments are not in this state, it follows that change needs to follow on from 'commitment to continuous improvement'. In the past the principal improvement sought has been an increase in efficiency by cutting costs. As a reason for changing the workforce this is immediately seen by staff in a wholly negative light. Such commitment to continuous improvement is not shared by junior staff or, more likely, the changes are not seen as an improvement but rather a deterioration of service.

A second important factor in the success of any organisational change is that the staff affected should contribute to the change and have a sense of control over it. The introduction of automation is usually viewed by all staff as an improvement to the service which helps to create a share commitment. This inherent success factor needs to be built upon by involving the staff in calculating the impact on staffing. It is essential that any major capital purchase, such as automated analytical equipment, should be justified by a full option appraisal which looks at the impact on all levels of staffing. By including service delivery staff in drawing up the analysis of staffing requirements and proposals for dealing with necessary changes, it is possible to provide them with the feeling of involvement and in control of the change process, thereby creating the climate for successful change.

Assessment of staffing requirements

In order to assess the need for change a complete job audit should be performed. This should include identification of the following:

- all current tasks targeted for automation;
- processing time;
- performance of tasks by grade of staff;
- required level of supervision;
- current workload;
- workload trends;
- capacity (staff) within other areas.

24

Discussion of the effects of the proposed purchase of automation on the audited area allows the development of a logical and justifiable course of action which is also agreed with the service providers.

Case study

Introduction of an automated blood culture analyser into a microbiology department

Job audit

Table 2.3.1 *Assessment of introduction of automated analyser*

Function/task	Current Semi-automated		Proposed Fully automated	
Loading analyser	MLSO 1	0.2 wte	MLA	0.05 wte
Reading results	MLSO 1	0.1 wte	N/A	
Administration	MLSO 1	0.2 wte	MLA	0.05 wte
Quality assurance	MLSO 1	0.1 wte	MLA	0.1 wte
Supervision	MLSO 2	0.2 wte	MLSO 2	0.2 wte
Processing positives	MLSO 1	0.1 wte	MLSO 1	0.1 wte
Reading plates	MLSO 1	0.2 wte	MLSO 1	0.2 wte
Quality issues	Slower detection Radioactive		Faster detection Continuous monitoring	
Staff requirement				
MLA	0		0.2 wte	
MLSO 1	0.9 wte		0.3 wte	
MLSO 2	0.2 wte		0.2 wte	

Workload
It is clear from the assessment (see Table 2.3.1) that following implementation there is a reduced requirement for MLSO 1 time and an increased requirement for MLA time. However, before final staffing can be decided upon, workload trends and their effects on required time should be investigated and identified, as should staffing capacity in related work areas. In this particular case the effect of an anticipated 10 per cent rise in specimens received was considered negligible for the proposed analyser in comparison with the current analyser.

Staffing
The staffing requirements for the analyser were identified as 0.2 wte MLA and 0.5 wte MLSO. The 0.2 wte MLA capacity was identified in another section while the rationalisation and merging of two other sections allowed for the required 0.3 wte MLSO capacity to be identified.

Achieving the staffing reduction
A time limit of one year for reduction in workforce of 1 wte MLSO was set and was subsequently achieved through natural wastage.

The opportunities ahead

The case study above demonstrates how implementation of automation can be used constructively to drive a review of skills required within a single pathology discipline. The principles can be applied to any of the disciplines but an awareness of where real opportunities are likely to arise is useful.

Microbiology departments are now facing a technological revolution in a number of areas, notably in the automation of blood culture and viral/non-viral serology. In the near future automated methods for the reading of antibiotic sensitivity testing will be available. The departments that are already highly automated, haematology and biochemistry, should be reviewed during purchase of replacement equipment.

However, the real opportunities lie in the development of automation which crosses the historical barriers. It is clear that a new generation of analysers is under development that will perform assays which will transcend microbiology, biochemistry and haematology testing. Such developments must go hand in hand with a complete review of staffing, organisational and training needs if full efficiency is to be realised. Another factor in the utilisation of automation is its interaction with information technology and the introduction of IT should also be considered as an opportunity for review.

Dealing with change

Having seen the opportunity and identified the necessity for change leaves the problem of dealing with such change. Many of the resentments that potentially can develop during a period of change should have been minimised by ensuring that service providers have been consulted and have contributed fully to the assessment and subsequent conclusion. Within the case study a time limit was used to identify by natural wastage a move towards the desired skill mix. A tactic such as this is well supported if fixed-term contracts are held by staff.

Using automation as a lever for changing skill mix provides a subtle move towards achieving the organisation's objectives as opposed to wholesale reprofiling, thus avoiding the demoralising effect of a high number of simultaneous job losses. However, it is inevitable that as the skill mix changes within pathology departments the overall number of MLSO staff will reduce and the number of MLA staff increase. The effect on staff morale must be considered. However, MLSO staff must also come to terms with the dilemma they face in wanting a more rewarding job while retaining current staffing mix and levels. The effect of reprofiling should be to optimise both the activities of MLSO staff and their MLA counterparts, but an undoubted consequence is a reduction in MLSO numbers.

Summary of key points

1. Understand the workforce and the environment.
2. Use the introduction of automation as a lever for change.
3. Ensure presentation of full job audit: who, what and for how long.
4. Identify capacity in associated areas.
5. Agree with service provider the required operational skill mix and levels.
6. Agree with service provider a time scale for attainment of agreed levels.
7. Be like Gary Lineker: smile, be a good team member, listen, but never miss an opportunity.

References and further reading

Audit Commission (1993) *Critical Path. An Analysis of the Pathology Services*, HMSO, London.

Dyson, R. (1991) *Changing Labour Utilisation in NHS Trusts: The Re-Profiling Paper*, University of Keele for NHSME BU, April.

Gourlay, Robin (1992) 'Reprofiling the labour force', *NHS Management Executive Trust Network*, 18, appendix 7.

IMLS *Medical Laboratory Assistants – Their Status in the Laboratory*, IMLS, London, August.

IMLS Gazette (1994) Readers write, September.

Mobey, Nigel (1992) 'Utopia is possible', *IMLS Gazette*, November.

Mobey, Nigel (1994) 'Open all hours', *IMLS Gazette*, July.

If Your Hospital Did Not Exist, How Would You Create It?

Peter Homa and Helen Bevan

Achieving more from less is an increasing preoccupation for hospitals. The rapidly changing environment in which hospitals operate creates the simultaneous need to improve both quality and efficiency.

Business process re-engineering is defined by Hammer and Champy (1993, 32), as 'the fundamental rethinking and radical redesign of business processes to achieve dramatic improvements in critical, contemporary measures of performance such as cost, quality, service and speed'. 'Process' may be described as a set of logically related tasks formed to achieve an outcome valued by customers. Processes in healthcare may include outpatient, inpatient and emergency care.

Hospitals do not usually invest responsibility for a complete process in one person. Responsibility is generally allocated by functional contribution to a process, for example, contracts or estates. Patients travel through hospitals metaphorically (and sometimes physically) horizontally, and yet hospital management structures are organised vertically (see Figure 2.4.1).

The Leicester Royal Infirmary's interest in business process re-engineering began with its Single Visit Neurology Clinic (see Table 2.4.1), the inspiration of Dr Paul Millac, Consultant Neurologist. This transformed a service that previously took up to twelve weeks with multiple patient hospital visits into a single visit. It cut administrative costs by 39 per cent. The single visit concept is now well established and a number of such clinics now exist, including hypertension, vascular, chest pain and back pain.

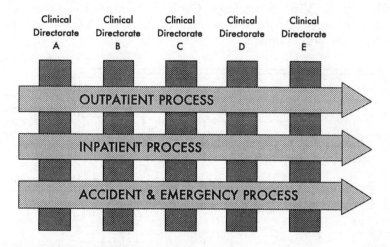

Figure 2.4.1 *Hospital healthcare process*

Table 2.4.1 *The Single Visit, problem-solving Neurology Clinic*

Target	September 1992	April 1993	August 1995
Organising tests and investigations 100% of appropriate patients will finish their consultation with all diagnostic investigations complete and reported within one visit.	0%	100%	100%
Availability of information 100% availability of notes and results at consultation.	93%	100%	100%
Timeliness 100% of patients to be seen within 30 minutes of appointment time.	50%	100%	100%
'Did not attend' (DNA) rate Elimination of follow-up DNAs.	10%	0%	0%
Report to GPs 100% of patients' GPs receive a same-day report of consultation	0%	100% next day	100% next day

The Single Visit Neurology Clinic epitomises the potential of business process re-engineering. Figures 2.4.2 and 2.4.3 contrast the old and new process maps.

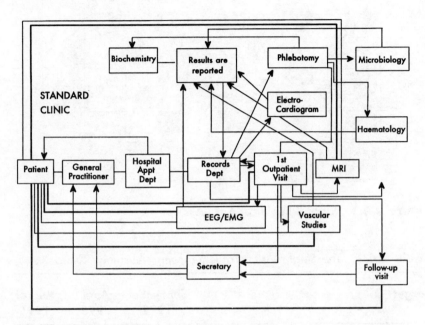

Figure 2.4.2 *Conventional Neurology Clinic*

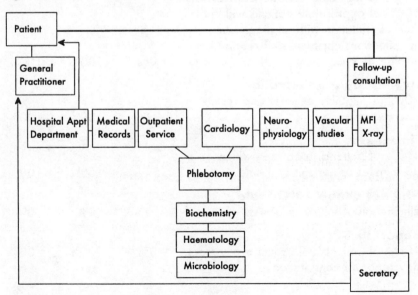

Figure 2.4.3 *Single Visit Neurology Clinic*

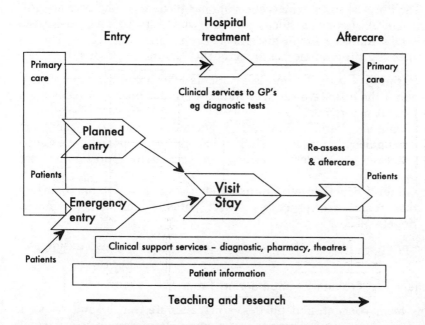

Figure 2.4.4 *The Leicester Royal Infirmary process map*

A key message emerged from analysis of the single visit clinic: *it is not possible to create excellence across hospital services without fundamental redesign of core healthcare processes.*

A 'scoping study' in May 1994 identified the biggest opportunities for improvement. The hospital's core process provides the framework for re-engineering (see Figure 2.4.4).

The hospital-wide re-engineering programme was launched in June 1994 to end in May 1996 and is one of the first of its kind. Hospital processes comprise:

- **patient visit process**: from referral by general practitioner through the hospital's outpatient, daycase or ambulatory service and return into the care of general practitioner.
- **patient stay process**: from referral to the hospital by general practitioner and admission for an inpatient stay and return home to the care of general practitioner. Patients enter the hospital either through 'planned' or 'emergency' routes. 'Planned entry' describes the elective process, whilst 'emergency entry' describes patients referred as emergencies by general practitioners via ambulance service or through the Accident and Emergency Department. Clinical support services include pathology, radiology and operating theatres. Teaching and research is embedded in these processes.

31

The hospital's re-engineering work has focused on the patient visit, and clinical support services process, which are redesigned by the hospital's full-time (multi-disciplinary) re-engineering teams. The re-engineering programme has three quality assurance groups:

- **Patients' Council** comprises patients who previously complained about the hospital's services and now critique proposed redesigned patient processes.
- **Academic Panel** comprises a number of the hospital's most distinguished academic staff who review proposed redesigned processes to ensure teaching and research opportunities are optimised.
- **General Practitioner Council** comprises family doctors to ensure that redesigned processes reflect patients' and general practitioners' needs.

The progress of two of the re-engineering teams is now considered.

Patient Test Process Re-engineering Team

This team concentrated on delivering accurate, timely and relevant information to assist clinicians in diagnosis by improving the speed of diagnostic tests. It created an integrated patient test facility for outpatients (Balmoral Test Centre), combining high-volume phlebotomy, ECG, pathology and radiography in a single centre close to outpatient clinics. Staff are multi-skilled and able to carry out a range of tests. Providing a service in 34 minutes that used to take 3 days, whilst also saving £50,000 per annum, the performance of the Balmoral Test Centre has exceeded targets (see Table 2.4.2).

The Balmoral Test Centre allows clinicians to redesign outpatient clinics, as illustrated by the Back Pain Centre (see Figure 2.4.5).

Patient Visit Process Re-engineering Team

The objective of this team is to optimise patient, GP and purchaser satisfaction (see Table 2.4.3) by:

- making the patient's journey through the outpatient process free from unnecessary activities and delays;
- ensuring excellence in clinical outcome and service quality;
- facilitating excellent research and its application;
- increasing teaching opportunities, subject to the patient's agreement, during patient visits.

Table 2.4.2 *Targets for the Balmoral Test Centre*

Measures	Nov 1994 Baseline	Feb 1995 Target	Aug 1995 Achieved
Time between test request to receipt of results	79 hours	60 mins	34 mins
Number of 'hand-offs'* of test information	16	5	5
Distance patient must travel for tests	650 paces	90 paces	90 paces
Patient waiting time for tests	90 mins	10 mins	8 mins
Patient second visit eliminated (estimate)	0%	5%	12%
Average number of patients seen daily	0	40	120
Proportion of outpatient tests performed by Balmoral Test Centre	0%	78%	82%

*A 'hand-off' is a task passed from one person to another

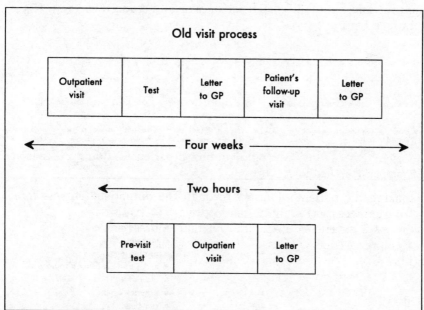

Figure 2.4.5 *Back Pain Centre*

Table 2.4.3 *Improvement targets*

Measure	Baseline Sept 1994	Target Feb 1995	Achieved Aug 1995
Outpatients benefiting from Patient visit re-engineering	0%	10%	100%
GPs benefiting from Patient visit re-engineering	0%	10%	100%
Number of 'hand-offs' in referral process	7	2–3	1
Mean time between referral letter received and appointment made	14 days	2 days	1 day
Medical time spent doing non-medical duties	35%	5%	5%
Mean clerical time per visit	34 mins	<25 mins	18 mins

Clerical support efficiency has improved through combining five roles into one – that of 'clinic co-ordinator'. This has resulted in improved accountability, staff satisfaction and reduced costs by 15 per cent (see Figure 2.4.6).

Old Process

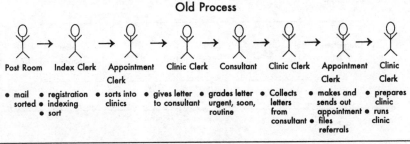

New Process

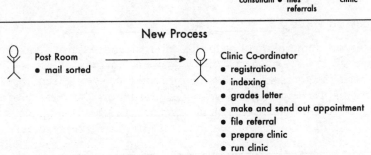

Figure 2.4.6. *Reduction of hand-offs in new referral process*

Follow up outpatient visits are reduced through the new patient visit process and fast test results provided by the Balmoral Test Centre. Patients and their doctors receive diagnostic tests and results on the same occasion as the patient's first consultation with the hospital doctor, whereas conventionally this would require two visits by the patient.

Re-engineering critical success factors

Prior to commencing the programme, The Leicester Royal Infirmary spent twelve months researching into re-engineering best practice. The time spent on this research has served the hospital well as the re-engineering effort has progressed and enabled us to identify critical success factors which are outlined below.

Leadership

The hospital's leadership must be committed to initiate, sustain and achieve successful business process re-engineering programmes. Strong visible and invisible support of the hospital's powerful groups is essential.

Hospital staff must understand why the organisation is to go forward with a re-engineering programme. The Leicester Royal Infirmary's experience is that a well-communicated strategic vision provides the context within which large-scale organisational change can take place.

Communication

Communication with interest groups inside and outside the hospital is essential to prepare for a business process re-engineering programme and to sustain organisational tolerance and understanding once it has commenced. A detailed stakeholder analysis should be conducted and internal and external stakeholders should receive focused information.

Focus on value

Focus on something of value to internal and external stakeholders: time and quality are both excellent targets. Cost reduction disassociated from quality improvement will discourage staff participation and without strong staff support, business process re-engineering programmes will fail. Business process re-engineering may offer significant additional productivity from existing resources, which is especially attractive for purchasers and providers faced with the apparently inexorable increase in emergency admissions and the need to achieve shorter waiting times for elective services.

Excellent re-engineering teams

Re-engineering teams should comprise the hospital's 'brightest and best'. This creates operational difficulties by removing staff upon whom the hospital depends, but re-engineering team members must be credible and influential people within the hospital. They must display an unusually wide range of skills and aptitudes as they work in a highly ambiguous, intense and stressful environment to develop creative process solutions.

Ownership of re-engineered processes

Line managers must be closely involved in the redesign and early testing of new healthcare processes. They are critical to any successful implementation so their ownership of the new processes is essential. As the re-engineering programme progresses, leadership must be transferred from the re-engineering teams to the general hospital staff. The ability to do this is an important test of sustainability.

Pay and reward systems

Redesigned work creates different jobs and requires different reward systems, as existing reward systems are almost certainly inappropriate to the revised nature of work. New reward systems facilitate and encourage changes in working practice. Reward system changes which occur too slowly, compared to the speed of process redesign and implementation, can result in faltering organisational performance.

Meticulous re-engineering programme management

Excellent programme management smooths the sequence of process redesign, prototyping and piloting, human resource management, negotiations with trade unions, outsourcing arrangements (if any) and overarching communications. Meticulous planning includes scanning the environment to anticipate obstacles and taking appropriate action. At present, there are more than thirty separate projects under the re-engineering umbrella at the Leicester Royal Infirmary. Each one has to be project managed to achieve activity milestones and deliverables.

Avoid premature outsourcing

Outsourcing non-core activities must not occur prematurely. Service specifications should be prepared after completion of business process re-engineering work. This allows appropriate service specifications to be prepared. Support service activities including porters and housekeepers are likely to change significantly by business process re-engineering so premature outsourcing may mean that the best results cannot be achieved without expensive variations to agreements.

Benefits realisation

Re-engineering healthcare processes requires a sophisticated benefits tracking system to ensure that all targeted benefits are achieved. Clinical and managerial leadership's reinforcement of the importance of achieving benefits is essential.

Bold targets

Bold, stretching targets for business process re-engineering teams are required, ensuring they break away from conventional assumptions and their solutions are as creative as possible. Results from the Patient Visit team exceeded original targets even though they were originally considered to be well beyond reach.

Conclusion

The future for hospitals will not be the same and more of the past as they seek increasingly to fulfil the requirements of patients, GPs, purchasers and staff. Business process re-engineering is a mechanism for radical change that breathes life into the excellent ideas which normally lie dormant within a hospital. To be successful, such programmes must harness the energy, creativity and ambition to improve patient care that bonds together those working in healthcare.

References and further reading

CCTA (1994) *BPR in the Public Sector*, HMSO, London.

Davenport, T and Short, T (1990), 'The new industrial engineering: information technology and business process redesigned', *Sloan Management Review*, Summer, pp 11–27.

Hammer, M and Champy, J (1993) *Re-engineering the Corporation*, Harper Collins, New York.

Newman, K (1994) 'The single visit clinic: a case study in process re-engineering', *The Journal of Corporate Transformation*, vol 2, no 2, pp 10–18.

2.5

Market Testing in the Healthcare Environment and Practical Implications of Rules and Legislation on Contracting Out Services

G.A. Evans

The NHS Executive remains firmly committed to the use of market testing as a proven and successful tool for achieving high quality and flexible services and for obtaining better value for money across the NHS.

(EL (95) 29)

This quotation from the recent Executive Letter makes plain the requirement for Health Service Managers to consider market testing all possible services. This comes after a series of instructions about market testing support services which began in the early 1980s and which from 1983 has required health services bodies compulsorily to market test Catering, Laundry and Domestic services on a regular basis. EL (95) 29 summarised:

1. states that market testing can secure better quality of services for patients as well as improved value for money;
2. states compulsory market testing of Catering, Laundry and Domestic services continues;
3. establishes that the NHS Executive requires more services, including clinical services, to be market tested in the future;
4. lists a range of services it considers to be appropriate to market test (see Appendix 1);
5. requires the active involvement of clinicians and other professional staff in the market testing process;

6. requires health service bodies to report regularly on market testing progress;
7. refers to guidance on regulations on market testing and safeguards to be applied.

Market testing benefits and advantages

The process and results of going through the market testing of a service can result in a wide range of benefits although there may also be some associated disadvantages. The benefits and disadvantages experienced are however largely controlled by the manner in which the market testing process is conducted. Conducted well it can be a useful refocusing exercise resulting in qualitative and financial benefits, but if done badly or incompletely it can be a demotivating experience which results in services no better than the ones which preceded them.

Experience of market testing a wide range of services in St Mary's Hospital, Paddington, has released significant amounts of money which have been reinvested in better support services and clinical services at the same time as improving the base quality of the services tested. Since the most easily market tested services are highly visible, eg catering, domestic, security, they can also have a competitive advantage and prove to be a differentiating factor when compared to other local hospitals.

Benefits

1. The opportunity for refocusing on what a service should provide. This should result in a clarification of the service need and a plan for changes.
2. The opportunity for competing bidders to look at innovative ways of providing the service, resulting in a better quality and/or reduced costs. This may result from the wider vision which outside bidders may bring to the issue.
3. Checking value for money — benchmarks the existing service against other ways of providing the service and the specification for the service required.
4. The quality of service may be improved.
5. Costs may be reduced.
6. The whole organisation receives a message that management is serious about testing the quality and cost of services. This should result, if relayed well, in all services reviewing their performance. There can be a positive morale benefit if the inhouse team wins.
7. Access to external backup. As the Health Service has fragmented, with the introduction of Trusts, the expert backup of district and

regional officers has disappeared. Contracting out of a service can mean access to a wider expert organisation.

8. Contractor's focus. A contractor providing one service will focus only on that subject which should result in incremental efficiency gains.
9. Access to capital. Private contractors may well have access to capital which can be spread over the period of the contract.
10. VAT can be reclaimed on contracted out services.

Disadvantages

1. Considerable time must be expended to achieve the most from market testing and if inadequate will result in no improvements in service or with a difficult contract to manage.
2. Staff in the service being tested may have their motivation damaged and this effect may spread to others in the organisation.
3. Mismatch of culture with new contractors. It is essential that there is a good relationship between the Health Service organisation and contractor if the most is to be achieved from the contract. The 'master/slave' relationship is inferior to that of partners with a common aim.
4. There is likely to be bad publicity from a market testing exercise however well handled.

Rules for market testing

Market Testing in the NHS − Revised Guidance was published in June 1993. Together with the EC Public Services Directive of 1992, TUPE guidance from the NHS Executive of November 1993 and local Standing Orders and Financial Instructions this makes up the framework of regulations which govern market testing.

1. The European Union rules apply to services of value greater than 200,000 ECU (c£140–150,000) over four years bought by state agencies such as the NHS. All contracts greater than this value must be advertised throughout the EU and the advert itself must comply with rules on layout, wording and placement. The timetable for advertising market testing of services is prescribed with a 37-day period in which interested parties can be requested to participate and a 10–42 day period for the tender review. Announcement of results is also covered.

   Procedures detailing rules for negotiation and justification for choice are laid down in Public Services Contracts Regulations 1993 (SI 1993 No 3228) as amended by the Public Supply Contracts Regulations 1995 (SI 1995 No 201). Compliance with these rules is not difficult but they must be adhered to.

2. TUPE – Transfers of Undertakings (Protection of Employment) 1981. The scope of this regulation is laid out in the EC Acquired Rights Directive 1977. This prescribes when a contracted out service is governed by the TUPE regulations. Essentially TUPE rules apply when an existing service is transferred to be run by a new body and determines that the staff providing that service must be transferred to the new body on the same terms and conditions. These remain in force until negotiated away. An equivalent pension, as assessed by governmental actuaries, must also be provided. Staff liabilities, such as redundancy rights and payments, bank holidays, etc, also transfer.

   Essentially staff will have the same terms and conditions after transfer as they had before. Guidelines have been provided – the Management Executive Letter of 5 November 1993 headed *Market Testing in the NHS – Revised Guidance* – Procedure Guidance on the Transfer of Undertakings (Protection of Employment) Regulations 1981 (TUPE).

3. The advice in *Market Testing in the NHS – Revised Guidance* gives good practical guidance on all aspects of market testing including background, strategy and planning, operational issues and sample working documents. There is detail on contracts, although expert advice should be sought, and guidance on issues of probity such as for when a 'management buy out' is possible. Probity generally is assured if local Standing Orders and Financial Instructions incorporating recent Corporate Governance guidance are complied with.

   Contract award must be made on fair and objective assessment of bids measured against the specification for the service, with the winning bid being the lowest evaluated bid. It is impossible to be categorical about how this is measured but the decision must be defensible if challenged.

The process of market testing

The flow chart in Figure 2.5.1 shows the market testing process for a service.

Critical points in the market testing process

1. The NHS executive recommend that a wide range of services be considered for market testing. The crucial action in making a decision is to carry out an objective assessment of whether the existing service provides what is required. This is not a question of how efficiently the service is currently running, but rather of whether all the current services contribute to significant patient

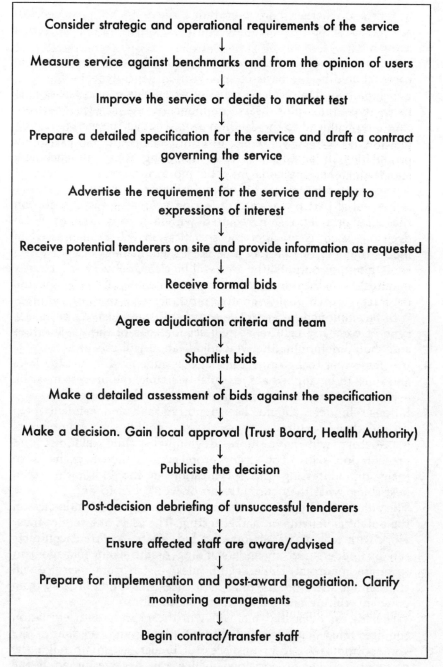

Consider strategic and operational requirements of the service
↓
Measure service against benchmarks and from the opinion of users
↓
Improve the service or decide to market test
↓
Prepare a detailed specification for the service and draft a contract governing the service
↓
Advertise the requirement for the service and reply to expressions of interest
↓
Receive potential tenderers on site and provide information as requested
↓
Receive formal bids
↓
Agree adjudication criteria and team
↓
Shortlist bids
↓
Make a detailed assessment of bids against the specification
↓
Make a decision. Gain local approval (Trust Board, Health Authority)
↓
Publicise the decision
↓
Post-decision debriefing of unsuccessful tenderers
↓
Ensure affected staff are aware/advised
↓
Prepare for implementation and post-award negotiation. Clarify monitoring arrangements
↓
Begin contract/transfer staff

Figure 2.5.1 *Market testing process*

benefit and whether more important services are not provided. All services develop incrementally and most often without objective assessment.

Consideration of what service is required, using feedback from users, should be the basis of specification development.

2. Benchmarking of a service against other outside services or against itself over time plus users' opinions of the service they are receiving will lead to the decision as to whether the market testing process is necessary. While market testing can be extremely productive, in a service already operating well by benchmark standards other methods may be more appropriate, eg use of service level agreements for users, further investment.

3. An essential part of the market testing process is the decision on the type of relationship required with a new contractor. Vital decisions such as whether the specification will be expressed in inputs (number of times an area is cleaned, number of staff to do something), or outputs (the area will be clean, delivery will be in x minutes); whether monitoring arrangements will rely on the contractor's own quality control processes or a team of monitors is to be employed; whether the contractor should have a particular type of company culture; all will set the tone of the specification and should determine the way adjudication will proceed.

4. It is important that a project manager is appointed. While the laws and rules to be applied are reasonably simple, the process must be actively managed to achieve the most from the process.

5. Inhouse bidders should be supported and independent help provided if required. There is no doubt that commercial contractors will have more developed public relations and presentation skills. The major problem for inhouse teams is to focus on addressing the specification in the bid, rather than describing what they currently do or would like to do.

6. The adjudication process and team have an important influence on the potential benefits of market testing. The users of a service must work with technical assessors of a bid. Visits to current contracts run by bidders and an understanding of the likely management team are important. Under TUPE rules all staff from a service will transfer and therefore the only differences will spring broadly from company culture and management organisation.

The lowest evaluated bid will win the process and legislation requires that unsuccessful bidders be given feedback. EU competition law allows unsuccessful bidders to go through the courts to challenge decisions, which can be overturned if the objection is upheld. Evaluation criteria should therefore be clear and objective and results defensible.

7. The period after a decision has been made can be traumatic. The

implementation period must be well planned and investment of time and effort by management and successful bidder will not be wasted. There may well be adverse publicity and there will undoubtedly be very considerable and understandable anxiety among staff. There is a danger of service delivery deteriorating before the new contract starts and contingency arrangements with a new contractor to begin the contract early if services break down are a useful backup.

The management process of market testing a service should ensure a reasonable implementation period, eg three months. Monitoring arrangements should be clarified at this stage and tied in with the contractor's quality assurance programme.

8. There is no doubt that the market testing process does not finish on the day of a new contract. New contracts will certainly take 6–9 months to settle and as terms and conditions of staff are protected under TUPE there will be tensions as new contractors really find out about the impact of customs and practice. Spanish customs will also become clear and may not be easy to remove. The contractor may well need support in this time and its provision will undoubtedly benefit the Health Service organisation which has let the contract.

Summary

Market testing of a wide range of services is being encouraged by the NHS executive and there is little doubt that it can be productive in qualitative and financial terms. However, the way the market testing process is carried out will, to a great degree, determine how successful it is.

The process of market testing is regulated but the recent legislation and guidance has clarified it and made it simpler, if not easier. Market testing must be considered to be a very useful tool in a NHS manager's toolkit because of its ability to review service standards and ensure they are met efficiently and effectively.

Useful information sources

Market Testing in the NHS – Revised Guidance (1993) NHS Market Executive.

Market Testing in the NHS: Update and Future Plans (1995) EL (95) 29, 7 April.

White Paper – 'Competing for Quality' – Market Testing and Revision of Guidance (1993), EL (93) 55, 24 June.

Market Testing in the NHS – Revised Guidance – Procedural Guidance on Transfer of Undertakings (Protection of Employment) Regulation (1981) TUPE.

EL(95)29 Annex A, Summary 1

Marketing Testing Database – Range of Services

Main services headings[1]

Admin, Information and Financial
Building and Engineering Services
Building and Equipment/System Maintenance
Hotel and Non-Clinical Support
Clinical and Clinical Support
Training

Groups of services under each main service heading[2]

Admin, Information and Financial

Advertising and Recruitment	Agency Staffing	Audit
Banking	Clerical and Secretarial	Computer
Consultants	Financial	Human Resources
Insurance	Legal	
Management Services	Micro-filming	

Building and Engineering

Building & Engineering	Design	Electrical
Energy Management	Estates management	Fire Systems
Flooring	Repairs and maintenance	Gas Supply
Glazing	Lighting	
Painting	Water Services	

Building and Equipment/Systems Maintenance

Building Equipment/Systems	Building & Engineering	Estates

Hotel and Non-Clinical Support

Accommodation	Car Parks	Catering
Courier	Creche	Domestic
Environmental Health Mng	Facilities Management	Gardening
General Patient Services	Hotel Services	Laundry/Linen
Pest Control	Portering	Security
Supplies	Switchboard/Reception	Transport
Waste Disposal		

Clinical and Clinical Support

Anaesthetics	Bio-Engineering	Chiropody
Clinical Coding	Continuing Care – Elderly	CSSD[3]
Dental	Clinical Genetics	HSDU[3]
Haematology	Infection control	IVF Services[3]
Lithotripsy	Medical Physics	Mobility Provs.

Medical Photography	Nuclear Medicine	Ophthalmology
Magnetic Resonance Imaging	Occupational Health	Orthotics
Occupational Therapy	Oxygen Therapy Units	Prosthetics
Pathology	Pharmacy	Physiotherapy
Patient Appliance	Radiology	Speech Therapy
Termination of Pregnancy		

Training

Education	Fire	Staff

Notes

1. There are no recognised standard definitions or lists of services. Those listed above are the interpretations used by Provider Units in the returns submitted in response to EL(93) 37.
2. Service headings such as 'Hotel Services' and 'Facilities Management' can include a wide range of individual services (catering, portering, security and car parking). Again, there is no set pattern of which services make up Hotel Services etc, but relates to individual Provider Units' interpretation.
3. Abbreviations
   CSSD   Central Sterile Supply Department
   HSDU   Hospital Sterilising & Disinfecting Unit
   IVF   In-Vitro Fertilisation

Risk Management

The changes seen in the NHS over the last decade have brought issues of risk and its management to the fore. Trusts function in an increasingly demanding and litigious world. Patients and employees expect to enter a safe and healthy environment in which all reasonable steps have been taken to minimise the untoward and unforeseen. Society and regulators will not tolerate unnecessary hazards to people or damage to the environment.

Over the last 30 years an increasing number of industries have adopted formal risk management methods and strategies to deal with these issues. The three basic steps in producing a risk management strategy are *identification* of risks, *assessment* of those risks and selection of options for *managing* them. Once the strategy is developed there are three further steps; *implementation, monitoring* and *review.* It is important that each of these steps are undertaken correctly using available methodologies to ensure a comprehensive and balanced approach. The benefits of a good risk management system are that managers can operate with confidence and use resources more efficiently.

Risk Management Services for Health Care Providers

AEA Technology is a science and engineering services business which solves risk management, technical and environmental problems for industries and governments around the world.

To find out how we can help you implement best practice contact:

Neil Griffiths
Healthcare Business Manager
AEA Technology
Culham, Abingdon
Oxfordshire   Telephone 01235 464342
OX14 3BD   Facsimile 01235 463389

Risk Management: A Practical Strategy for Hospitals

Ron Steed

Introduction

This chapter outlines the latest Health and Safety legislation to affect hospitals and describes a practical sequence of actions to set up the necessary systems to comply with it.

Healthcare is a risky business

Every working day throughout the UK there are over 6000 work-related injuries and 2 deaths. Most accidents occur as a result of an unsafe system of work. A lack of clear policies, poor working practices, vaguely defined responsibilities, and inadequate communications are all parts of an unsafe system that may lead to a wide range of injuries that occur by accident rather than design. In 1992 the cost to the NHS of nurses permanently leaving the profession due to musculoskeletal injuries was estimated at £120m per year (National Back Pain Association, 1992).

The Health and Safety at Work Act 1974

The HSW Act provides general requirements to you as employer to do what is 'reasonably practicable' to ensure the health, safety and welfare of persons at work. This includes people who:

- work for you, including casual workers, part-time workers, trainees and sub-contractors;
- use workplaces you provide;

- are allowed to use your equipment;
- visit your premises;
- may be affected by your work (eg your neighbours or the public);
- use products you make, supply or import;
- use your professional services.

The Act applies to all work activities and premises and everyone at work with five or more employees has responsibilities under it.

European Council Directive of 12 June 1989 (89/391/EEC)

This Directive relates to the introduction of measures to encourage improvements in the health and safety of workers at work. This so-called Framework Directive gave birth to six daughter regulations, while the Manual Handling Operations Directive of May 1990 (90/296/EEC) was introduced as the Manual Handling Operations Regulations 1992. These are known collectively as the Six Pack (see Table 2.6.1.). They are implemented by the Management of Health and Safety at Work Regulations 1992 and became effective as law on 1 January 1993.

Table 2.6.1 *The Six Pack*

THE SIX PACK
• Management of Health and Safety at Work • Display Screen Equipment at Work • Manual Handling • Personal Protective Equipment at Work • Work Equipment • Workplace Health, Safety and Welfare

Responsibility of directors and managers

The implementation of the Six Pack has reinforced and extended the responsibilities and liabilities of directors and managers under the HSW Act. Directors and managers can be held personally responsible for failures to control health and safety. Accidents are costly to workers but can financially cripple or kill a company. The British public is becoming increasingly predisposed to take legal action. Awards are increasing and come not only from patients or clients but from employees. In 1992 a Birmingham Nursing Assistant was awarded £203,000 damages for a back injury she incurred while lifting

Attaining the standard

The establishment of the Clinical Negligence Scheme for Trusts (CNST) has stimulated interest in the techniques of risk management and claims handling in healthcare.

In order to ensure that the interests of the members of the fund are protected the CNST has issued a set of Risk Management Standards. Trusts which attain the relevant Standards over a three-year period will be offered significant discounts on their contributions to the Scheme.

The ten Standards (plus an additional one for Trusts undertaking mid-wifery or Obstetrics) are concerned with organisational issues; systems of risk management (including Clinical Incident Reporting); training and induction arrangements; and record-keeping.

The CNST has appointed Assessors who will visit all Trusts in the Scheme in order to make a formal assessment of the degree to which they have attained the Risk Management Standards. This process will replace the informal self-assessment mechanism used for calculating the 1995/6 discount.

In order to attain the required standard many Trusts will have to engage in significant work. While activities like issuing a clinical risk man-agement strategy are relatively straight-forward, operating an effective Clinical Incident Reporting system is not. Members of the Scheme will be expected to obtain comprehensive clinical risk assessments and to demon-strate that the findings of such assessments have been implemented.

The CNST will expect members to have excellent Claims Management systems for handling clinical negligence claims.

It is our experience that the decentralisation of management to Clinical Directorates is not always linked to central policy-making and standard-setting. While it is important that the many gains of the Directorate system are not reduced, it is also imperative that standards are maintained. This is true not only in order to meet the CNST standards but also to obtain King's Fund Accreditation.

Cross-Directorate co-operation and co-ordination are vital. Managers and clinical staff at every level will need to work together if effective sys-tems are to be established. This will require the same degree of corporate commitment that is needed to undertake effective clinical audit and high quality care. This is not surprising as quality, audit and risk management share many common themes.

Bevan Ashford Solicitors and the joint venture company QRM Healthcare Limited (in association with Willis Corroon Limited) are ideally placed to assist Trusts in meeting both the clinical risk management standards and the claims handling requirements.

a patient. In addition to the costs of personal injury claims, far greater costs may be incurred by damage to equipment, property, lost production, fines, or destruction of corporate image; all of which lead to deteriorating quality of product (or service provision).

Cost to the company

Can you and your organisation afford to ignore or to implement only half-heartedly a risk management programme? By complying with the laws and regulations you may avoid fines, damaging publicity, reduced quality of care and legal action against you and your organisation (see Table 2.6.2). There are four basic steps to practical risk management.

Table 2.6.2 *Practical risk management*

PRACTICAL RISK MANAGEMENT

- **Identify risks**
- **Organise control measures**
- **Implement training**
- **Monitor and audit**

Identify risks

The primary aim of risk management is to be proactive in the reduction of risks to the lowest level 'reasonably practicable'. The Management of Health and Safety at Work Regulations 1992 require managers to undertake formal risk assessments of the workplace. To do this you must identify hazards and assess the risk involved.

- A *hazard* is something with the potential to cause harm.
- A *risk* is the likelihood of the hazard occurring.

Essential risk management responsibility is usually devolved to the line manager but identification of risks may come from several sources. These may include:

- **Questionnaires**: where anonymity is provided staff will often respond with open and frank answers and comments.
- **Analysis of accident figures**: analysis of occupational health department accident forms may indicate a large number of similar-type injuries occurring in a particular area. Investigation may reveal that the injuries are caused by inappropriate work methods.

- **Analysis of sickness figures**: analysis may indicate that staff in a particular work area are frequently ill. Investigation may reveal hazards inherent in that work area.
- **Observation by staff with specialist skills**: during inter-departmental visits specialists may notice hazards and risks. A manual handling adviser may notice poor lifting techniques in use on a particular ward.
- **Review of policies already in place**: reviews may highlight several versions of the same policy with no dates or with varying dates of enforcement. They may also highlight areas that have already been addressed with varying levels of success.
- **Formalised risk assessment**: this must be carried out if there is a risk of injury and should be performed by specialists with expertise in certain areas of interest or line managers and staff specifically trained by those specialists. With the removal of Crown Immunity in 1991, it has become increasingly important to seek advice from specialists. Specialist advice should come from those experienced in areas such as Health and Safety, Manual Handling, Fire Prevention, Radiation Emission Control, Occupational Health, Crime Prevention Officers and Infection Control.

Organise control measures

Organising control measures will help make your risk management strategy change your organisation into a proactive health and safety culture. The control measures should include:

- policy;
- safe systems of work.

Policy

A written health and safety policy is not only a legal requirement but can also bring many benefits. If you employ five or more people you must, by law (HSW Act, Section 2 (3)) have a written, up-to-date statement of your health and safety policy that is accessible to all staff and drawn specifically to their attention. Your policy should fulfil the following requirements (see Table 2.6.3).

The policy should be written by a multi-disciplinary team including specialist advisers such as manual handling adviser, radiation emissions control officer, fire prevention officer, etc. (See Health and Safety Executive, 1991.)

Table 2.6.3 *Written health and safety policy*

State your general policy on health and safety.
- Describe the organisation and arrangements for carrying out your policy.
- Bring your written policy to the notice of all employees.
- Revise your policy whenever appropriate, with every revision brought to your employees' attention.

The policy should include:

- **Resources available for implementation**: funding; high-quality guidance and training for directorate and department managers; time available; assessment and monitoring tools.
- **State clear responsibilities for implementing the policy**: which senior officer is responsible for seeing that it is implemented and kept under review; clarification of the responsibilities for all levels of the organisation and the feedback mechanisms.
- **State who is responsible for specific areas of health and safety**: safety inspection programmes; training programmes; fire training programmes; first aid training programmes; accident investigation reports, etc.
- **Provide clear understanding that employee co-operation is essential**: how employees will be involved; what duties the employee is responsible for.
- **State an expressed commitment to health and safety**.

A policy that is thoroughly thought out and has the backing and firm commitment of the organisation should lead to a proactive health and safety culture which will eventually be reflected in a better quality of patient care.

Safe systems at work

Under the HSW Act, employers have a particular duty for the provision and maintenance of safe systems of work so far as is reasonably practicable. A safe system of work is needed when a hazard cannot be eliminated and an element of risk remains.

A safe system of work is one resulting from a formalised and systematic examination of a task to identify hazards and their risks (see Table 2.6.4) It provides recommendations to ensure that safe methods are implemented to eliminate hazards or reduce or eliminate the risks involved.

Table 2.6.4 *Safe system of work*

- Task assessment
- Hazard identification
- Define safe methods
- Implement
- Monitor

The system should be applied to all tasks in all areas of work and to all personnel, including contractors and agency workers not directly employed by you but working on your site.

Implement training

Under Section 2 (2)(c) of HSW Act the employer is obliged to provide 'such information, instruction, training and supervision as is necessary to ensure, so far as is practicable, the health and safety at work of his employees'. (See Table 2.6.5.) The Management of Health and Safety at Work Regulations 1992 reinforce this obligation: 'Employers should take account of the employees' capabilities and the level of training, knowledge and experience. ... Training is an important way of achieving competence and helps to convert information into safe working practices. It contributes to the organisation's health and safety culture and is needed at all levels, including top management (Health and Safety Executive, 1992a).

Table 2.6.5 *Provision of Health and Safety training*

Health and Safety training should be provided for employees:
- when recruited into the employer's undertaking;
- before being exposed to new or increased risks because of
  - transfer or change of responsibilities
  - introduction of new equipment or change respecting existing work equipment
  - introduction of new technology
  - introduction of new work system or change of existing work system;
- repeated periodically where appropriate;
- adapted to any new risks or changes to current risks;
- occur during normal working hours.

Because of increasing litigation it is advisable to maintain detailed records. Who is responsible for maintaining these records should be clearly identified. These should record:

- what training was provided;
- when provided;
- the course contents;
- who was the instructor;
- how many students were in the class;
- verification of the employee's attendance and his/her statement confirming he/she feels competent to meet the required performance as trained.

Monitor and audit

'Monitoring provides the information to enable you to review activities and decide how to improve performance. Audits ... complement monitoring activities by looking to see if your policy, organisation and systems are actually achieving the right results' (Health and Safety Executive, 1994).

- Monitoring begins with recording and assimilation of data from various sources including incident forms that allows patterns to be observed. Monitoring information recorded on incident forms provides an early warning system that a decrease in standards may have occurred and a continued rise in the number of incidents may lead to litigation. Once normal patterns have been established, trends may be identified by comparing information of a specific nature.
- Auditing should tell you how reliable and effective your safe systems are. You should establish a risk management feedback loop. See Figure 2.6.1.

Identifying hazards and their associated risks will help to indicate the extent of risks which your organisation is taking. Organising control measures helps change your organisation into a proactive health and safety culture. Providing training will help to increase an employee's capabilities and provide better quality services. Monitoring and auditing ensure that your organisation is achieving the right results. As a practical strategy for risk management these policies should help to reduce the running costs of your organisation, decrease litigation and increase quality of care standards.

KEY ELEMENTS OF A RISK MANAGEMENT
PROGRAMME FOR HEALTH AND SAFETY

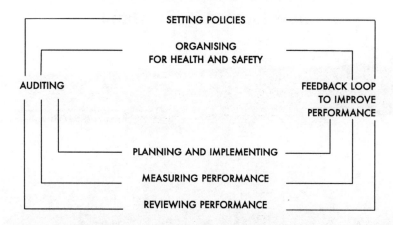

Figure 2.6.1 *Risk management feedback loop*

References and further reading

Chamings, A and Keady, P (1995) 'Safety First', *The Health Service Journal*, 9(4): 28–9.

Health and Safety Executive (1991) *Successful Health and Safety Management*, HS(G)65, HMSO, London.

Health and Safety Commission's Health Advisory Committee (1992) *Guidance on Manual Handling of Loads in the Health Services*, HMSO, London.

Health and Safety Executive (1992a) *Management of Health and Safety at Work*, HMSO, London.

Health and Safety Executive (1992b) *Manual Handling: Manual Handling Operation Regulations 1992, Guidance on Regulations*, HMSO, London.

Health and Safety Executive (1994) *Five Steps to Successful Health and Safety Management*, IND(G)132L C1000, HMSO, London.

Health and Safety Executive (1995) *Management of Health and Safety in the Health Services*, HMSO, London.

National Back Pain Association (1992) *The Guide to Handling Patients*, National Back Pain Association, Teddington.

NHS Executive (1992) *Risk Management in the NHS*, Department of Health, F50/065 1639, HMSO, London.

If you could achieve the same efficacy in reflux for £5.21 as you could for £93.50, would you?

0800 556606

(24-hour recorded message)
**Call Freephone
for the Humberside Report.**

The Humberside Report is a comprehensive review of two clinical papers analysing the efficacy and cost of different treatment pathways for patients suffering from gastro-oesophageal reflux disease.

Sponsored by Reckitt & Colman Products Limited

liquid: **sodium alginate BP, sodium bicarbonate Ph.Eur., calcium carbonate Ph.Eur.** tablets: **alginic acid BP, sodium bicarbonate Ph.Eur., aluminium hydroxide BP, magnesium trisilicate Ph. Eur.**

Gaviscon is indicated for the treatment of gastric reflux

Further information is available from Product Licence Holder:
Reckitt & Colman Products Limited, Dansom Lane, Hull HU8 7DS.

Gaviscon is a trademark. **Legal category:** GSL (PO).

G11/95

Hospital Records and Clinical Negligence

John Hickey

True story

The letter before action has arrived. It alleges that, following a carpal tunnel release, the patient, a 33-year-old concert pianist, suffered a severe web space infection in the hand which has severely impaired his ability to perform. A five-figure sum is demanded. You know that only rarely can it be proved that post-operative wound infection results from negligence so that, in theory at least, this one may be defensible.

The medical record arrives. You open it confidently knowing that your Trust has invested heavily in a risk management programme, with state-of-the-art software, an advanced incident reporting system and, most important of all, a real change in the cultural attitudes of the clinicians with a positive approach to risk management processes.

You are unable to find the operation note. The entries dealing with the outpatient follow-up are sketchy. It appears that the patient was admitted to hospital when the post-operative infection was diagnosed but the entries are barely legible and many are unsigned. Worst of all, the microbiology reports showing antibiotic sensitivities are missing. Your heart sinks. A defensible case seems to be turning into a non-negligent loser.

Why? Theoretically it should be possible to defend such a claim, but you know that without a complete record a defence may be very difficult. The claim settles for over £50,000.

Aren't we good at clinical risk management?

Clinical risk management has a very high profile at present, especially since the advent of the Clinical Negligence Scheme for Trusts (CNST) and the introduction of the risk management standards for member Trusts. The practice of medicine can be a risky business at the best of times and it is right that clinical risk management should form an integral part of the day-to-day processes of any hospital or unit which undertakes patient care. While an element of risk is an intrinsic part of modern clinical practice, and little progress would be made without a willingness to take carefully considered risks, nevertheless patient safety within the system must be considered a priority, and steps taken to minimise avoidable risks.

Incident reporting systems are extremely valuable, software designed for handling incidents, complaints and claims can be a very useful tool, risk management audits are of great importance, and all are excellent investments for the future. However, there are some extremely simple steps which can be taken at little cost, which can save much money in the short term. So often simple measures for minimising risks are forgotten or dismissed as irrelevant.

An important but often forgotten area is the quality of the medical record. The complaints software is singing, the adverse incident reporting system is dancing, and yet the medical record remains a Cinderella. In one study of 64 closed obstetric claims, just under 50 per cent of claims had to be settled because the cardiotacograph (CTG) traces had been lost or shredded. Of that 50 per cent possibly half might have been defensible if the trace had been available. What a poor return on the investment in a shredding machine!

Getting the basics right

What steps can we take to avoid the problems associated with poor medical record practices? We are not suggesting a major investment in sophisticated storage and retrieval systems, nor are we expecting a complete reorganisation of the way in which the record is constructed and maintained. The following measures are suggested.

Education

Education should be provided for all staff, but particularly medical staff, on the importance of:

- Writing legibly – the medical record is a means of communication both as an *aide-mémoire* for the author when he or she is again involved in the patient's care, and as a means of communication with others who have a role in the patient's care. Clearly an illegible record is useless as a means of communication and shows a lack of professional care.

- The need to sign, date and time each entry — so often liability in a claim is dependent on a number of separate episodes, the timing and relationship of which may be crucial.
- The absolute requirement of never altering a record with intent to deceive — if changes are made because, for example, an opinion changes, this should be recorded as such and dated and timed appropriately.
- The avoidance of wit, invective or sarcasm — records should be constructed on the basis that it is likely that, at some stage in the future, the patient will read what is written there.
- Making records of each contact with the patient — if staff are conscientious enough to perform a particular examination or procedure, they should be conscientious enough to record that they have done so. If challenged at a later date the record will provide evidence of the performance of the procedure.
- Recording negative as well as positive findings, particularly on examination.
- Making a note of what the patient has been told when giving consent in addition to the signing of a consent form — in this context and at current settlement rates, the phrase 'warned re risk of sterilisation failure' written in the record may be worth £10,000 per word.
- Remembering that notes should be written in the knowledge that one day they may be read out in court.
- Getting clinical directors to take a few hours, perhaps spread over a month or so, to write down what they expect staff in their directorate to record in the patient's notes. Each directorate should identify acceptable abbreviations.
- Where abbreviations or symbols are used regularly (for example, in ophthalmology) and which may not be understood by other practitioners, it is helpful if a typed explanation sheet precedes the first entries for that specialty.

An educational programme

What does an educational programme cost? At most a clinical director or chief of service needs spend only an occasional half hour at induction courses and unit meetings to enforce the message about good clinical record-keeping. Such a programme is not difficult and not expensive and it will save you money.

Signature banks

Tracing witnesses can be difficult at the best of times, more so if you are unable to identify the witnesses! The most complete medical record may not be sufficient if a claim arises many years after the event and you are unable to identify the author. You should remember that there are many claims currently being pursued in which the events occurred ten, twenty or even thirty years ago. It is therefore of immense value not only to maintain forwarding addresses of former staff, but to keep on record the signatures and concurrent status of those staff. Given that reasonable scanners can be purchased for a few hundred pounds it should not be expensive or difficult to maintain a record of signatures.

Destruction policies

How long records should be kept is a perennial question to which the only safe answer is indefinitely. Delays between clinical incident and subsequent litigation are lengthening rather than shortening and changes to the statutory limitation periods have made it easier for prospective plaintiffs to commence proceedings many years after the clinical event that gave rise to them. Storing records indefinitely is a counsel of perfection but as storage space is usually limited, microfilming or other imaging techniques may be of value. At present, it is recommended that records should be stored for a minimum of eight years after the last entry for adults, and until at least the twenty-fifth birthday in the case of minors. For those who are intellectually impaired so that they are legally incompetent, medical records should be kept indefinitely. It is also helpful if health records in which litigation is thought possible are marked in some way so that the records are not destroyed.

Laboratory and radiography reports

Simple systems can be set up at little expense to ensure that laboratory and radiography reports are not filed in the medical records unless they have been read by an appropriate member of staff. However to ensure compliance, it is important that regular audit takes place. In rare instances it may be appropriate that disciplinary measures are invoked should it be shown that these procedures are being wilfully ignored.

ECG and CTG traces

Such traces should be stored in some permanent fashion, stapled or otherwise safely secured to the main medical record. The loss of such traces may make an otherwise defensible claim difficult to defend.

Disclosure policies

Although the Access to Medical Records Act 1991 has rightly given patients almost complete freedom to inspect their own medical records where these were created after 1 November 1991, we still hear of prospective plaintiffs encountering difficulties in obtaining copies of records created prior to this date. We also hear of trusts who automatically pass requests for disclosure to their solicitors. This is an expensive way of responding to a straightforward request. In most cases, it would be entirely reasonable to agree to disclosure, provided that certain safeguards have been met. A climate of openness prevails, and there is only rarely a good reason why a patient should not have full access to records if requested. There seems little justification for trying to hide the facts from most patients, and most of us would surely want to know the full details if we or one of our relatives had a medical problem. We estimate that only 20–25 per cent of requests for disclosure result in claims of negligence. Time and effort expended in resisting disclosure would be better spent in investigating the circumstances of those requests which are likely to become claims. Your claims manager should be able to identify a large proportion of these.

Regular audit of the records by the risk manager

It is all very well to have simple systems such as those suggested in this chapter but can you be certain that they are being implemented? A regular audit of a sample of records across the clinical directorates is the easiest way of ensuring compliance. Your risk manager can assist in this process by checking some of the process aspects, for example, that entries are signed legibly and dated. The clinical directors will also need to be involved in checking the content of records. A trust which has achieved the culture change necessary to implement a full risk management programme will find this relatively easy. To include a record audit in the clinical audit system is good practice. If there are difficulties in auditing records, it may indicate that you have not made sufficient efforts to persuade your staff of the importance of accurate record-keeping. The record issue may be a good first step towards creating a risk-management friendly environment as most of your clinicians will agree that good records are an essential ingredient in the care of the patient. So if you have problem records, a high profile campaign to educate all your clinical staff through the use of workshops, training and induction courses, letters to staff and poster campaigns in appropriate areas should raise standards very quickly. Good examples of the effects of poor clinical records are relatively easy to come by (talk to your claims manager!) and cause and effect are easily demonstrable.

Conclusion

Clinical risk management is currently a fashionable topic, but many of the issues are basic ones which can be solved with just a little effort and minimal expenditure. Before you launch into sophisticated incident-reporting systems and risk management assessments, think for a minute.

- Are the records in your hospital being correctly completed with a full account of the management of the patient?
- Are all the entries dated and signed?
- Can you recognise the signature and can you trace the individual?
- Are the laboratory and radiography reports read before they are stuffed into the record?
- Are CTG and ECG traces firmly affixed to the patient's notes?
- What are your policies on disclosure?
- Are your clinicians on side?
- Are your records audited?

If you can answer yes to all these questions, then you are ready to proceed to more sophisticated risk management techniques. Get the basics right first.

2.8

Quality: What Effects Will Hospital Performance Tables Have?

Amanda Stokes-Roberts

The creation of an internal market, the Patient's Charter and increasingly detailed purchasing specifications have brought pressure upon the NHS to adapt and improve. Purchasers have become concerned with the wide variations they find in the quality of healthcare, particularly when there is little evidence that higher cost services are of higher quality. As a result, there has been a demand for the adoption of measurement-based approaches to quality assurance.

The quality agenda began developing at the end of the 1980s with Total Quality Management (TQM) projects and an increasing emphasis on the patient's point of view. The use of accreditation schemes and quality awards, such as King's Fund Organisational Audit and BS5750, has gradually gathered momentum but there is still no single quality framework in place that will allow comparisons across the whole NHS.

Measuring performance in non-clinical areas is relatively straight-forward. However, in the clinical arena, meaningful data are hard to find and difficult to interpret. The Department of Health Service Indicators (HSIs) were developed in the 1980s and heavily criticised for saying next to nothing about quality. More specific patient-based data such as those coming from medical audit studies were difficult to aggregate meaningfully to a level that would be of use in strategic planning.

The development of consumerism and rising public expectations have led to a desire for increasing amounts of information to be made available. A constant diet of sensationalised stories of failure, mismanagement and erosion of health services has been fed by the media to an increasingly concerned public. As a consequence, the NHS needs to take responsibility for publishing data in relation to what it is doing and why, what it costs and the benefits to individuals and local communities. This was the backcloth against which the first performance tables were published in June 1994.

Performance tables 1993–4 – first impressions

Inevitably the publication of NHS comparative data was the occasion for a good deal of heady rhetoric. Political commentators of both left and right used the occasion to promote their respective agendas. From the public point of view, where the results were good, it is likely that they were found to be generally reassuring; where poor, it is probable that they were either unsurprising or worrying. The rationale of the performance tables was to provide the public with information to help them make informed choices. Their effectiveness in achieving this remains to be proven.

From the provider point of view a very clear patient-focused agenda was identified. However, the simplicity of the indicators raised concerns about the risk of misinterpretation, lack of comparability and the fact that data represented a snapshot rather than a picture of performance trends.

To purchasers, community health councils and general practitioners, the tables were undoubtedly seen as useful levers for engineering change. Issues for discussion were highlighted and in some instances stimulated purchasers and providers into useful collaboration in order to find solutions.

Benefits and risks of performance tables

Although not exclusive, five areas which may be influenced by the development of performance tables are discussed below:

1. **Explanation, discussion and debate.** Publishing such data should stimulate discussions with local communities to help develop understanding of the meaning of the data and the issues involved. Such discussions may offer opportunities to raise wider issues of health consciousness and give Trusts the chance to play a larger role in terms of the health of their local populations. In due course, such dialogues potentially could influence the marketing strategy of an organisation, whether it is targeting local or national organisations and charities as well as local voluntary organisations and communities.

2. **Data quality and use.** Issues of validity, comparability and credibility surrounded the publication of the 1993–4 performance

tables. Of necessity, the measures chosen were simplistic in order to be easily measured and acceptable to a lay audience. They were a snapshot focused largely on acute hospital provision and need to be recognised as a facet of quality, not a definition of it.

In due course, as experience and expertise in collecting and interpreting data develops, there should be an understanding not only of the limitations but also a recognition of their value in raising issues for investigation. The risk at present is that, because of organisational sensitivities, energy is put into defending or disputing the data rather than taking responsibility for improving performance. The value of focusing on measurement is to learn, not to select and blame.

3. **Competition.** In their efforts to be seen to perform well, there is a risk that organisations may focus on indicators in the public eye and attempt to 'quickfix' difficulties. Developing an understanding of problem-solving methodologies and making changes in management skills takes time and should be an integral part of a quality improvement system. Being able to respond quickly in this context is very different from fixing something superficially for short-term gain. The consequence of the latter approach may be severe damage to the motivation and morale of staff.

Local sharing of information, exchanging ideas and benchmarking are valuable benefits of a mature, constructive use of this data. Used purely competitively, there is the potential to inhibit such developments and further fragment services and organisations.

In addition, such data may create perverse incentives. For example, hospitals may increase throughput by cancelling fewer operations and speeding up assessments in Accident and Emergency (A&E) at the expense of some other aspect of care or health outcomes.

4. **Handling strategies.** The more data that are published, the more organisations will need to address how they handle a good or poor showing. Success may be sweet, but it should be handled pragmatically with an explicit recognition of the contribution made by staff and the fact that there is no room for complacency. There are many public relations opportunities in success, but it is worth remembering that there will always be someone with an alternative view of your performance.

Poor performance requires positive, constructive handling both internally and externally. Efforts that have been made to achieve a target should be recognised and an explanation given as to why, on this occasion, they were unsuccessful. A clear plan of action should be publicised internally and externally and followed up by reports containing demonstrable proof of progress that has been made. Such handling strategies are essential for building the credibility of an organisation in the eyes of staff, service users and purchasers alike; the publication of performance tables may act as a stimulus to putting such strategies in place sooner rather than later.

5. **Organisation development.** The culture of the NHS has perhaps encouraged the adoption of inspection and standard setting imposed from above, but there is a revolution occurring in human relations and attitudes that is as much a part of the quality approach as the techniques, disciplines and systems.

Top management through chief executives must develop organisations where the reaction to comparative data is not defensive but questioning, so that it is possible to address genuine issues and assist progress towards better performance.

Leaders who can nurture improvement in complex systems understand the deep and important nature of intrinsic motivation, the will to learn. They are also skilled in helping people to learn how to resolve conflicts. Continuous quality improvement has to be driven by the service provider, not purchasers nor even performance tables.

Case study

An organisation that performs well will have done so because of a great deal of hard work by staff from every discipline and every level of that organisation. The experience of St George's Healthcare NHS Trust is a case in point. There were four significant factors that contributed to the Trust's success in the tables.

1. **Infrastructure.** The organisational structure is arranged around clinical specialities specifically geared towards service delivery. Each unit of management is led by a clinician/manager partnership which is accountable for the financial, managerial and clinical management of the unit.
2. **Quality strategy.** Striving for quality is part of everyone's daily business. Three dimensions of quality are encompassed by the strategy; the patient's perspective, the professional perspective and the managerial perspective. Achieving a balance between these three dimensions is crucial to the delivery of high-quality care.

Since its implementation in 1991 the quality strategy has been underpinned by a number of basic principles including:
   - Building on what was there – many quality initiatives already existed within the Trust and these were encompassed within the overall framework.
   - Making sense of 'quality' – the approach adopted had to be simple enough for everyone to understand. In addition, time and effort were put into explaining and convincing staff why

quality was important and the benefits that could be achieved by adopting such a philosophy and the methodologies that accompanied it.

- Developmental approach – the objective was to seek continuous incremental improvement, not just one of quantum leaps which could not be repeated. There was a recognition that this would take time.
- Clearly defined responsibilities – everyone at every level of the organisation understood their own personal responsibilities for achieving improvements in quality.
- Integration – for the approach to be systematic, it had to be an integral part of daily life and the management agenda as a whole.

3. **Performance measurement systems.** Helped by an effective organisational structure and business manager support at speciality level, a range of performance measurement systems have been developed to enable the Trust to identify trends and highlight problem areas. Combined with a knowledge of problem-solving techniques and skills in change management, services are able effectively to address areas of concern.

4. **Performance management culture.** The commitment of the Chief Executive and other senior clinicians and managers ensured progress against the targets which were discussed regularly in a wide variety of forums. Achievement of targets was incorporated into the Individual Performance Review (IPR) system of general managers and business managers as well as monthly performance reviews with individual specialities. In addition, the Quality Assurance Directorate acted as a catalyst to identify areas of weakness, translate good practice from one area to another and ensure progress was sustained across the whole Trust. The Trust enjoys a collaborative relationship with local purchasers, which facilitates areas of difficulty being addressed constructively in an atmosphere of openness and honesty.

Future directions

It may not be long before the performance tables include data on hospital acquired infection, pressure sores and other clinical issues which are of concern to service users and purchasers alike. The recent introduction of published death rates in Scotland demonstrated a clear intention to move in this direction. Interestingly, the data were issued with a proviso that the information should be treated with care.

Concern to shift the focus of the Health Service from activity or process to a greater reliance on health outcomes has stimulated much work on measurement of health outcomes (for example CEPOD,

CASPE, UK Clearing House). It will take time to develop sensitive, accurate outcome measures that are widely accepted and which combine both patients' and clinician's perceptions of outcome. A greater awareness of outcomes may increase patients' appreciation of the dilemmas in current clinical practice; the danger is that lack of confidence in the data or inappropriate use may discredit the value of outcome information.

Over time, disease management indicators are likely to become the principle measure of clinical quality. As measurement and tracking methodologies improve, purchasers will expect providers to document that they are able to treat disease (across a continuum of care) in a way that produces the best outcomes at the lowest possible cost. Whether such indicators will be included in performance tables remains to be seen.

Conclusion

A holistic view of quality is one that emphasises the results of addressing trends and improvements over time. Although past performance is not a predictor of future performance, it is relevant for purchasers when combined with an assessment of quality assurance systems and other subjects. Performance tables are a beginning; their use must act as an incentive to influence the measurement process and generate more awareness of why information is being used. While the market may eventually focus on only a handful of key outcome measures, it must be clear that this does not imply that the remainder do not matter. Ultimately, the most valuable contribution of quality data will be to help providers to determine the correct cost and quality trade-offs in the provision of care.

If an organisation is committed to pursuing continuous quality improvement, it should be able to handle performance tables. The focus of activity should not just be a response to a particular indicator but the development of an organisation capable of responding to indicators as they arise.

Further reading

Department of Health (1993) *Improving Clinical Effectiveness*, EL(93)115, December, HMSO, London.

Department of Health (1994) *Improving the Effectiveness of the NHS*, EL(94)74, September, HMSO, London.

Department of Health (1994) *Patients Charter Hospital and Ambulance Services (Comparative Performance Guide 1993–4)*, HMSO, London.

Department of Health (1994) *Priorities and Planning Guidance for the NHS 1995/6*, EL(94)55, July, HMSO, London.

Drummond, M F, Maynard, A (eds) (1993) *Purchasing and Providing Cost Effective Healthcare*, Churchill Livingstone, Edinburgh.

Hopkins, A (1990) *Measuring the Quality of Medical Care*, Royal College of Physicians, London.

Hopkins, A, Costain, D (eds) (1990) *Measuring the Outcomes of Medical Care*, Royal College of Physicians/King's Fund Centre, London.

Koch, H (1994) *Implementing and Sustaining Total Quality Management in Health Care*, Pearson-Longman, London.

NHSE (1993) *The Quality Journey — A Guide to Total Quality Management in the NHS*, HMSO, London.

Ovretveit, J A (1991) *Health Service Quality*, Blackwell Scientific Press, Oxford.

Ovretveit, J A (1993) *Measuring Service Quality: Practical Guidelines*, Letchworth: Technical Communications, Letchworth.

Health and Safety

Your statutory obligations and how to put them into practice

Steve Goodchild

Introduction

The Health and Safety at Work Act 1974 was a milestone for the NHS in two ways. It was the first comprehensive attempt to rationalise the law in respect of Health and Safety, incorporating many earlier statutes and imposing several important new duties. It was also the first major legislation to challenge the concept of Crown Immunity. Although it was 1991 before the law applied consistently inside and outside the Health Service, Health and Safety Executive (HSE) staff have always had rights of access to NHS property, records and staff, and have had the power to curtail dangerous practice.

Recent years have not only seen the removal of Crown Immunity and its attendant ambiguities, but also the introduction of a range of EU-influenced directives enacted within the framework of the Act. These are important in that they break new ground, removing the concept that strict compliance with a set of defined standards is all that is required to meet the legal duties, and introducing instead the concept of risk assessment. This is both a blessing and a curse. On the one hand, it frees managers to make reasoned and rational decisions on addressing identified risks to health or safety in the workplace. On the other hand, it removes the shield of protection which the standards give. It requires a proactive approach to health and safety management by a committed and knowledgeable organisation. It also requires that managers can demonstrate that actions they have taken are reasoned and rational. This will require the support of written records.

Responsibility for ensuring that adequate policy and procedures for

Health and Safety management exist rests with the chief executive, who will be called to account by the HSE in the case of a breach of the law. Responsibility for implementing policy will be delegated; though it may be that in some specialist areas the detail of policy will be left to the specialist, the general rule must be that policy should be debated and approved by the board before it is implemented. They will need to take a view on the appropriateness of the proposals, the effects they may have on the organisation, and the resource implications. It is not reasonable or helpful for specialists to adopt a 'shroud waving' stance in these matters. The essence of the system should be to allow diverse risks to be evaluated, to enable limited resources to be targeted at areas of greatest benefit. The list of topic areas is enormous, but the following need to be considered as a minimum:

- Management of health and safety
- Food safety and hygiene
- Fire
- Lifting and handling
- Infection control
- Waste management
- Electricity
- Substances hazardous to health
- Display screen equipment
- Radiation (radioactive, X-ray, laser equipment, etc)
- Noise
- Pressure systems
- Asbestos
- Legionella
- Flammable and explosive substances
- Personal protective equipment
- Workplace health, safety and welfare
- Work equipment
- Construction design and management

In addition to these, there need also to be well understood policies in four areas which can be considered to be the tools of Health and Safety management:

- Training
- Health and safety audit
- Risk assessment
- Incident reporting

SAFECODE

A Health and Safety management software system has been developed by the Management Executive of the NHS in Scotland. Called SAFECODE, it is designed specifically to address NHS issues. It contains four modules. There is a document reference database, with comprehensive key word search facilities. There is a safety audit system, which meets statutory needs, and measures performance in Health and Safety. There is a prioritising system to help generate an investment programme to remedy identified deficiencies in order of importance, and there is an incident recording system, which will produce management information on accidents and incidents. The use of SAFECODE will ensure that operational issues are adequately addressed, as part of an overall strategy for compliance.

Health and Safety Policy

It is a legal requirement for an organisation to have a written safety policy. This will normally consist of a general policy statement which sets out the organisational framework, duties and responsibilities, and the systems to be used for discharging those duties. This general statement must be supported by statements of policy for specific topic areas (see above) and for particular site-specific problems. There are five essential elements to any statement of Health and Safety policy:

- What is the objective?
- Who is responsible for implementing it?
- How is it to be implemented?
- How are procedures to be audited?
- A reporting system, reviewing success.

The objectives are normally straightforward. They will generally relate to maintaining the occurrence of incidents at an acceptable level. This can be defined in many ways. The complete eradication of incidents is generally very difficult, and costly to achieve. To attempt the complete removal of risk is not normally feasible.

If a policy is introduced it must be applied throughout the organisation and the person named as responsible for implementing it must have both the professional competence to have a clear grasp of the issues and the authority to enforce compliance consistently. Policies must apply to every department without exception and the named person must be able to enforce this.

Any policy needs resources to implement it. This may mean purchasing expertise, training staff to undertake specific duties, or a combination of the two. There must be procedures which are understood and followed.

Auditing is simply the process of checking that a policy is being implemented in accordance with the set down procedures, and that these procedures enable objectives to be achieved. The final part of a policy is a regular report, to a specified format, reviewing progress of compliance with objectives and examining the procedures to ensure that they remain valid.

Health and Safety Audit

Specific topic areas form the specialist area of Health and Safety policy. The generalist area is the province of the departmental manager, who has the responsibility for ensuring day-to-day compliance with policy, and for ensuring that the workplace is a safe one. There are a wide range of duties expected, but the most important one is the Health and Safety audit, which is a comprehensive examination of the workplace and working practices to ensure that they are safe and comply with established procedures. The audit is an important formal review, which should look for and carefully document all observed hazards, making considered recommendations for their reduction or removal. Many can be implemented immediately. Others will need reference to specialists to determine the extent of the potential problem, or to higher management for funding consideration. Auditors hold a key role in Health and Safety policy. They must be well trained and well versed in local policies and procedures.

Risk assessment

The underpinning principle behind Health and Safety policy is risk assessment. This is the process of identifying hazards, evaluating the risks associated with them, and selecting appropriate solutions. The solutions may involve avoiding the risk by changing procedures or minimising the risk so that the hazard becomes acceptable. Risk assessment should be carried out formally and the assessment record retained. It is important to realise that hazards cannot be removed completely, only controlled to a level considered to make the risk acceptable. In the event of an accident, the HSE would wish to satisfy themselves that the potential problems had been properly considered and evaluated. The difficulty in assessment is being objective about very subjective issues. A number of topic-specific assessment systems are available (eg for lifting and handling) which score specific aspects of the activity, enabling a judgement to be made by summing weighted scores. Generally, assessments will attempt to categorise hazards as low, medium or high severity, and low, medium or high probability. High-severity, high-probability items demand immediate attention. Low-severity, low-probability items can be discounted as risks. High-severity, low-probability items rank equally with low severity, high probability.

Guidance

Judgements on Health and Safety issues will always be made against compliance with published guidance. This may come from many sources, but for the NHS the most important general sources are:

- Health and Safety Executive – a wide range of guidance notes and Codes of Practice
- British Standards Institution (BSI)
- NHS Estates – Health Technical Memoranda

Additionally, Barbour Index publish a microfiche library containing copies of most of the documents relevant to Health and Safety, which links to the ENCODE software.

Making the Clinical Audit Happen: Base Metal into Gold

Robin Stott

We must no longer wait for tomorrow. It has to be invented.

Gustav Berger

How will medical audit affect or be affected by the ongoing changes in the NHS?

As a clinician manager, I am committed to the efficient equitable use of resources, whether human or material. This aspiration accords with my Green political perspective and, being of a charitable disposition, I assume this to be the imperative behind the Health reforms. So I welcome any initiative which allows us critically to evaluate all we do. This is what audit is supposed to do, but I believe it has not been effective. To quote a few favourite lines from T.S. Eliot:

> Between the idea
> And the reality
> Between the motion
> And the act
> Falls the Shadow
>
> T.S. Eliot
> *The Hollow Men*

In the rest of this chapter I shall try to suggest what the shadow is, and how to get rid of it. Clearly, if audit is to have any role in the future Health Service it has first to survive, and the prospects are not that good. I am frankly worried about it. Indeed, some people liken the trajectory of medical audit to the life cycle of a giant star, growing to rapid prominence, undergoing cataclysmic explosion as a supernova on its evolutionary pathway to a black hole into which huge resources are poured and nothing comes out. I have a less apocalyptic view, but feel that unless there are substantial changes in our approach to audit, we will all be in danger of getting first-hand experience of the inner working of a black hole – my astronomical knowledge does not encourage me to relish this prospect. So, first, I shall look at how our understanding of audit will have to change, and then discuss, with examples, what implications these changes will have for the structure of audit in our health care institutions.

The survival of audit has, of course, to be in the framework of the reformed NHS, and should bolster the worthy aspirations of the reforms. So I shall put forward a clinician manager's view of a strategy which will, I hope, not only ensure survival, but allow audit to function within the service as it should. In essence, this strategy has three dimensions:

- conceptual
- organisational
- implementational

So first the concept. I am sure that medical audit must be extended rapidly and irreversibly to clinical audit, involving all members of the healthcare team and addressing all aspects of health care. Clinical audit then becomes the patient's friend, a stimulus to research and education, a tool for commissioners (or purchasers) so that healthcare changes are not driven by money alone, a management tool for providers to enable them to make sensible change in the way they record and organise their care, indeed, central to what is presently called total quality management (TQM).

Why is it necessary for this alchemical transmutation from the base metal of medical audit to the gold of clinical audit to happen? To understand, we need to go back to what we believe the Health Service should be. I imagine everyone will share my belief that a public Health Service should be underpinned by a strong ethical framework, an ethic which might be expressed along the following lines.

1. **Preservation of the autonomy of the individual** – this underlies the principal of democratic consent – whatever policies are decided upon should be supported by a broad consensus of those engaged in the finance, provision and delivery of health care.
2. **Doing no harm** – non maleficence – what steps collectively or individually we should take to ensure that our treatment is doing no harm.
3. **Doing good** – beneficence – as above to make sure that our

treatments are doing good.
4. **Justice** – explaining the basis on which personal health need/due is calculated. Given that all needs cannot be met, this will illuminate the principles of resource allocation.

Table 2.10.1 *Four principles which underlie healthcare*

Four principles which underlie health care

- Preservation of the autonomy of the individual.
- Doing no harm – non maleficence.
- Doing good – beneficence.
- Justice – explaining the basis on which personal health due/need is calculated.

With this ethic to guide us, we could readily identify characteristics which such a service should have. Tables 2.10.2, 3 and 4 illustrate some of these characteristics. The optimistic view is that they will be more in evidence when the reforms are in place. But how can we accurately assess, in all areas of health care, what is going on at present, identify deficiencies, seek ways of rectifying these and then monitor whether the suggested solutions are working in practice? This enormous but essential task can only be achieved either for providers or purchasers, through a critical systematic and continuing evaluation of all aspects of our work which is as good a definition of audit as one might wish.

Table 2.10.2 *Characteristics at a national level*

---

1. What principled basis is used for determining the total spending on health care within the public budget?
2. When the amount is allocated, how do you get to know how the public want to spend it? Are you trying to create informed public debate about allocation resource?
3. Is there a clear policy of desirable and attainable standards of service in the main area of spending? If so, how is the view communicated to and discussed with patients, providers and the public?

Table 2.10.3 *Characteristics at an institutional level*

1. Which groups will gain or lose by the decisions you are making on allocation?
2. How do you make your criteria of choice publicly understood?
3. How does your performance compare with other similar institutions? What can you learn from them?

Table 2.10.4 *Characteristics at a personal level*

- How far do I press sectional versus overall interests?
- Do I know the cost of my treatments and overall practice?
- Are my therapies effective and how often do I review the evidence for this?
- How do I decide not to treat?

The Standing Committee on Professional and Medical Education (SCOPME) has expressed this more formally on the following headings:

- Audit should be directed at quality of care.
- Audit should include setting of standards.
- Audit should compare performance with these.
- Audit should lead to beneficial change.

Audit as so defined is, as Russell and Wilson (in *Quality in Healthcare*, volume 1, 1992) have so eloquently told us, a branch of clinical science, a tool which can be used to examine any aspect of health care, whether organisational or clinical. Their idea of an extended audit cycle clarifies my own understanding of what audit is all about, and makes explicit this conceptual change. (See Tables 2.10.5, 6 and 7.) So to reiterate my first point: To be an effective agent in driving forward the beneficial aspects of the Health Service reforms, medical audit as presently viewed and practised will have to change in the ways I have outlined. We need to instil these ideas into the collective conscious of the health service so that audit moves from being a tedious additional burden upon an already harassed medical profession to centre stage in the task of all healthcare workers in all our healthcare institutions.

Table 2.10.5 *Extended audit cycle (1)*

1. Choose a general topic for audit, and a specific hypothesis to be tested.
2. Develop a standard.
3. Disseminate the standard.
4. Implement the standard.

Table 2.10.6 *Extended audit cycle (2)*

1. Design unbiased and precise methods for sampling patients.
2. Collect valid and reliable data on performance.
3. Compare these performance data with the standards by careful statistical analysis.

Table 2.10.7 *Extended audit cycle (3)*

1. Feed a clear summary of this comparison back to participants.
2. Ensure that this process generates beneficial change.

Organisational change

This conceptual change is not sufficient. It needs to be coupled to an organisational change. The organisation of audit within most institutions is, to pursue the thespian analogy, akin to a bit part, rather than the lead – Elaine Paige as a chorus girl rather than Elaine Paige as Evita. The transformation of Elaine Paige came about through good luck, hard work and an eye for the main chance. What worked for Elaine can work for audit. The good luck we have is that many of us have in place competent audit teams, as a result of central funding. The chance we need to grasp is the crying need to co-ordinate the action of the innumerable committees set up to advance the cause of quality, only one of which is the medical audit committee. The hard work we need to do is to devise, in each of our institutions, a new structure to deliver the goods. My view as a clinician manager is that there should be one group in the hospital, chaired by a senior clinician supported by the Chief Executive, which has three limbs; one service department, one research and evaluation and the final one educational.

Rather than having an organisation pulling in different ways, we can have one pulling together. An idealised structure is outlined in Table 2.10.8 and Figure 2.10.1.

Table 2.10.8 *Suggested membership of Quality Management Group (QMG)*

- Senior clinician interested in research and development (R&D).
- Chief Executive.
- Senior person in hospital with track record of getting things done (Project manager).
- Executive Director of R&D – person with research experience as well as managerial and organisational skills.
- Clinical Tutor – representative of Postgraduate Medical Centre (PGM).
- Senior Resource Management Initiative (RMI) representative.
- Two 'implementers' drawn from any place in the unit.
- General practitioner.
- Professional allied to medicine rep.
- Senior nurse (hopefully doubling as one of the above).
- Audit representative.
- Records/coding representative.

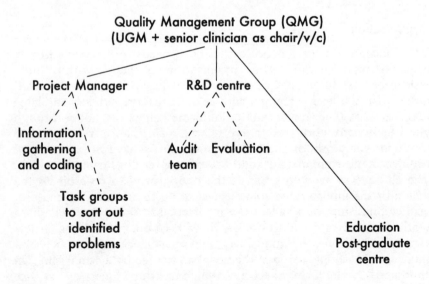

Figure 2.10.1 *Project-orientated approach to quality*

This structural change should allow us to analyse need and identify problems, develop a standard, implement the standard, feedback the information to the participants, and ensure beneficial change, in short, complete the extended audit cycle within a single coherent management organisation.

These principles should apply to both preventive medicine and first contact healthcare settings. The organisational structure needed here may well be different from that applicable to larger healthcare institutions, but both should facilitate the auditing of care across traditional divides.

Implementation and ethics

So we need to change our perception of audit and strengthen the organisational framework within which it is developed. Under the general umbrella of implementation, I now want to discuss three other aspects of audit. Even if we implement the above two recommendations (for that is what they are), we will face the problem that our initiatives will be perceived as being driven by the government's desire to cut costs in health care. Audit is sometimes seen as an ogre. I have no doubt that this is the motivation for some, but as I have suggested before, there is a much more important reason for the involvement of doctors and to ensure the support of medical colleagues. We must articulate this clearly.

We need continually to stress the ethical value of audit, to recognise that those healthcare workers who have primary responsibility for individual patients are confronted with very difficult decisions. The tension between individual advocacy for a particular patient and corporate responsibility for the group is never going to go away. Therefore we need to discuss at all levels of our organisation the ethical base upon which we offer treatment – to share with all involved the principles which I outlined earlier. In practical terms, the move towards clinical directorates is essential, as it locks those who have traditionally been healthcare leaders – the doctors – firmly into this important debate. It is not difficult to persuade people that the only reasonable resolution of these complex problems is to ensure that we only do what we know to be beneficial. How do we get to know what this is? Only through extended audit.

So emphasising the ethical basis for audit is essential if we wish to get the commitment of professionals, which all of us believe to be necessary to the effective implementation of audit. Many professionals still feel uncomfortable with the notion of clinical audit, not because of professional confidentiality, but because they are not convinced of the relevance of, let us say, organisational audit to patient care. How do we convince them otherwise? If we ask patients what for them are the most important determinants of quality of care, they include both service and clinical markers. An apparently excellent clinical episode may be marred by having to wait in an unfriendly, uncomfortable and information-free environment and vice versa. There is abundant evidence that this is the case, and we need to heighten professional awareness of this reality. Whatever we professionals feel, from the patient's point of view it is as important for the process of health care to run smoothly as to get the diagnosis and treatment right. Hence, if we want to improve health care, audit must address both service and clinical issues – in short be clinical rather than medical.

Purchaser's role

Finally, what is the role of the purchaser? How can they support the implementation of audit? Paradoxically, at the present time the purchasers are blinkered in the opposite direction to clinicians. They concentrate on service issues almost to the exclusion of clinical ones. (As long as it looks nice it doesn't matter too much about the outcome.) If audit is to illuminate the shift in healthcare provision that we are told is about to take place, this attitude must change. I sympathise with purchasers – setting clinical service standards is relatively easy, whereas setting specific medical intervention standards is difficult. We know from audit of audit that unless those standards are owned, they will not be implemented effectively. There are, however, many examples of established best practice which purchasers should discuss with directorates, within an audit and evaluation framework, and then implement at the time of contract setting. Because of the exemplary research of Chalmers at the Cochrane Centre in Oxford, this task is relatively easy for obstetrics and perinatology, but can also be applied readily to many other interventions, such as coronary artery disease, shared care in asthma and diabetes, and the relative virtues of different ways of enabling people to stop smoking.

Patient involvement

In implementing and making audit effective there is one final problem that I want to discuss, which to me is the most interesting and the most difficult. The health reforms suggest that patients will have a greater say in all aspects of their health care and ultimately if our patients are not satisfied, we cannot claim to have done a good job. Audit will never be truly effective until we integrate the patients' views into health care in a much more effective and immediate way than we do now.

There are a number of ways in which patient views may be obtained for audit purposes:

- focus groups;
- patient panel;
- exploring different perspectives and understanding of outcomes;
- elected representatives to healthcare boards;
- election from a panel of people drawn up after discussion with interested parties in the local community, and elected at local election time. See Table 2.10.9.

Table 2.10.9 *Possible patient involvement*

- Whose outcome is it?
- Patient panels
- Elected representatives to health boards
- Elected representatives to quality groups
- Involvement in choosing topics

Central to making audit work is the engagement and commitment of all our healthcare colleagues. In this respect making audit work is no different from any other management initiative, so I will conclude with the two pieces of management advice which I have found to be most useful to me over the years. They represent the best in the tradition of devolved, enabling and participatory management, and it won't surprise any of you to know that they were formulated by the school of Lao Tzu flourishing in China in the 6th century BC.

Go to the people,
Live amongst them.
Start with what they have
Build on what they know.
And when the deed is done, the mission accomplished
Of the best leaders,
The people will say
'We have done it ourselves'.

Lao Tzu

So to summarise:

- conceptual change – clinical audit
- organisational change – centre stage
- implementation – good management

In case you feel I am being naïve, I do recognise the importance of financial incentives which may modify the behaviour of even the most august of us – private practice.

References

Russell, I.T. and Wilson, B.J. (1992) *Quality in Healthcare*, Volume 1, pp. 51–55.

PART THREE

MANAGING FINANCE

ONE DAY, ALL BANKS WILL HAVE A CONICAL STRUCTURE SURROUNDED BY PERICARDIUM AND POSSESSING FOUR CHAMBERS AND FOUR VALVES.

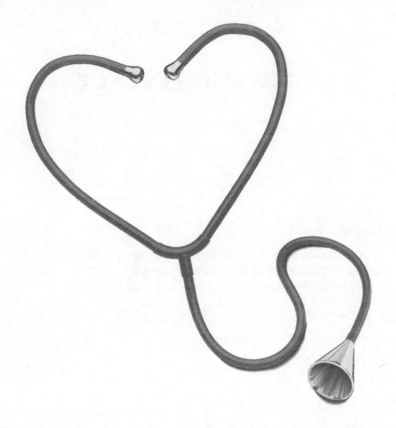

TILL THEN, THERE'S *ALWAYS* THE ROYAL BANK.

In a rapidly changing health service, running the finances of a busy practice can give you heartache.

That's why The Royal Bank offers specialised financial guidance and support for Medical Practices and GP Fundholders. From simple overdraft facilities to Doctors' Surgery loans, our dedicated managers are always on-call with help and advice to meet the needs of today's healthcare professionals.

For more details about Royal Bank services for Doctors' Surgeries, phone free on 0800 121121.

The Royal Bank of Scotland

3.1

GP Multifunds

Jean Roberts-Jones

What is a Multifund?

The simple answer to this question is: a collection of practices that have agreed to pool part of their fundholding management allowance in order to facilitate a central administration system for fundholding purposes within their practices. How this takes place in practice terms can vary from Multifund (MF) to Multifund but the reasoning behind why practices have chosen to take this path will probably share three important factors: economies of scale; shared information; and, most importantly, strength in numbers. There are now at least 22 MFs in or about to enter fundholding.

There are two models of pooling the funds. One option is to have all management funds paid to the central administration office for distribution to practices to pay for expenses such as data clerk time and office items (eg photocopying, postage, etc). The other is for individual practices to agree to pay a set amount into the central office for their expenses and to retain the remainder for their own use.

Both systems have advantages and disadvantages and the exchange of invoices between the central administration office and practices cannot be avoided. However, the practices in an MF feel this is a small price to pay for having the management responsibility taken away from overworked GPs and practice managers, leaving time to manage day-to-day matters and for wider issues.

The central administration system oversees all activities that relate to fundholding, the extent depending on individual agreements and the needs and strengths of the practices involved.

Economies of scale

The achievement of economies of scale can affect practices at various levels, but the three main benefits are:

- to reduce the burden of the extra administration;
- to employ proficient managers;
- to ensure the balance of power is tipped away from the large providers, thus increasing the influence of fundholders.

Although individual practices have to ensure that the data collection exercise for fundholding occurs, administration of the scheme can be removed to a greater or lesser extent, depending on the degree of involvement in fundholding required.

A business or mega-fund manager is employed by the central office to oversee all activities related to fundholding, rather than each practice having to employ its own manager. The fact that these managers are working across practices and probably have offices separate from them, helps to avoid potential problems, including possible conflict with existing practice managers about perceived overlap of duties. The problems of employing and finding space for an extra member of staff are thus also circumvented.

By pooling part of the resources of individual practices, MFs are able to employ business managers of a calibre to match those in the contracting departments of major providers. The salary of such managers will be often in excess of £30,000 per annum, beyond the budget of most individual fundholding practices but affordable to a large group with shared costs.

Equally important on a practical level is the knowledge that the business manager who works in co-operation with practices will also cover issues which cross practice boundaries such as systems, recruitment and training. GPs and practice managers will agree common policies with the business manager, not only on data collection and reconciliation but also on issues such as employment and staff support. Training can be bought as a group and targeted to meet individual needs.

Considerable benefits can be gained from the possession of common computer systems, including access to data in the same format and data clerks who are able to support each other. New team members can be trained by existing Multifund staff. Computer systems can remain separate or become networked (having different GMS clinical systems is not necessarily a problem).

Shared information

If an MF has a standard computer system the common data format is shared. This will allow the practice to analyse trends as well as to monitor budgets. The business manager will be able to use the information to make predictions and to work closely with GPs to develop services.

However, it is not necessary for all practices to develop the same clinical services nor to run them in the same way. The group will probably be large enough to run its own pilot schemes, allowing one practice the opportunity to try someone or something different.

Another major advantage in an MF is the facility of the business forum, where GPs can get to know each other and talk about mutual areas of concern. Most MFs are linked across a locality and therefore have shared knowledge of the area. They may even share practice boundaries, thus being in a position to have a wealth of local interest, both medical and social, which they can bring to bear on all issues.

This knowledgebase should occur at other levels within practices, such as practice managers or practice nurses. Multifunds should allow all team members opportunities to get to know each other at a local level where many of their problems will overlap. These forums facilitate general discussion on how day-to-day issues are managed and encourage good practice.

Multifunds help to address the problem of professional isolation often felt by GPs who by nature are extremely individualistic. However, they can, and do, work closely together. Practices that have been working in the same area for years may know little about colleagues and their practice methods. The sharing framework in an MF will bring doctors together, even in simple ways such as by holding meetings in each other's surgeries.

Strength in numbers

The purchasing power that comes from being an MF, and the size of budget it carries, is perhaps the most powerful argument for practices to come together. Providers can be slow to change existing policy, slow to react to new ideas, reluctant to look at the way in which they provide services. If one fundholding practice wants to make a significant change to the service they get and the provider is reluctant or unwilling to listen to argument, the only option would be to look to another provider. This is easier in some areas than in others.

However, as a Multifund the withdrawal of all budgets for a particular service would mean a large loss of income for a provider and could even destabilise a department, leading to possible cuts in the levels of consultants. Few practices would want to do this but at least arguments would be listened to. Providers may still be unable to help because of reasons beyond their immediate power, but this approach will have brought the issue into the foreground for open discussion.

Established in 1980, the AAT is the recognised professional body for Accounting Technicians and is sponsored by the five major accountancy bodies in the UK.

With more than 90,000 members and students, part of the AAT's remit is to provide formal qualifications for accounting support staff, through its NVQ-based Education and Training Scheme. As the only professional body to provide NVQs in Accounting, the AAT also prepared its students for membership.

The West Cheshire NHS Trust led the way within the NHS in February this year by becoming an AAT Approved Assessment Centre. There are now four NHS Trusts registered with the AAT to provide its Education and Training Scheme in-house, with several other sites in the process of applying for accreditation.

By becoming an AAT approved work-based assessment centre, Trusts can either provide the complete qualification to their staff, or can work in conjunction with a local training provider. Call the contact number on this page for further information.

However, threats to change providers should not be made lightly and referral patterns may need changing and services moving if providers refuse to co-operate, or all credibility would be lost.

Potential problems

Although there are advantages to being a Multifund, the government programme was not designed to cover joint working arrangements. The fundholding rules were not written to accommodate the differences between MFs and individual fundholders, hence the inability to move budgets within an MF. Rules which apply to individual fundholders have to apply to MFs and sometimes they do not fit well. These rules are contained in numerous government White Papers, but all health authorities have produced their own guides for prospective fundholders. Such documents will be central to most planning and operational decisions.

Despite potential outside threats to fundholding in general from political uncertainty on all sides, the general feeling seems to be that primary-care-led locality purchasing will still be in favour, whichever party is in power. An MF is ideally suited to adapt accordingly. The Association of Independent Multifunds (AIM) is a newly formed body representing MFs throughout the country with the aim of being heard at national level and making people aware of the advantages of having a locally sensitive service.

However, there may be problems nearer to home for most MFs. Local providers may see a large group as intimidating if there is talk of moving services away. Health commissions can also see MFs as difficult to deal with and as a possible threat to their own contracting departments, whose workload could be cut back with possible reductions in employment levels. Misunderstandings or lack of adequate information exchange could mean that fundholders may upset long-term strategies, unless sufficient consultation has taken place. Problems may even lie within the group. Although there are advantages in being a large group there is also an additional level of commitment and everyone needs to feel sufficiently involved to accept that they will not always get their way.

A good communication network within the MF and within practices is vital. All parties involved should know what is expected of them, and be aware of the timetable. It is also beneficial to keep everyone informed of developments with other agencies in order to avoid duplication or misunderstandings. Without this information exchange, trust cannot be maintained, goodwill breaks down, misinformation from third parties abounds and people quickly become unhappy and disillusioned. They may even break away.

Where it is necessary for smaller practices to link together to form the minimum required list size, it cannot be overstated how important it is for them to have a good relationship and similar referral patterns. They will need to agree over many issues and the process will take less time if they are comfortable with each other.

Advantages

There are a considerable number of advantages in practices joining forces as briefly outlined above, and others that do not relate to fundholding. The concept of bulk purchasing can cover anything from flu vaccines to couch rolls. Regular MF meetings are an excellent forum for exchanging ideas on practice matters. Time restraints on a fundholding practice can be eased in an MF as all practices do not have to be involved with every aspect of fundholding. An MF will have a lead GP who will take on a specialist area, such as physiotherapy or mental health provision. The lead GP will work with the business manager in supplying clinical input into the contract negotiations on behalf of colleagues. They will report regularly back to the main group and check for consensus views.

Conclusion

There are many positive reasons for fundholding practices to join together, but the key to an MF's success is GP co-operation and a business manager who can pull the group together and work closely with the practices. Maintenance of trust between practices is essential and this can only be done through a communication network which includes all members of the primary health care team. Despite being strong individuals, GPs can work together because they have the same aim – to improve the quality and efficiency of health care in their locality.

3.2

Contracts for Health Care
Analysis of new trends and types of contracts

Barbara Ghodse

Introduction

Since the introduction of the internal market in 1991, contracts have been the mechanism for:

- purchasers (health authorities and GP fundholders) to procure health care services to meet the identified needs of their population;
- providers (hospitals, community units) to secure the necessary funding for their continued operation.

At first, most contracts were nothing more than simple block contracts. However, against a background of new configurations of health authorities and trusts, the growth of GP fundholding, changed (and changing) allocation of funding and improved information systems, there has been a steady move towards more complex contractual arrangements which define more precisely the services being purchased/delivered, match payment more closely to the cost of the services and include incentives to providers to deliver the services that their purchasers want. Thus contracts have become more sophisticated in terms of their type, pricing structure, the use of different contract currencies and the range of services excluded. This chapter describes some of these approaches and discusses how they can be utilised to derive contracts that meet the needs of both purchasers and providers in a complex environment.

COURSES ON HIV DISEASE
for General Practitioners and Hospital Doctors

St Stephen's Centre, the Department of HIV/GU Medicine at the Chelsea & Westminster Hospital, London, offers a *2-day course on HIVDisease* which aims to improve knowledge about the presentation and management of HIV-related disease and develop a basic understanding of the relevant epidemiology, virology and immunology. The course also provides guidance on how to care for people with HIV, including diagnosis, treatment, referrals, necessary precautions and counselling around the antibody test. The St Stephen's/Chelsea & Westminster Model of care is described, and a Patient Panel give their views on their disease, their treatment, and their aspirations for health care. The course is organised by Dr Brian Gazzard, Consultant Physician and HIV Clinical Director and Dr David Hawkins, Consultant Physician, St Stephen's Centre. It is held six times a year, from September to May, and is PGEA approved and CME accredited.

The Department of Dermatology with St Stephen's offer a day meeting held annually which aims to look at dermatological manifestations in people with HIV. As well as a short introduction about the epidemiology of HIV disease, the course deals with clinical features and histopathology, and the management of dermatological manifestations of HIV. *HIV & The SKIN is* organised by Dr Richard Staughton, Consultant Dermatologist, Chelsea & Westminster Hospital and Dr David Hawkins, Consultant Physician, HIV/GU Medicine. The course is PGEA approved and CME accredited.

In addition, other courses on related issues, such as measures to improve the sexual health of patients in primary care settings, and meetings on topics relating to GU Medicine, are offered on an occasional basis. Please contact the number below for further details of these.

To apply for one of the above courses, or to receive more information, please contact:

Carol Whitwill, AIDS Course Co-ordinator, St Stephen's Centre, 369 Fulham Road, London SW10 9TH; tel. 0181-746 8234.

Chelsea & Westminster Hospital, Department of HIV/Genitourinary Medicine

HIV DISEASE AND THE G.P.

Approaches to the management of HIV disease has provided an opportunity to refocus on the provision of care for many other medical conditions. One fundamental issue is the balance between hospital and community care. To date, most AIDS care in the UK has taken place within the hospital setting. This is increasingly inappropriate with greater numbers of people affected spending more time in the community. A triangle of forces with the patient, hospital and community at each apex militates against a balance between hospital care and community care. Forces within this triangle include the marginalisation of the primary care team, the perceptions of patients that community care is less willing and able to deal with this infection, and the hospital's difficulties in appreciating the potential resource of the GP.

However, the primary care physician has a unique set of skills to offer the HIV positive patient. No other carers possess the combination of training in medical and communication skills and awareness of the social and psychological issues.

There are 5 principal areas in which the GP is involved. The first and most important is the prevention of HIV disease. Health promotion clinics are an appropriate time to discuss safer sex practices and recreational drug use. Second, the GP is commonly involved with patients who perceive themselves to be at risk of HIV infection. The doctor can make a realistic assessment of the risks and advise about testing as appropriate. Third, the GP may be involved in the maintenance of the patient who has HIV disease and whom may be symptomatic or asymptomatic. This is characterised by the patient requiring regular (but not necessarily frequent) health checks, looking for the stigmata of HIV disease and treating appropriately. Fourth, the physician may next be involved in the care of patients with AIDS, either with their initial diagnosis of subsequent opportunistic infections or tumours. Finally, the GP may be involved in the terminal care of such patients should they choose to die at home. The GP is able to offer help and support to the patient, their family and carers. It is this comprehensive care that is the characteristic of general practice.

The perspective of the primary care physician is often very different from the hospital physician. This important difference should not be underplayed by the GP who feels relatively inexperienced in HIV disease, as it is likely to be a perspective that is invaluable to the patient.

Types of contract

Simple block contract

A fixed sum is paid for access to a defined range of services; although an indicative workload may be specified, over- or under-performance does not affect the financial payment. Block contracts were appropriate at the start of the internal market because of their administrative simplicity and lack of dependence on sophisticated information systems. They carry no financial risk for the purchaser, who may however waste resources if anticipated workload fails to materialise. In the more usual context of increasing demand for healthcare services, it is the provider who is at greater risk with a block contract; faced with more and more patients who cannot be turned away because of the urgency of their condition, over-performance against the contract may occur with no corresponding (in year) increase in funding. The main disadvantage of simple block contracts from the purchaser's perspective is that, because of the lack of specificity, there is no leverage over the provider.

Cost and volume contract

Purchasers pay a fixed sum for an identified volume of service; beyond that level an additional payment is made for each episode of care usually at marginal or variable cost. A volume (and therefore a financial) ceiling is usually agreed to limit the financial risk to which the purchaser is exposed. The provider's risk is reduced by being paid for what is delivered, although it can be difficult to balance many similar contracts.

Sophisticated block contract

This type of contract has emerged as a practical response to the reality of the internal market in which purchasers have cash limited budgets which are usually insufficient to meet all potential demand. It is a hybrid of simple block and cost and volume contracts in which an agreed sum is paid for access to a defined range of services or facilities. Indicative volumes for workload are included, usually specifying the casemix (for example, by specialty in a contract for acute services). The contract may be monitored on activity and/or the value of the completed workload, with variations exceeding an agreed tolerance level triggering joint action by purchaser and provider. This may include curtailing/increasing elective workload, increasing the indicative volumes of the contract by purchasing additional activity,

Johnson & Johnson

MEDICAL COMPANIES

Introduction

Walk into any hospital in the UK – and in most countries of the world – and you will be in an environment where Johnson & Johnson is known and respected.

Johnson & Johnson

MEDICAL

Johnson & Johnson Medical provides a wide range of essential products for the operating theatre, intensive care, medical and nursing staff. Its products embrace wound management, infectiion prevention, surgical specialities, patient monitoring equipment and vascular access products.

Johnson & Johnson

INTERVENTIONAL SYSTEMS

Johnson & Johnson Interventional Systems provides interventional cardiologists, interventional radiologists and vascular surgeons with devices used in the treatment of cardiovascular disease.

We are the leading suppliers of stents – scaffolding devices designed to restore blood flow through otherwise occluded vessels.

Johnson & Johnson

FINANCE LIMITED

Johnson & Johnson Finance Limited offer financing alternative which address the unique capital requirements of our health care customers, including the NHS under the Private Finance Initiative, for the acquisition of capital equipment, medical products and services.

Johnson & Johnson

PROFESSIONAL

Johnson & Johnson Professional provides advanced quality, cost-effective devices and services to orthopaedic specialists, spinal surgeons and neurosurgeons. Products supplied include precision surgical instruments, orthopaedic, spinal and neurosurgical implants, and innovative fracture repair products and braces.

Our innovative product range also includes specialised neurosurgical equipment used for neuroendoscopy and electrosurgery, disposables, hand-held micro surgical instruments, implants for the treatment of hydrocephalus, intracranial aneurysms and spinal instability and single-use products used in neurosurgical and spinal surgical procedures.

THERAKOS

Therakos specialises in innovative advances in extracorporeal disease management through photomedical therapy.

Johnson & Johnson Medical
Customer Service, The Braccans, London Road,
Bracknell, Berks. RG12 2AT
Tel: 01344 864000   Fax: 01344 864001

(often at preset marginal rates) or refunding the purchaser for under-performance (again at marginal cost).

Cost per case contract

As the name suggests, the purchaser pays a predetermined price (as specified in the tariff) for particular treatments as and when they arise. This exposes Health Authority purchasers to potentially unlimited financial risk and, to circumvent this, a call-off contract may be preferred, specifying the upper financial limit against which individual cases can be charged. From the provider's perspective too, cost per case contracts can be risky, because fixed costs may not be covered if the anticipated workload fails to materialise. GP fundholders often utilise cost per case contracts for inpatient and daycase Finished Consultant Episodes (FCEs), but the associated administrative costs are high.

Tolerance/variance

Both cost and volume and sophisticated block contracts usually specify a tolerance (or variance) of a few percentage points which, if exceeded, triggers joint action by purchaser and provider. This tolerance may operate on activity levels or financial value and, by offering flexibility, helps to offset the difficulty of delivering the contract precisely on target in the face of unpredictable demands and pressures.

Traditionally, a tolerance above the contract baseline is matched by a similar tolerance below the baseline, with the range depending on the value of the contract. For example a £1 million contract with a tolerance of 5 per cent has a value range from £950,000 to £1,050,000. A similar percentage tolerance on a much larger contract (eg £60 million) would expose the purchaser to an unacceptable risk if referrals increased above anticipated levels and therefore tolerance levels are usually lower on the main host purchaser/provider contracts than on smaller contracts.

Variable/marginal costs

The introduction of variable/marginal costs is closely linked to tolerance levels. If activity on a cost and volume contract exceeds the upper tolerance level, additional payment will be required. However, if the provider's fixed costs have been met by the agreed contract sum, marginal cost pricing can be utilised for the additional workload to reflect the variable costs incurred, sometimes offering a significant discount to purchasers. However, if over-performance is substantial, requiring, for example, the opening of additional beds and/or the employment of more staff, the variable element of the cost may increase and marginal prices may be stepped to reflect this.

Duration of contracts

Traditionally, the vast majority of contracts are placed for one year at a time, even when both parties are sure that a similar contract will be placed the following year. This very tentative approach arises from purchasers' uncertainty about future budget allocations and a consequent reluctance to commit funds. Nevertheless, it seems likely that longer term arrangements will become more common, perhaps in the first instance for contracts of small value and of limited strategic importance either to purchaser or provider, and later for more significant contracts with adjustments for inflation and efficiency each year. This would carry an added advantage of spreading the financial risk of over-/under-performance across a longer time frame.

Contract currency

The traditional contract currency for inpatient and daycase workload is the Finished Consultant Episode (FCE) and, in the early days of the internal market, all costs related to a particular specialty were rolled up into an average cost for an inpatient FCE for that specialty. Now, with improved costing, more contracts are built up using a variety of currencies and, for acute services, the hallmark of more sophisticated contracts is that activity is specified in terms of both inpatient and daycase FCEs with outpatient activity separately identified as the number of appointments. Additional refinements, often introduced by teaching hospitals with a complex casemix and a diverse contract portfolio, include:

- inpatient and/or daycase prices, grouped into bands to reflect more accurately the cost of different treatments;
- separate prices for different outpatient clinics within a single specialty;
- different prices for new and follow-up outpatient appointments;
- separate identification of elective and emergency episodes.

A wide variety of different approaches has been adopted for classifying the workload in a particular specialty into bands according to its complexity. In order to facilitate comparisons between providers, Healthcare Resource Groups (HRGs) are being adopted nationally. These assemble conditions and procedures, identified by recognised coding systems (ICD10, OPCS), into 'iso-resource' groups that consume similar quantities of resources.

Increasingly, too, it is being recognised that an FCE is an inappropriate unit of measurement for much clinical activity and new currencies have been developed, such as:

- yearly/monthly programmes of care for those with chronic illness (eg chronic renal failure);
- delivery episodes, to cover the whole cost of obstetric care;
- bed days for intensive care (neonatal, paediatric and adult);
- fractions for radiotherapy, to reflect actual usage of accelerators;
- units of factor VIII to reflect actual usage by individual haemophiliac patients.

Contract exclusions

Most tertiary referral centres offering a wide range of services now have a number of contract exclusions. These are usually for highly specialist and high-cost areas of medical care (eg bone marrow transplants, intensive care, implants) for which there is considerable uncertainty about the level of activity that will arise. Contract exclusions are also utilised as a mechanism for obtaining funding for new service developments previously financed by research monies.

If these high-cost services are included in the contract, small fluctuations in activity can make the rest of the contract very difficult to manage. However, if they are excluded, purchasers may retain excessive financial reserves to meet unpredictable activity, thus reducing the sums available for contracts. Clearly contract exclusions can be high-risk areas for both purchasers and providers and a jointly agreed approach is required to sharing this risk equitably.

A more recent trend is the specification of contract exclusions by the purchaser. Whole specialties may be excluded from some contracts if the purchaser wishes to commission these only from preferred providers – perhaps to achieve economies of scale or to ensure that cases requiring a particular expertise are managed in centres with a critical mass of patients. Sometimes particular procedures, to which the purchaser accords low priority, may be excluded. The implementation of different exclusions by different purchasers poses administrative problems for providers who have to check the contractual status of individual patients before embarking on treatment.

Contract terms and conditions

Although of great significance, the financial and activity agreements outlined above are not the totality of the contract and other terms and conditions are also important. In particular, requirements for information are often specified in some detail, as well as specific standards for the quality of care to be provided. Sanctions (usually financial penalties) may be included to ensure compliance although incentives and rewards are utilised more rarely. These measures are often adopted to ensure that Patient's Charter standards are met. Although this is a practical approach to implementing national directives, achieving Charter standards relating to waiting times (ie for a non-urgent outpatient appointment and for admission to hospital) is intimately related to the volumes being purchased and such terms should not be included in contracts without careful joint (ie purchaser/ provider) consideration of whether sufficient investment has been made to permit stringent targets to be met.

Although it appears eminently reasonable for health authorities and GP fundholders to specify particular quality standards for the services they are purchasing, the diversity of their requirements poses problems for providers, especially if a particular standard is not a priority for the host purchaser. In practice, therefore, the standards for information and quality of care agreed with the host purchaser are usually accepted by all other purchasers. However, in some areas of quality, such as waiting times, differential standards may be implemented if individual purchasers wish to make additional payments to purchase bigger volumes and prompter access.

Discussion

In this brief account it has only been possible to identify some of the ways in which contracts and contracting have developed since the introduction of the internal market. However, this is a dynamic process and further changes and developments are certain. For example, the increased sophistication of many contracts is a direct consequence of real improvements in data collection and quality which, in turn, are permitting and encouraging the momentum towards more and more detailed contracts. This trend is being reinforced by the growth in the number of GP fundholders who, because they deal with much smaller populations than health authorities, can handle (and require) much more detailed information on individual patients. Cost per case contracts therefore seem likely to occupy an increasing proportion of a provider's portfolio – with the attendant risks outlined above.

Sophistication has also developed in other, perhaps less obvious ways. Along with improved negotiating skills on the part of both providers and purchasers, confrontational relationships, which were common at first, have given way to more co-operative approaches and an understanding that many problems can only be solved jointly. Achieving Patient's Charter standards for waiting times is a simple example, with purchasers having a responsibility to invest adequately and providers having to manage waiting lists competently. However, with growing emphasis on the importance of health authorities to develop a commissioning strategy to improve the health of their population, there are other significant areas where purchasers and providers are likely to work together more closely in future.

Of immediate, practical importance, is the need for a collaborative approach to an equitable sharing of financial risk so that costly facilities, such as intensive care units, are adequately resourced and available when needed, without purchasers having to retain excessive financial reserves for expensive Extra Contractual Referrals (ECRs). Any such collaboration will have to extend beyond a single purchaser/ provider relationship and joint working between a number of purchasers is likely to become more common.

Second, sophisticated contracts, with detailed quality standards, may be impressive but they are only useful if they are monitored to ensure compliance and/or to identify any variance. Even with bigger and better information systems, all such monitoring is time consuming and may divert resources away from patient care. It is essential therefore that purchasers and providers reach agreement on a limited number of core monitoring requirements so that a correct balance is achieved between adequate and excessive monitoring.

Finally, with increasing emphasis on outcomes, it seems likely that contracts will become more disease focused, and that packages of care for particular conditions will become more common as contract currencies. This is an immensely complex area and one which can only be taken forward in conjunction with clinicians with specialist expertise. Thus the involvement of clinicians in contracting, as yet in its infancy, looks set to increase.

3.3

Business Planning in the NHS, or Re-engineering Purchasing Strategy

Nick Owens

Introduction

Traditional business planning approaches

The NHS has been plagued in recent years by many exhortations for business planning. In the early 1990s, having a business plan was regarded as a key indicator, it seemed, of a would-be NHS Trust's readiness to apply for the then hallowed status. Many of the leading consultancies espoused their own methods adapted either from private sector methods, or from American 'management engineering' concepts of the factors that hospitals should be able to control. Some such forays into business planning, it must be admitted, were either more complex than the market was or indeed is ready to apply, or not well tailored for the block contract market conditions and largely fixed labour force that characterises the NHS.

It is becoming ever clearer that the market-based structure of the post-1991 NHS does not serve patients well. Volumes of 'consultant episodes' are perhaps increased, but competition between Trusts tends to prevent important options for service rationalisation being considered. These options may include more appropriate use of capital stock and modes of service delivery that are more attuned to patients' and their GPs' preferences. Thus a new paradigm of care is required, which takes a fundamentally radical approach to business planning across as well as within NHS organisations. This chapter describes one such method that is being adopted in parts of the NHS today.

New paradigm of healthcare management

The proposed new paradigm of healthcare management is not new in concept but in method of execution. It requires planning of healthcare delivery which takes account of the needs of patients in terms of quality care by doctors, nurses and paramedical staff who are all experienced in dealing with both the patient's clinical condition and with the type of care required at that moment in time. This multi-agency requirement in the planning process must therefore include:

- health commissioners, in their planning and purchasing roles;
- GPs as both purchasers of care and as representatives of patients;
- NHS Trusts of all types to advise on options for improvement or on their capability to do more or to do it differently.

Creating winners and winners

The overall goal must be to improve services for patients. This may mean that individual Trusts change in their scope of work, and many employees may feel threatened by such changes. But properly planned and executed, the actual threat should be minimal or nil:

- Provision of jobs can be ensured even in a period of change if people are willing to retrain and (within reason) to change work location.
- This may require a group of Trusts to work with each other and their local health commissioner to manage the change process responsibly.

Such changes cannot be implemented at no cost. The commissioner may need to wait over a period of time for planned and agreed benefits to be realised. It requires the health service to act maturely in its treatment of both staff and patients, and build in quality to its management decisions. This is almost certainly the only way to escape the worst excesses of both the pre-1991 'planned economy', and the post-1991 assumptions that market forces and management by strength will deliver better patient care.

Strategic objectives

How then, do these ideals and principles relate to business planning for a better health service? There is a basic sequence that needs to be adopted, as set out in Figure 3.3.1.

A business planning team

A business planning team must be brought together which includes decision-makers from all the principal organisations within the scope of the planning programme. Organisations not willing to participate

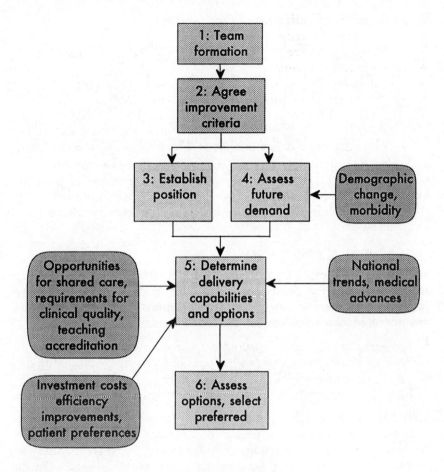

Figure 3.3.1 *An approach to business planning*

will tend to lose out by failing to promote their own people and development initiatives in the appropriate timeframe and/or forum.

Steps may need to be taken to promote teamworking among this group if they have not worked together in this way before, and the availability of change management and facilitation skills is likely to be important in achieving successful outcomes.

Agreeing strategic objectives

Second, the appropriate strategic objectives and criteria by which improvements in healthcare delivery will be judged should be identified and agreed, by consensus wherever possible. These criteria should include, for example, definitions of:

- appropriate and effective quality of care;
- good access to facilities;
- well-integrated care, working across organisational boundaries;
- efficient care delivery;
- care delivery that is economical in its use of resources;
- what is required to provide good teaching facilities;
- what is a good use of skills, in particular allowing service availability and quality to be maintained by creating a setting and way of working that is attractive to potential recruits in the future.

Assessment of current position

Third, the present position should be identified as regards levels of demand experienced by each provider. It is important that this assessment identifies throughput and capacity by site and by type of care, so that differences in resource availability and use can be considered. In acute care settings, differences in bed and theatre utilisation will be apparent. In community care, there are frequently identified mismatches between the locations in which care and treatment is available, versus the locations of demand by centre of population and social need. Thus the work to establish current service delivery patterns must be quite detailed.

An important component of this position assessment is the documentation for each specialty and care group and how they rate against the previously agreed criteria. This step is not easy. In each case, the views of the Trust concerned may differ from those of outsiders. Previous differences over strategy or execution of policy may mean that the views of some team members cannot be readily reconciled. In this case, it is important to refer to relevant available material, such as King's Fund and other clinical audits of care quality, Royal College views as to the suitability of a facility for training accreditation, or other impartial views as may be available. Local differences should not be allowed to stand in the way of the overall objective of improving care quality.

Forecast of future demand

Fourth, and if need be in parallel with the previous step, a first-cut view of future demand should then be projected from current demand by reference to changes in demography, trends in morbidity, committed changes in the physical fabric of Trusts (for example, if new departments are opening or sites are already scheduled to close). Changes in healthcare priorities, for example planned increases in screening rates better to enable Health of the Nation targets to be met, may also be injected into the future demand scenario at this point. This first-cut projection is important in the aggregate, as the sum of healthcare demands to be met.

Delivery options

In the fifth step, delivery options can be considered. In planning changes from the status quo, the multi-agency team should work together as far as possible. It must be clearly stated, that in developing a vision of future service delivery, redundancies other than voluntary are not the permitted means of adjusting staffing in line with expected future needs. The need for this rule is simple and fundamental: not to do so creates planning blight and damages morale and operational effectiveness. It is essential for unfettered assessment of options and because the types of change being considered will generally take several years – often three to seven, sometimes longer – to implement.

Because of the complexity of multi-organisational, multi-site scenarios, many options are possible. The planning team must therefore be rigorous in dropping from further analysis those options which are clearly inferior to others being considered.

This step five also considers the present delivery capabilities of the NHS Trusts or other organisations which are involved in meeting current demand. There will often be identified a mismatch between delivery capability, and expected demand. This mismatch can take many forms:

- facilities appear materially too small/too large;
- resource cost (based on present service delivery modes) exceeds anticipated resources;
- mismatch between location of demand and the available supply.

Problems such as these form typical inputs to process–redesign programmes undertaken by individual trusts. This aspect is considered below.

Selecting the preferred option(s)

The sixth and final step is to assess what is the preferred option or options. In making this assessment, the guiding light is always how well does a particular option meet the initial criteria set out. In assessing options, the planning team may wish to give preference to ways of treating patients near to their homes, or of returning the patient promptly to a home setting, if this does not prejudice care quality. Outcome assessments are important for determining whether reduced inpatient length of stay is beneficial or detrimental to patient care, though the quality and quantity of available data on this issue is limited at present. The cost of additional community care from earlier discharge, ie releasing higher dependency patients, must also be carefully analysed to assess whether such an option is viable and/or desirable. Comparative benchmarking of neighbouring Trusts (or of a Trust against itself) for like types of care can be helpful in determining where operational improvements are likely to be found.

Finally, and unfortunate but true, both capital and revenue cash limits have to be the ultimate arbiter of whether particular options can be accepted as the preferred basis. The Private Finance Initiative gives some additional flexibility as to sources of funding and in options for satisfying demand that cannot currently be met, though how business planning should respond to PFI is a large topic which merits a chapter in its own right. The outcome of this sixth step is potentially threefold:

1. Most certainly, a shared understanding in both Trusts and healthcare commissioners, of what ought to be the goals for care delivery, what can be achieved now, and what types of change are needed.
2. It provides what in many cases for Trusts is a much-needed opportunity to set out ways that services can be developed, and how the commissioner's goals can be met. In addition, it reduces the frustrations of delay and inaction that can result if issues and problems are not shared.
3. If conducted openly, with trust between organisations, it can result in significant acceleration in achievement of practical steps to improve services and deliver better care.

In conclusion, this chapter has outlined a new approach to business planning. It proposes that the planning effort should be led by health commissioners, with the active collaboration of Trusts. Data must be shared; and the means of implementation must also be set out and agreed in order that results can be achieved. A planning process of this nature is not an end in itself. For many Trusts, it is only the beginning, for it will set new challenges for the Trust to achieve step-changes or 'break-points' in organisational performance, and require each Trust in turn to re-engineer its means of care delivery to achieve new standards for the NHS into the twenty-first century.

3.4

The Private Finance Initiative

Paul Nash

Ever since its launch in 1992, the Private Finance Initiative (PFI) has generated continual interest both within the national press and the House of Commons. The PFI encompasses all government departments and even the Treasury building has been offered for sale. Much of the interest in the initiative has been in the area of health and this can be attributed to a number of reasons. Historic underfunding has led to a large backlog maintenance requirement. However, capital was now needed to meet the requirements of new technology. The Department of Health thus made an early commitment to PFI and has pushed forward more quickly than many of the other departments, such as Environment. More important is the fact that Health is one of the most politically sensitive departments of government and this has led to all sorts of claims of privatisation and Treasury plots to provoke a hiatus in NHS spending. Not unnaturally, the Labour party has a paternal affection for its most favoured child, but perhaps also recognises the ability to score easy political points in front of a concerned public. All of these factors have helped to ensure the continued coverage of the PFI within the NHS.

Despite the exhortations of the government and the Treasury, progress has not been as fast as initially hoped. A number of projects are registered as completed on the Newchurch PFI database but, with an average of only £1.5 million capital, it is recognised that the majority of these are small projects. Total capital of around £100 million has been raised so far but, in the context of an annual capital spend of £2 billion, this is not significant. It is the signing of the first major District General Hospital (DGH) project that the sector is waiting for with eager anticipation. This day is approaching with schemes at Carlisle and South Buckinghamshire entering final stages of negotiation and, with a fair wind, we could yet see half a dozen major completed schemes by the end of 1995. Should this prove to be the case, the news will be most welcome, as some evidence of major success is now becoming a priority if the PFI is not to lose momentum.

The initiative itself has catalysed a number of more fundamental questions in relation to such things as models of service delivery; the asset base of the NHS; legal boundaries of Trusts and the role of the commissioning agencies. What began as an initiative has become part of a much more fundamental change in the delivery of health care.

PFI teething problems

Not surprisingly, in the context of this fundamental change in the provision of health care, a number of issues arise.

Clarity within the NHS

In the early days there was much confusion within the NHS as to the requirements and rules for the use of private finance. The rules relating to its use were laid down in a number of Treasury and NHS Executive documents which gave some guidance and generally encouraged its use. However, despite this encouragement, the use of private finance appeared to remain purely a matter of choice. This was clarified, to a degree, by the issuing of the new Capital Investment Manual in July 1994. This clearly laid out a requirement for investigating private finance but did not fully describe the process for doing so. It was not until HSG(95)15 was issued in March of 1995 that a clear lead was given.

Commitment

The level of commitment to the initiative has been varied, both within the NHS and the private sector. Sections of the NHS have embraced the initiative wholeheartedly and one chief executive has claimed that he wants to run the first Trust with no assets on the balance sheet. At the other end of the spectrum there are claims of Trusts running sham processes, designed merely to jump through the hoops required to obtain Treasury funding.

A few projects have reached an advanced state and consumed large amounts of resources only to be thwarted by a purchaser, who belatedly had second thoughts about commitment to the Outline Business Case. While the need to get the strategy right before committing to it cannot be doubted, disruptions such as these only lead to doubts, in private sector minds, as to the real commitment of the NHS to the initiative.

Nevertheless, a number of projects are now nearing completion and Chief Executives are seeing that, despite any earlier concerns they may have had, an alliance with the private sector can bring extra rewards not envisaged. As projects are completed which have significant additions to their original requirements, the pleasure of those Trusts' directors must prove to be infectious among Trusts still waiting for Treasury funding.

Construction bias

Many of the initial consortia responding to the PFI were led by, or solely consisted of, construction companies. While many of these organisations have much experience in the building of healthcare facilities, few have any real knowledge of how to run them, even if they desired it. The construction industry has suffered in recent years and the apparent loss of the health section of the market left it desperate to find work. Unfortunately few of these organisations are prepared to wait twenty or so years to recover their investment and therefore still offer proposals to finance and leaseback facilities on terms which will never be acceptable to the Treasury. Some of the more astute concerns have developed partnerships with facilities' managers and hospital operators, who can not only bring the required expertise to the fray but are also prepared to take a longer term view in recovering their investment. Increasingly, we are seeing consortia, led by healthcare experts, with no construction content at all. These consortia aim to agree designs with the Trust and then tender for the actual construction at the appropriate time.

Lack of a UK healthcare industry

Due to the lack of any real private sector healthcare industry, UK funding organisations, unlike American institutions, do not, on the whole, understand health care. Consequently they are hesitant about investing in hospitals when they read in the papers of more closures with each passing day. This position is exacerbated by the fact that Trusts cannot mortgage their assets or own equity. Political considerations, also, can not be overlooked and the intentions of a potential Labour government are high on the list of concerns in the City. These factors have combined to make funding institutions take a very cautious approach.

Again, this is a problem which is starting to resolve itself. The banks, recognising the size of the market, are keen to be involved and are putting themselves through an intensive learning process, which hopefully will lead them to the conclusion that health care, far from being under threat, is the safest industry in the country.

Flooding the market

At the time of writing, during the summer of 1995, the market is positively awash with PFI projects and there is just not the capacity within the private sector to respond to all of them. Projects have been turned down by companies who would like to respond but quite simply do not have the manpower. The situation is exacerbated by a requirement on Trusts to test all capital projects for PFI. This further tries the patience of both the private sector, that suffers continuous requests to bid on projects which have no chance of success, and of wretched NHS managers who must test the options for privately financing items such as a new roof or replacement windows.

The result has been claims that the private sector is cherrypicking the best projects in which to be involved. What is surprising is not that the private sector is cherrypicking, but that anybody is surprised that it should do so. Naturally, limited resources should be invested in the best way possible. This is the whole point of the PFI: the private sector will fund those developments where it can add value, the Treasury those where it cannot.

The experience of the private sector in responding to the Private Finance Initiative is growing rapidly. Organisations and partnerships that have a good understanding not only of the necessary financing but more importantly of health care are springing up. Nevertheless, it seems likely that there may be a shortage of bidders of sufficient quality with whom the NHS may form partnerships for some little time yet.

EC public services procurement laws

The whole process for testing PFI is not hastened by the use of the EC public services procurement process, which is vague and lengthy, confuses most lawyers and is designed for works or services. In reality, Private Finance partners fall into neither of these categories and strict adherence to the rules can lead to such bizarre situations as shortlisting potential joint venture partners for the next twenty-five years on the basis of the number of mechanical diggers they have available.

Despite these shortcomings, a fair competitive process has to be undertaken. The EC procurement process is a proven method of doing so and one which is well understood by the private sector. The negotiated procedure allows for the flexibility required by the PFI and it therefore seems unlikely that another process will be adopted.

The future of the Private Finance Initiative

Many of the concerns highlighted above are merely the sort of

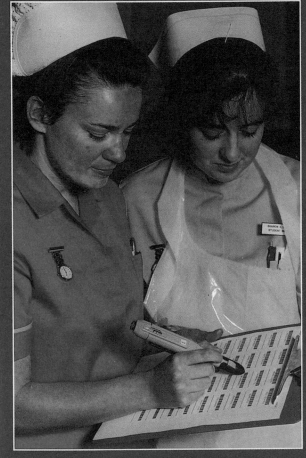

Data collection for Skillmix Monitoring

Many Trusts undertake Nursing Activity Analysis and Workload studies using the NISCM methodology (Nursing Systems for Change Management; JDM Management Services). Data capture for the Activity Analysis is achieved with Diary Cards maintained manually by staff throughout each shift they work over a seven day period. The information is then sent to the Consultancy who process the data and return the reports, within 8-12 working days. The cost is £800 per ward (including in-house costs and VAT) with a total turn around period of approximately six weeks from completion of the Diary Cards at ward level to the return of processed information to the Ward Sister.

On implementing the system more widely, the data is processed in house. Inputting takes thirty-five hours per ward for one operator. The turn around time for the information is two weeks. The costs are in the region of £300 per ward.

Purchase of the Tel-PARS barcode and light pen system has drastically reduced the cost. The data for one ward is inputted into the computer within ten minutes. The turn around period for the data from commencing downloading to production of the finished report, including user defined graphics, not available from the previous system without extra processing time, is now six hours.

In addition to the financial benefits of this system accuracy in data collection has increased markedly. This is due to:

1. Real time aspect of data capture prevents retrospective data entry ie with diary cards nurses would fill in a mornings activity at the end of the morning.

2. Ease of use and convenience means staff are more conscientious in the process of data capture.

As with any new system there were initial problems with the Tel-PARS software, not least being the project Nurses limited experience of Information Technology and complete ignorance of the Microsoft Access Data-base. Telford Management Services provide a high level of support, ensuring the efficient use of their product. Any difficulties are promptly addressed and resolved, with site visits being initiated as and when required. It should be noted that use of the Tel-PARS System for Activity Analysis in the form required involved significant modification of the application.

CONCLUSION

Tel-PARS has proved a cost effective data capture system which enhances accuracy and significantly reduces turn around time. Telford Management Services have provided an effective and efficient support service to complement a polished product.

Tel-PARS for skill-mix monitoring is just one of many applications. Others include outpatients waiting time analysis, junior doctors activities, pharmacy, theatre utilization, patient satisfaction surveys, community and PAMS etc.

For more details contact:–
Healthcare Application
Telford Management Services
The Cedars, 39-41 Compton Road,
Compton, Wolverhampton WV3 9DW
Tel: 01902 20999 • Fax: 01902 20666

teething problems to be expected from the birth of such a major change in the method of financing the delivery of public services. As the fog of uncertainty clears, the NHS is increasingly speaking with one voice. The private sector for its part is developing a greater understanding of health care and has learned to adapt to the needs and culture of the NHS.

The greatest apprehension over the future of the initiative at present stems from the actions of the Labour party. Fears have been expressed, both within the NHS and the private sector that, once in power, a Labour government would halt the initiative and rescind any deals already completed.

From much of what the Labour party has published, however, it would appear that they are heavily in favour of the initiative and it is difficult to see why they would back away from this. Labour is committed to public–private partnerships and has even criticised the government for its lackadaisical management of the Private Finance Initiative. The latest Labour health document, *Renewing the NHS*, talks about removing the compulsion on NHS organisations to enter into partnerships with the private sector, but makes no mention of scrapping the PFI. Removing this compulsion could immediately alleviate many of the problems of a flooded market, lack of players and concerns at any lack of real commitment from the NHS.

Testing only those projects where the private sector is realistically likely to be able to add value would increase the interest of the private sector, as an acceptable solution would be rather easier to develop. The limited resources of the private sector would not be spread so thinly and thus more real competition would be developed for those projects tested. This can only result in better value for money for the NHS. As mentioned earlier, concerns have been voiced that the private sector is cherrypicking the best projects. Perhaps then, it is time that the NHS once more took the driving seat and did the cherrypicking for them.

What will ultimately decide the fate of the Private Finance Initiative will not be politics but the commerciality of the deals. If the private sector can add value and transfer risk on terms which are acceptable to the Treasury, while meeting their own requirements to make a satisfactory return, then the initiative can look forward to a rosy future.

PART FOUR

MANAGING PEOPLE

4.1

Assessing Labour Productivity in the Healthcare Workforce

David Cochrane

The recent unit labour cost initiative by the NHS Executive has demonstrated wide variations in staff costs between similar providers. Unit labour costs express the cost of the staffing input for every unit of output achieved. In the NHS this has been largely measured as consultant episodes of care – the standard Korner measure of activity which is used in most NHS contracts for hospital care. The extensive database which is now available to NHS Trust managers shows these costs by major specialty and also shows the relative position of each Trust. The process through which managers assess their own performance in relation to that of other similar organisations is called comparative analysis or, as in the USA, benchmarking.

Productivity has become a central issue in health services management over the last two years. A major factor in this has been the government's pronouncements on public sector pay which have allowed only small increases in allocations to the NHS to take account of wage settlements. Anything over and above the allocation was to come from local productivity arrangements. This has converged with the move to local pay bargaining in the NHS. Although local pay allows NHS employers to tune reward more closely to individual performance and local labour markets, dynamic implementation requires money to be freed up to be available for redistribution.

Of course it should not need these initiatives to engage Health Service managers in the issue of productivity. Like any service industry, staffing is the major cost in the NHS, averaging 70 per cent of the nearly £40 billion that taxpayers spend on health care. In a service that is constantly pressed to keep up with demand (and often lagging behind) it should be a key role of management to ensure that staffing is achieving optimum value for money. Improving productivity offers more opportunity to release existing resources than any other single factor in NHS providers.

How can we measure and assess productivity in NHS providers?

The answer lies in a systematic approach to workforce planning, ensuring that it is an integral part of the business planning process operating within the management and service delivery structure of the provider. In most NHS Trusts, sub-units of service or clinical directorates exercise management authority for a given service area devolved from corporate management. Workforce planning should operate at this level but should also allow for corporate management to set an overall framework which reflects the Trust's strategic priorities and takes account of the cost, volume and quality parameters set by the contracting process (Watts *et al.*, 1993). We can look at the process in six major stages:

- Setting objectives.
- Setting out the current profile.
- Developing a supply-based forecast.
- Developing measures of productivity.
- Demand modelling and target setting.
- Setting strategic targets.

Setting objectives

Initially, objectives are developed at both corporate and clinical directorate level. Typical objectives that emerge could include using projected activity growth as an opportunity to increase productivity, or setting out the staffing implications of planned investment in capital and new equipment such that staff savings offset additional capital charges.

It is important that corporate objectives should be formulated at the outset to provide a framework within which the objectives of the clinical directorates are set. This avoids the common occurrence at clinical directorate and departmental level where initial objective setting can have the format of shopping-list proposals with little consideration of the resource implications.

Setting out the current staff profile

No planning process can proceed without accurate information about the starting position. Therefore the next stage is to set out a systematic inventory of all staff, relevant budgetary and activity information by clinical directorate. The staffing information should include detail of both skill mix and grade mix. Skill mix is the proportion of qualified staff to unqualified staff in any given staff group. Grade mix is the proportion of staff in each of the grades, particularly within the qualified staff. Data also need to be collected on use of bank and agency staff, use of overtime and absence data since all of these add to staff costs.

The data should be developed to provide a common format between directorates to enable valid comparison and should also allow aggregation across directorates, departments and staff groups so that summary information can be presented to the corporate level. It is also essential that the database is agreed between all participating parties, including the clinical directorates and relevant corporate departments (usually finance, human resources and contracting).

Developing a forecast of staff turnover

At this stage, trend data on supply indicators are generated. The data here include annual leavers, and wastage rate, annual joiners and recruitment rate and hence net rate of change. Once gathered, they are studied to produce a forecast of future supply assuming no proactive intervention. This has important implications. First, it will reveal actual potential change through natural wastage and thus inform later decisions about pace of change towards agreed planning targets. Second, it shows the extent to which current training initiatives are consistent with need for qualified staff. Third, it reveals whether high vacancy factors in a given grade are due to high turnover or simply difficulty in recruiting staff. The staffing profile can then be reappraised to reflect supply more logically.

Developing measures of productivity

The directorates and corporate management must agree a basis for measuring productivity. Measures of productivity can be developed for each major staff group and directorate by relating staff numbers to unit volume of output and to costs. The measures of productivity need to be meaningful to managers and staff within the service directorates. They should also be linked to activity, skill mix, levels of staff input and thus unit labour cost so that they facilitate comparison of the directorate's performance both between directorates within the Trust and externally with similar organisations.

Ratios that set the measures of activity against overall staffing levels in the staff group are a useful starting point. The directorates themselves should be involved in the selection of activity measures to go into productivity ratios. To ensure consistency, all directorates should use at least one set of parameters that is common to all and has a denominator which is an activity measure used in the business planning and contracting process. Examples might include:

- **Surgical specialities – nursing.** Nursing staff (wte) per occupied bed.
- **Medical staff by specialty.** Consultants (wte) per 10,000 finished episodes.
- **Physiotherapy.** Total qualified staff per 1000 first patient contacts.

Once the ratios have been agreed they can form the baseline for any discussions about changes to overall staffing levels.

Demand modelling and target setting

Current productivity is then analysed and targets for the next three years are developed through top-down modelling and what-if analysis.

Top-down modelling

The principal output from this stage is a statement of the scope of change for each directorate. This is the amount of change in levels, skill mix and grade mix, by staff group which the directorate would need to implement in order to be comparable to other similar units. A major element in this process is a comparative analysis. This shows the position of each directorate relative to some reasonable external comparators. A number of sources of comparative data can be used including examples of current best practice in the service and national and local comparative data.

Best practice planning is a strategic model and cannot be seen as a substitute for detailed local work to build up a staffing profile in a given hospital. However, it can provide the framework for more detailed scrutiny at directorate level. For example, a given model could indicate a skill mix in nursing in surgical specialties of 55 per cent qualified staff, to 45 per cent support staff. This can be compared with the current position in the unit and questions asked about the appropriateness of any divergence. Some analysis is also made of the comparative position of the unit with national and local averages. The Department of Health's Health Service Indicators and Unit Labour Cost data can both be useful sources. Alternatively, indicators can be derived from nationally aggregated workforce data (Department of Health, 1991) and nationally aggregated activity data such as the *Hospital Episode Statistics* (Department of Health).

What-if modelling

Having established the scope for change, each directorate can model the implication through what-if analysis. To minimise the workload, this should be based on a spreadsheet that allows the user to vary productivity ratios, skill, grade mix and also the staff group mix if, for example, multi-skilled support workers are being introduced. The spreadsheet is designed to compute the cost per grade and total cost to the directorate by staff group, showing the variation between current and planned staff, and the variation between current and planned expenditure.

By inputting a range of staff planning assumptions, various scenarios can be explored while the cost implications are made explicit throughout. This is often a revealing process for the business managers and clinical directors involved. The scope for savings from relatively marginal shifts in staffing levels, skill mix and grade mix are significant and can become substantial when aggregated to the total hospital level.

Setting targets and incentives

Once a clinical directorate has produced a set of proposals for future staffing these are fed back to corporate level for assessment and any amendments made to derive the planning targets. In this way, future workforce usage is projected on the basis of agreed productivity, skill- and grade-mix targets and any planned changes in service activity. Thus the business plan and the workforce plan run side by side.

Targets for change should be set at one-year intervals. Initially year one changes may leave the unit some distance from the optimal position. Although some directorates will be shown to be unduly tight for staffing and require investment, it is the common finding that Trusts have scope to release resources from the staffing profile of between 10 per cent and 20 per cent.

Resources so released can be used to relieve financial pressures. However, account should also be taken of the need to provide enhanced volume and/or quality of service for patients and not least to fund the emerging local pay systems. If staff within the directorates see this taking place they will become motivated to take a dynamic approach to workforce planning. This can accelerate the process as experience of the changes demonstrates that additional resources can be freed up within a directorate with no loss of service quality. Moreover, a culture change takes place wherein service and professional managers, aware that proposals for more staff will be closely reviewed through the workforce plan, dramatically reduce the number of bids for additional staff they would have otherwise routinely made to central management (Watts, 1994). An overview of the process and incentive structure is shown in Figure 4.1.1.

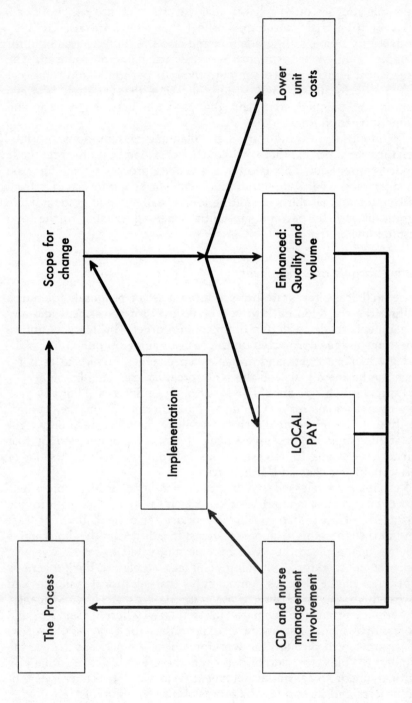

Figure 4.1.1 Overview of process and incentive structure

Productivity versus quality

When productivity issues are raised by managers it is not uncommon for clinical staff to raise concerns about quality. This is partly because some managers have tended to see productivity as an exercise in saving money. By the same token, some clinical staff view quality strictly as their territory and not the province of lay management. To resolve this tension, it is important to focus on a process of productivity review that also addresses quality issues. Years of experience in total quality management in other industries in the UK and in healthcare management in the USA and Canada have shown that quality and unit labour cost reduction can go hand in hand. Indeed it should be a fundamental objective that each time a process and/or staffing profile is reviewed with a view to achieving greater productivity, a quality gain is also achieved.

Health process re-engineering

A number of NHS Trusts have begun demonstrating how this can be achieved through a radical reappraisal of the process of care and staff roles. Sometimes called 'patient-centred care', health process re-engineering (HPR) seeks to streamline patient care processes, eliminating any unnecessary stages and administrative work, particularly as some of these can increase patient waiting-time, be detrimental to good clinical care and (not least) create substantial 'hassle factors' for staff. Quality is thus kept centre stage since it is defined in terms of both clinical inputs and outcomes and patient satisfaction.

Among other objectives, HPR seeks to reduce both the number of individuals coming into contact with patients and also the number of different types of staff involved in the care process. Thus, the boundaries of the traditional professional territories or role demarcations which are replete in the NHS are called into question. Working directly with the staff delivering the service, new roles emerge which are radically different from traditional working practices. By making better use of the skills and experience of qualified nursing staff in support of medical staff and removing from them much of the hotel and other routine work which nurses have traditionally performed, the job of the professional nurse can be greatly enriched. The work that does not require extensive training and specialisation transfers to support workers who are able to combine the roles of nursing assistants, with some of the more routine functions of physiotherapy and occupational therapy, as well as hotel services, and administrative tasks. The support workers' roles are designed around the needs of a given specialty or programme of care such as orthopaedics or accident and emergency and undertake competency-based training programmes overseen by professional staff.

The benefits of HPR include increased productivity through reduced length of stay and a revised staffing profile with fewer administrative staff and some reduction in nursing skill mix. Unit costs can therefore be reduced while quality is either maintained or, as in most cases to date, enhanced. The experience for staff can be greater job satisfaction and, where dynamic reward strategies are being developed, a direct share in the benefits of lower cost.

References

Department of Health, *Hospital Episode Statistics*, vols 1 and 2, published annually.

Department of Health (1991) *NHS Workforce in England*, HMSO, London.

Watts, John (1994) *Presentation of Northern General Hospital*, Association of Healthcare Human Resource Managers Annual Conference, October.

Watts, J, Cochrane, D and Conroy, M (1993) 'What about the workers', *Health Services Journal*, 11 November: 28–9.

4.2

Right-sizing and Redundancy

Lew Swift

Right-sizing, or the process of tailoring the workforce to the needs of the organisation, has for one reason or another become an important aspect of management in the NHS. In the minds of the staff at least, it has become linked with redundancy and job loss. It is important to appreciate, however, that right-sizing is not always a negative process and actual job loss will not be the inevitable result. In the wider sense, it is best seen as a change management process out of which some people may be displaced and some may lose their jobs, but only as a last resort. Conversely, other jobs may be enhanced, providing enriched employment to the mutual benefit of both management and staff.

Therefore redundancy is not a single and simple issue to be applied in isolation but part of an overall approach to achieving the best fit of workforce to organisation. If redundancy does eventually become necessary, it should be approached positively, decisively and in a constructive way.

The context

First, a definition: to paraphrase section 81 of the Employment Protection (Consolidation) Act 1995, redundancy occurs when the employer ceases to carry on the business for which the employee was employed or ceases to carry on the business in the place where the employee was employed. It also occurs when a requirement for a particular kind of work either ceases or diminishes or a requirement for a particular kind of work in a particular place either ceases or diminishes.

Behind these rather impersonal words, however, lies a whole range of human hopes, fears and aspirations. Partly because of this and partly because of the wide range of subtleties involved, there is a high potential to get it wrong. On this issue, like so many others in the field of Human Resources, it is extremely important to do the simple things well. It is also necessary to work within a sound procedural framework.

The framework

Organisational change involving displacement and possible redundancy should be anticipated, at least to the extent of the production and maintenance of a clear procedure for dealing with the Human Resource issues. The approach should, as far as possible, be agreed with the staff through whatever local machinery exists for this purpose. The procedure should contain the following elements:

- **The scope.** This is a clear indication of those staff to be covered. If there are to be any excluded categories, temporary, casual or bank staff for example, these should be identified and listed. Such staff may not in any event be entitled to redundancy payments because of their length of service, but they may or may not be given the benefits of other aspects of the process.
- **Measures to avoid redundancy.** The whole point of the procedure is to try and avoid compulsory redundancy. Some of the measures outlined below can go a long way in this respect:

    (a) Elimination of uneconomic working practices wherever this is practicable.

    (b) Positive enforcement of the Trust's Retirement Policy.

    (c) Natural wastage, which will include restrictions on recruitment in affected and related staff groups/disciplines. This could involve the use of temporary contracts if a service has to be maintained for an interim period.

    (d) Positive commitment to retraining and redeployment of staff within the Trust.

    (e) Consideration of requests for volunteers for redundancy where this is appropriate and where management has identified a need for manpower reductions or other grounds for redundancy.

    (f) Identification in forward planning of any possible future redundancy situations, with an immediate action plan designed to minimise the effect on permanent staff.

    (g) Full discussion with staff interests whenever any possibility of future redundancies is foreseen.

- **Consultative agreements.** These provide for consultation with staff's side interests and also the way in which it should be carried out. If the consultation is to be only with recognised staff organisations and only within the context of an established machinery, the arrangements should be clearly set down and followed. Any other arrangements should be similarly identified.
- **Selection procedure.** If it becomes necessary to choose between staff, either for redeployment or for compulsory redundancy, some form of agreed approach is necessary. The usual first step is to invite those who wish to retire on a voluntary basis. After that if there still remains a problem, the criteria for selection must be established. The most common method for this is length of service, last in, first out (LIFO). While this is generally satisfactory and will often be applied by industrial tribunals in the absence of agreed criteria, it is not always the most reasonable method to use. It may not be entirely appropriate, for example, where new skills have to be acquired, or where there are measurably increased responsibilities. In such cases, it may be more acceptable to base the selection on experience, skills and knowledge, in preference to length of service. In any event, length of service begins to be less relevant when the employees in the group at risk all have long service and where the length of the service varies individually by a relatively small amount. Additionally, length of service can either be in that particular Trust or in the NHS as a whole and this should be established.
- **Payments.** This sets out the way in which compulsorily redundant or downgraded employees should be paid, usually by reference to the Whitley Council provisions or to alternative arrangements maintained by the Trust.
- **Appeals.** Aggrieved employees usually have facilities for appeal, either by way of the established grievance procedure or by using an alternative specifically set up to deal with these matters.
- **Redeployment.** An employee offered a new post to avoid redundancy should be provided with full details of the alternative employment. Section 84 of the Employment Protection (Consolidation) Act 1978 provides an entitlement for a trial period in the new job, of four weeks, or for a longer period as agreed between the parties.

It is also important to have rules about the way in which vacancies are filled by redeployed staff and to ensure that these are consistently applied. For example, employing managers should clearly understand that displaced staff should only be rejected for alternative employment if they are unsuitable for the new position. They should not be rejected simply because a better candidate may be found elsewhere. The procedure should demand that unsuitability' be shown to be justified and not simply contrived by an unwilling manager.

- **General assistance.** This should describe the arrangements which an employer might make to assist the situation generally. These could include paid time off to seek alternative employment, retraining/educational facilities, in-house 'job shops', financial advice and help with the production of applications and CVs.

The process

Right-sizing is a process of change management. As such, individuals will perceive it to be threatening to their status, power base, economic and social needs, and to their general well-being. Managers affecting the change will have few friends as a result, even amongst those who remain in the organisation.

This can be minimised however if the following principles are observed.

- **Ensure early involvement.** This will go a considerable way towards reducing resistance and easing the traumatic effect that the process produces. It implies a very heavy emphasis on communication, not least to counter the spread of misinformation and rumour. It helps to provide as much information as possible at this stage, it is also extremely important that managers be very clear about the objectives of the exercise and display a positive attitude about the anticipated outcomes.
- **Work at gaining commitment.** This is very difficult when staff fear the worst, but still a legitimate management objective. In the long term it is best achieved by joint agreement on the way in which the exercise is to be carried out. It comes from a common understanding on the change vehicles to be used and centres on the operation of the overall procedure. Producing and agreeing an organisational change procedure is one thing, making it work in practice can be quite another. Joint monitoring arrangements will help considerably so that when specific issues arise they can be dealt with quickly and to the satisfaction of both sides.

   Once the rules are agreed, they must be consistently applied, even if on occasions some managers concerned do not perceive a particular situation to be in their best interests. Industrial tribunals, if involved, will not look kindly on an idiosyncratic interpretation of an agreed approach. On the other hand, they tend to accept joint agreements in practice, even if these might vary from established norms, provided the outcome is generally fair and consistent.
- **Keep it simple.** In the emotional environment created by

organisational change and right-sizing, the potential for misunderstanding and confusion is immense. The need to do the simple things well is therefore paramount. The use of an organisational change procedure will throw up an endless series of problems, some of them quite subtle. Direct lines of communication, together with simple rules and simple steps will go a long way towards solving the problems in a satisfactory and helpful way.

- **Provide help.** This covers a number of activities. It means making sure that people understand why the process is necessary in the first place and that the jointly agreed procedure is there to minimise the effect on the staff concerned. It also means providing direct help with redeployment and accepting that this is a management obligation and not a privilege for the staff. Do also bear in mind that 'suitable alternative' employment is not an absolute concept but requires definition in the light of the needs and expectations of both parties. Post-redundancy help may be very useful and is something that good employers will do naturally as an essential aspect of their overall approach.

If right-sizing is necessary, bringing all of this together can be carried through successfully if the following steps are taken:

- Have a clear view of what you want to do and keep your eye on the objective throughout.
- Set out the new arrangements and identify those jobs no longer required. Decide on the extent to which surplus staff may be redeployed.
- Involve staff at an early stage, the earlier the better.
- Communicate like never before.
- Draw up a procedure to facilitate the changes, agree this with the staff. Apply it consistently.
- Deal with any casualties sympathetically but positively, offer help and assistance.
- Provide any retraining/reorientation required.

Achieving organisational change and right-sizing in an efficient and fair way is never an easy process. It can be iterative and messy. Those involved, particularly those to be displaced, will be fearful and resentful. Even those left in the organisation are likely to be lukewarm about the exercise. Given this degree of difficulty, it is not surprising that things sometime go wrong. Following some of the basic approaches set out above, however, can go a long way towards the achievement of a successful exercise.

4.3

Outsourcing: The Flexible Route to Success

Iain Herbertson

Contracting out is not a symptom of recession-hit times but a positive shift in working practices. Offering greater flexibility and efficient utilization of resources, it is fast becoming an integral part of increasing productivity and providing excellent quality service to patients.

When the Wiltshire Health Care NHS Trust began preparing for the Measles/Rubella immunization campaign in November 1994, it soon became clear that they did not have the number of clerical staff needed to support the initiative. With the programme running only for five weeks recruitment was out of the question. A different approach was needed. Instead of spending time solving the problem internally, the task of finding and supplying the 14 clerical staff required was contracted out to an employment services agency. Not only was the agency able to provide a fully trained team ready to go from day one, but in agreeing a fixed rate for the duration of the campaign the Trust was able to identify in advance how much the additional staffing would cost.

Wiltshire is just one of the many NHS Trusts now utilizing the very real benefits of outsourcing staff to achieve a more flexible working structure. This new approach not only helps them deliver an excellent quality of service but also facilitates more exacting cost control.

Pressure to cut costs while delivering better quality service has forced everyone to look at workplace structuring – and the Health Service is no exception. One of the key facets of this change has been a reassessment of the way human resources are organized and deployed. With labour as the most expensive commodity, a more flexible staffing strategy means increased productivity with reduced costs. More and more organizations in the public and private sectors are now turning to outsourcing as a solution to shift in demands.

Contracting out enables an organization to respond to and plan for changes in work patterns with the advantage of being able to predict the unpredictable in terms of cost and productivity. A professional and responsible contractor can be held to firm cost estimates against agreed specifications, with a direct and positive impact on budgeting and cost control. Whether redeployed from one department to another, or recruited for a particular duty, be they intensive care nurses or clerical support staff, means additional training, often the source of spiralling budgets in the past. By using staff as and when they are needed, and paying on the basis of skills rather than length of service, running overheads can be significantly reduced.

In an area such as the health service, where cost effectiveness can only be truly measured against the quality of the service provided, outsourcing staff ready to work from the moment they arrive not only maximizes productivity but ensures this quality of service can be delivered at a continuously high level of excellence.

But implications for productivity do not stop there. In assessing the workplace structure, many organizations have found that full-time staff are underused, spending time on duties for which they are overqualified. Using contract workers to fill either specialist roles or those peripheral to the main business, frees up permanent employees and enables them to put their skills to better use, so helping them to achieve greater motivation and job satisfaction as well as productivity. For managers, the practicalities of passing on more administrative duties are self-evident: delegating and outsourcing wherever possible releases more time to focus on key priorities such as identifying core skills and activities essential for survival and growth.

As more and more companies make use of outsourcing, its traditional role of emergency measure is also changing. Over the last few years the service has increasingly been utilized as a key adjunct to full-time staff and is now seen as an integral part of business strategy for long-term development.

Manpower has been at the sharp end of this shift in approach for some years. In the 1980s, their management skills were focused on recruitment, selection, assessment and training to provide highly productive temporary workers for sickness and holiday cover or meeting sudden workload peaks. Now they are increasingly working in partnership with companies at a strategic level and helping develop more flexible solutions to staffing requirements. The work varies in scale from supplying small numbers of administrative staff to staffing and managing complete (large-scale) mail room operations. Staff are supplied to work in a wide range of areas from medical to industrial positions and from driving to office support.

Restructuring staffing profiles

For example, four years ago Manpower contributed to the restructuring of the administrative support functions of a major service based company with tasks very similar to those within the Health Service. Analysis revealed that 85 per cent of costs was labour, 20 per cent above the benchmark ideal, and that there was no correlation between better quality and increased costs. Manpower was asked to look for ways to improve quality, gain greater flexibility and reduce costs.

A comprehensive study showed that staff spent a large part of the day on duties for which they were overqualified, there was a high turnover of staff due to promotion to other areas and a sense of being undervalued. Productivity was poor in relation to the number of people available and many resources were underused. By clarifying the skills available and ensuring tasks were matched to the appropriate person, permanent staff could be deployed more usefully in roles that fully utilized their extensive business understanding. The proportion of contract staff was increased including the introduction of evening and night-shift teams to make best use of the available technology. The contract staff were also trained in different tasks so they could be redeployed into different departments or locations, thus providing an increased flexibility.

As a result, productivity has increased by an average of 26 per cent each year for four years, quality of service (measured by users of the service) has improved by 12 per cent and general costs have been reduced by 25 per cent each year.

In addition to work at a strategic level, contracting out can also solve ongoing staffing issues, providing fully trained contract workers, to supplement the core work force. For example, Forth Valley College has been using Manpower to source additional administrative and clerical staff as required on a monthly basis since 1994. At Hairmyres Hospital, the company is providing temporary field staff to work across the different areas in the supplies section as well as clerical assistants, secretaries, personal assistants and storeroom staff throughout the hospital.

Staff training

Contracting out does not necessarily end with supply of staff. Many contractors offer experienced training services and will take responsibility for client staff development, especially in the areas of new technology. For example, Manpower were able to provide a northern acute hospital with a four-part programme to develop the skills of 30 secretarial staff and provide smooth transition from typewriter to word processing technology.

The hospital's new Trust status put a premium on high standards of cost-effective performance and the medical directorate wanted to benchmark quality in administration and customer service. Manpower identified the training needs of medical secretaries in both medical spelling and specialist terminology.

Further quality and productivity assessments were then made. Until then, it was impossible accurately to measure productivity levels and production costs, because benchmarking had not previously been available to the hospital. Manpower's predictive assessments thus provided the first opportunity accurately to determine the performance of this group. What was revealed was that the unit cost of producing a standard set of medical documents ranged from £4.05 to £8.65. There was no correlation between cost and age, ethnic origin, length of service, medical spelling ability, knowledge of medical terminology or clerical skill of the staff involved.

With this benchmark established, the staff were further trained in appropriate word-processing software to a consistent standard.

Integrating staff groups

As with any managerial system, the success of contracting out relies on the way in which it is used and integrated within an organization. The key to gaining maximum business benefit is threefold. First it is imperative to find the right business partner who can understand management needs and has a proven track record in supplying well-trained and high quality staff. Equally important is the manager's ability to identify and be clear about what those needs are and how best to put them into action. Establishing a successful working relationship also relies on preempting and addressing possible staffing issues. Under TUPE the law protects the pay and conditions of the new workforce, but the aim should be to go beyond the basic legal requirements to establish best practice. Industrial relations and union implications need to be thoroughly explored and managed. The responsibilities of the client company and contractor must be also be clearly identified, such as who will bear the financial responsibility for contract staff training and management.

Finally, if the increase in contract workers is to be viewed positively within the organization, it is vital that the impact they will have on permanent staff is fully considered. A key priority must be to decide how a temporary workforce is to work with the existing one. Is it to be complementary and analogous, or an entirely separate managed activity? Whatever the scenario, it is essential to draw up a realistic working strategy – before the staff arrive!

Communication across all areas of the permanent workforce is also crucial. The prime objectives in supplementing the workforce must be made clear if it is to be taken on board and accepted. Managers must have a clear picture of their particular areas of responsibility and more junior staff must understand the reasons for third-party sourcing, particularly if the decision to contract out follows a period of de-manning and restructuring – they need to know their jobs are not under threat. In communicating the motivation for this shift in policy it is also helpful to highlight the benefits: that increased flexibility can bring greater job security to workers, and, in some cases, even facilitate room for career development.

Finding the right outsourcing partner

To gain maximum benefit from outsourcing, it is critical to find the right business partner. Not all companies tendering will be the same and there are wide variations in style, ability, resources and experience. It is important to assess these differences before making a decision:

- Can they demonstrate a successful track record within your industry and do they have recognized quality accreditation? Ask what client references they can provide.
- Are they financially sound and able to complete the term of the contract?
- Do they know your business? How do they evaluate your needs? Do they ask relevant questions?
- Will they be able to offer a high level of pre-work training? If so, will this minimize the amount of internal training required from you and so keep costs down?
- What investment has the contractor made in its own training systems – do they have experience in providing customer training material if required?
- Will the temporary team to be supplied fit your corporate culture?
- Can they provide high-quality project management skills to manage an independent team if necessary? Is the company structured to provide local support and fast decision making? Do they have dedicated management to work on your account? Can they provide a total managed service if required?
- Check the availability of flexible contractual terms (eg hourly billing with cost advantages for early completion).
- Will they take on full employment responsibilities for the staff they provide?
- What guarantees and indemnities do they offer – a personal liability cover or fidelity bonding for example?
- What systems are in place to ensure confidentiality of your information?

A recent survey conducted by Manpower and the Institute of Management shows that 74 per cent of senior managers expect to see an increase in flexible working. The Institute of Personnel and Development predicts that by the end of the decade nearly 50% of workers will be working flexibly for leading organisations in the public and private sector.

4.4

Managing Staff Absence

Karen Baker

Why has absence management become so topical?

The growing interest in absence management relates primarily to sickness absence and over the past year staff sickness absence levels and the possibility of managing them more effectively have become issues of considerable debate in many hospitals. This does not seem to be because the incidence of sickness absence is increasing, but is probably a result of five (sometimes interrelated) factors:

1. Trust Boards identifying absence levels as an area offering potential savings without negative impact on patient care.
2. An increase in the amount of survey work (and published results) being carried out on absence within Trusts, and, indeed, across a broad range of organisations in the UK economy.
3. Some Trusts seeing an opportunity for linking locally negotiated 1995–6 pay settlements to productivity increases, including reductions in absence levels.
4. Growing media interest in NHS staff absence levels, their causes, and the action being taken by Trusts.
5. The government's abolition in April 1994 of reimbursement of Statutory Sick Pay to larger employers, who had previously been able to reclaim 80 per cent of the bill.

What are Trusts doing to reduce sickness absence levels?

Individual Trusts have introduced a wide range of initiatives aimed at reducing sickness absence levels. Several have reported on the methods they are adopting and their initial impressions of success or otherwise, but it would be true to say that few are at a stage where results over a sustained period can be assessed. Action seems to fall into five categories:

- 'carrots'
- 'sticks'
- health promotion
- improved record-keeping
- increasing responsibilities of line managers for absence control

'Carrots'

A number of Trusts have introduced reward schemes for employees with good or perfect attendance records. Included in these are additional annual leave or cash bonus arrangements, air miles incentive schemes, study tour schemes, and personal letters of appreciation from senior management. Costs and administrative input vary considerably, and some Trusts see the prime purpose of such schemes as being to reinforce a new culture of rewarding 'good behaviour' rather than driving down sickness rates.

'Sticks'

Rather fewer Trusts have reported in detail on their efforts to toughen up on those with poor sick records. However, it is clear that a considerable number of organisations are adopting a much firmer line than has been taken historically. Some are simply being more ruthless in terminating the contracts of long-term sick employees who have run out of sick pay and have little hope of returning to work (and where appropriate of encouraging retirement on grounds of ill health), or of treating employees with a history of persistent short-term absence through the disciplinary process where the problem seems to be one of conduct rather than capability. Others are negotiating with trades unions on linking reductions in absence levels to pay awards and/or reducing the amount or availability of occupational sick pay in certain circumstances.

Health promotion

Many Trusts are approaching absence management in a rather different way, by putting a great deal of effort into health promotion and education for their workforces, in the belief that this will produce gradual but sustained reductions in sickness absence levels. Linked with such campaigns is the introduction of a wide variety of services for staff, ranging from relaxation classes to chiropody to free eye tests. The development of confidential staff counselling services, either inhouse or via external agencies, seems to be a growing trend.

Improved record-keeping

One of the major stumbling blocks to effective absence management has traditionally been poor data collection. Many Trusts are in the process of overhauling staff absence record-keeping and looking at upgrades to their computer systems to enable absence information to be collected more effectively and accurately and analysed more speedily.

Line managers' responsibilities

Much published research suggests that the key factor governing the absence level in any given work area of any given organisation is the attitude of the relevant line manager towards absence management. Given this factor, many Trusts have been actively promoting absence management training, issuing fresh management guidelines on absence control, and introducing requirements such as the line manager interviewing every employee returning from sick leave and referring cases where assistance is required to the Occupational Health or Human Resources departments at an early stage.

How can the line manager tackle the problem of sickness absence?

The starting-point for any line manager has to be a thorough review of the facts. He or she needs to know how great a problem (if any) is being faced, and how the pattern and levels of sickness absence compare with other departments in the hospital and (if the data can be obtained) with similar departments in other hospitals.

Checklist

In your own area do you know:

- What percentage of working hours is being lost through sickness?
- Whether the situation is improving or deteriorating?
- Whether some groups of staff (by professional background, seniority, shift pattern etc) have worse records than others?
- What percentage of staff is going off sick each month?
- How long, on average, people are staying off when they report sick?
- How much of the absence is a result of long-term sickness?
- What are the most common incapacities causing sickness absence?
- What percentage of sickness is a direct result of industrial accidents?
- What were the direct costs of sickness absence over the last year?

Many Trusts are focusing almost exclusively on the financial consequences of high sickness absence levels, and these can indeed be worrying, but of equal concern to the line manager who is trying to run a quality service are the indirect effects of staff absence, including loss of expertise, disruption to continuity of patient care and time wasted in orientating temporary staff. Once he or she has established the nature and pattern of absence in his or her area an action plan needs to be drawn up to address problems. For any such action plan to prove successful it needs to be 'owned' by the people who are going to be putting it into effect – probably the first line managers – and it is therefore essential that they are involved in the process from the outset. If absence management is perceived as a high priority in the department this should be reflected in managers' objectives, with clear, realistic and quantifiable targets for improvement being identified.

Checklist

In putting together an action plan:

- Involve line managers and your director/clinical director from the outset.
- Analyse the situation carefully before developing the plan.
- Enlist the help of your Human Resources, Occupational Health and Health and Safety Advisers with planning your strategy and to advise on specific problems.
- Agree with line managers how you are going to communicate your action plan to staff. Remember that absence management is an emotive and sensitive area and decide from the outset whether/ how to involve trades unions/staff representatives in the initiative.
- Ensure that all line managers are conversant with your Trust's absence management guidelines and receive proper training in absence management (contact your training department for advice).
- Reflect targets for improvement in line managers' objectives – make sure that these are stretching but realistic and are tailored to the areas concerned.
- Ensure that the systems are in place for proper record-keeping and data analysis, if necessary seeking help from your Human Resources and Information Departments to rectify any deficiencies.

Future trends in absence management

Absence management is likely to remain a topical issue for some time to come, and as growing numbers of Trusts are able to evaluate and report on the outcomes of the initiatives they have introduced, the bank of empirical data on absence management should become much more useful and accessible.

There are a number of areas where Trusts are likely to focus growing attention over the coming months:

- The impact on employees of stress at work (following the widely reported recent case of Walker-v-Northumberland County Council, in which the High Court awarded substantial damages to a former social worker).
- Lifting handling injuries and the health of those who operate VDUs, as the full force of recent European legislation begins to hit employers.
- The effects of passive smoking, as individual employees who believe their health has suffered increasingly turn to the legal system for redress.

It is also possible that Trusts will begin to look more closely at areas of absence other than sickness and introduce new guidelines or strategies for their control. These might include unauthorised absence, compassionate leave, special leave and the rostering and management of annual and study leave.

Further reading

Absence surveys

The Confederation of British Industry (1994) *Managing Absence – In Sickness and In Health*, London: CBI.

The Institute for Employment Studies (1994) *Health at Work in the NHS: Key Indicators*, Brighton: IES University of Sussex.

Absence management initiatives – general

Advisory, Conciliation and Arbitration Service, Advisory Booklet Number 5 *Absence*, London: ACAS.

Cole, Andrew (1994) 'Absent trends', *Health Service Journal*, 4 May.

Cole, Andrew (1995) 'Absence makes the bills grow longer', *Health Service Journal*, 1 June.

Impact of changes to Statutory Sick Pay regulations

Watkins, Ivor (1994) 'Sick excuses for swanning around', *Personnel Management*, April.

Stress at work

Hall, Liz (1994) 'Pressure gauge', *Personnel Today*, 17 May.

Paxton, Roger and Axelby, Jackie (1994) 'Is stress your occupation?', *Health Service Journal*, 10 November.

Industrial accidents

Health and Safety Executive (1994) *The Costs to the British Economy of Work Accidents and Work-related Ill Health*, London: HSE.

National Occupational Standards in the Health Service

Chris McMahon, Kate Arter

and Isabelle Cook

The National Council for Vocational Qualifications (NCVQ) was established by the government following the publication of the White Paper *Working Together – Education and Training*, July 1986, which adopted the recommendations of the *Review of Vocational Qualifications in England and Wales*, (HMSO, April 1986).

It was the government's view that the system of qualifications in existence was overly complex and not related closely enough to the needs of employment. Only 40 per cent of the working population held vocational qualifications. International competition has intensified and, as a strong link exists between the competence of the workforce and a nation's economic competitiveness and prosperity, the National Council's primary task was to reform and rationalise the provision of vocational qualifications, which it has done through the creation of the National Vocational Qualification framework.

National Vocational Qualifications (NVQs) are available in England, Wales and Northern Ireland, while in Scotland there are Scottish Vocational Qualifications (SVQs). For the purpose of easy reference all vocational qualifications will be referred to as S/NVQs. The National Council has overseen the development of S/NVQs, which are employment-related qualifications, based on competence in the workplace and assessed to nationally agreed standards. General National Vocational Qualifications (GNVQs) were designed primarily to assist 16–19 year olds by offering an alternative form of education. GNVQs are available in three levels that are broadly based and allow

Royal College of Midwives Trust

Registered Charity No: 275261
15 Mansfield Street
London W1M 0BE
☎ 0171-872 5170

Education and Practice Development

Director: Louise I. Silverton, MSc, BSc, SRN, SCM, MTD
Business Manager: Shân Millie MA (Cantab)

Corporate Mission

As part of the **Royal College of Midwives,** our mission is defined as advancing the art and science of midwifery and specifically:

- to advise and negotiate with government departments and other bodies on all matters relating to the maternity services in the UK
- to arrange educational courses and afford opportunities for exchanging ideas on subjects connected with the profession
- to ensure the exchange of information and ideas on the profession of midwifery throughout the world and to improve international understanding
- to promote research by midwives on all aspects of their work and to initiate the preparation required to enable them to undertake such research

As the primary constituent of the **Royal College of Midwives Trust,** which is a registered charity, EPD has an additional responsibility to contribute to the development of midwifery to carry forward the profession for the public benefit.

Our aims

- To spearhead professional development for midwives
- To safeguard the quality and standards of midwifery education
- To provide leadership to the midwifery profession
- To fulfil the educational function of the Royal College of Midwives
- To pursue efficient and effective business management and business development to the benefit of the RCM and its members without compromising the organisation or the charitable status of.the RCM Trust
- To seek worthwhile and appropriate collaboration with partners in government, higher education, clinical practice and the international community

About the Royal College of Midwives

The RCM is the oldest and largest professional association for midwives in the world. Beginning life as the Matron's Aid Society in 1881, it became the Midwives Institute in 1886, the College of Midwives in 1941 and received its royal charter in 1947. The RCM is a membership organisation largely funded by subscription. Membership currently stands at over 37,000 individuals representing about 90% of the UK's practising midwives. There are 230 or so RCM branches throughout the UK and a national headquarters in each country. Providing leadership and support in all professional, educational and employment matters affecting midwives and midwifery, the College is closely linked with the five UK statutory bodies, Central Government, other medical Royal Colleges and women's and consumer groups.

Continuing Professional Development from the Royal College of Midwives*
1996 PROGRAMME

Do you need guidance on the cost and other issues around Professional Updating for Midwives?

Are you looking for high-quality, unique educational opportunities for you and your midwife colleagues?

The 1996 Professional Development Programme from the RCM: ✓ takes the guesswork out of professional updating ✓ gives you access to innovative events that anticipate future needs ✓ puts you and your midwives in the bigger picture

Selected Highlights for 1996

April	Workforce Planning
May	Evidence-based Practice
June	Genetic Screening
August	Midwifery Care & Disadvantaged client
September	Workforce Planning
October	Neonatal Update
November	Parenthood Education
December	Midwifery & Changing Environment

Want a closer look? Contact us at the address and telephone numbers below for a <u>FREE</u> copy of the Programme Brochure, which also includes suggestions on how to plan updating.

Professional Development Programme 1996
Education and Practice Development
Royal College of Midwives Trust
15 Mansfield Street, London W1M 0BE
☎ 0171-872 5170   Fax: 0171-872 5101

Contributing to and leading professional development of midwives for the future of the profession, the maternity service and the general public.

*The Royal College of Midwives' educational and practice development mission is fulfilled by the Royal College of Midwives Trust, a registered charity.

progression into further education, either academic or vocational. By undertaking a specific GNVQ a person would acquire a background knowledge base and the capability but not the competence, in an occupational area. The GNVQ that reflects health care is Health and Social Care.

Competence in work activities should be recognised, however, and wherever it is acquired the framework can encourage individuals to accredit this and to continue learning and updating working practices throughout life. S/NVQs are seen as the future currency of the labour force, allowing employees to obtain a national qualification based on National Occupational Standards.

The Government White Paper *Education and Training in the 21st Century*, May 1991, made clear the intention that GNVQs and NVQs will eventually replace other vocational qualifications and become the main national provision for education and training. It is the overall aim of the government that by the year 2000, 60 per cent of the workforce be qualified to S/NVQ level 3, advanced GNVQ or 2 GCE A level standard, and that 30 per cent of the workforce have a vocational, professional, management or academic qualification at NVQ level 4 or above (National Advisory Council for Education and Training, 1995).

Structure and process of vocational qualifications

Lead Bodies, funded by the Employment Department and known as Occupational Standards Councils, undertake a functional mapping and analysis of specific roles within the sector and develop occupational standards that are linked together to form an award reflecting a specific occupational area. These work-based qualifications cover the breadth and depth of all the various occupations within the Health Service. The breadth includes the occupational work activities and can involve functional mapping, while the depth is dependent on the level of the qualification. (See Tables 4.7.1 and 4.7.2.) An ideal situation would be when all employees of an organisation could be offered the opportunity to gain an S/NVQ. The benefits to the individual and to the organisation would be increased motivation, allowing people to develop to their full potential and becoming a more efficient workforce, resulting in an increased standard of client care.

The National Health Service as the largest employment sector in the UK, offers many vocational opportunities. Many NHS Trusts are working towards the 'Investors in People' standard and S/NVQs, as they are based on standards of good practice, help to ensure that services provided to clients are of high quality and enable the training needs of employees to be identified.

When selecting the appropriate S/NVQ for an employee, it is

Table 4.5.1 *Areas of occupation*

Occupation	Level	Awarding bodies
Administration	1, 2, 3, 4	BTEC, C&G, RSA
Care: Health Care Assistants	2, 3	JAB (C&G, CCTESW)
Catering and Hospitality	1, 2, 3	BTEC, HCTC
Child Care and Education	2, 3	BTEC, CACHE, JAB
Customer Service	3	BTEC, C&G, HCTC
Engineering	1, 2, 3, 4	C&G, ETA
Maintenance and Estates	3, 4	IMBM, C&G
Management	4, 5	BTEC, HMC, ITD, OU
Operating Department Practice	2, 3	JAB
Physiological Measurement	3	BTEC
Training and Development	3, 4	BTEC, C&G, ITD, RSA, PEI

Notes:

BTEC	Business & Technology Education Council
CACHE	Including CEYA & NNEB, Council for Awards in Children's Care and Education
C&G	City & Guilds of London Institute
CCETSW	Central Council for Education & Training in Social Work
ETA	Electricity Training Association
HCTC	Hotel, Catering Training Company
HMC	Henley Management College
IMBM	Institute of Maintenance & Building Management
JAB	Joint Awarding Bodies: C&G and CCTESW
OU	Open University Validation Services
PEI	Pitman's Examinations Institute

Source: NCVQ (1994–5)

imperative that the award and the relevant units of competence reflect the specific work area of that employee. As S/NVQs are competence based, it is necessary for the candidate to have the opportunity to perform the role in order to gather the necessary evidence for assessment. Thus the principle of work-based qualifications arises from work-based performance.

The NCVQ National Database gives details of the current awards, including units of competence and possible routes for progression and transfer. This information can be used when advising employees about NVQ opportunities. The Central Council for Education and Training in Social Work (CCETSW) maintain a database for the awards in Care – CareMatch NVQ Database (see References). An alternative method

NATIONAL BOARD FOR NURSING, MIDWIFERY AND HEALTH VISITING FOR SCOTLAND (NBS)

Powers

The National Board for Scotland (NBS) was constituted in July 1983 as the statutory body responsible for the education and training of nurses, midwives and health visitors in Scotland. National Boards in England, Wales and Northern Ireland, and a United Kingdom Central Council (UKCC), were also established at that time.

The Nurses, Midwives and Health Visitors Act 1992 amended the Board's statutory responsibilities and led to the reconstitution of NBS as an executive Non Departmental Public Body, with prescribed regulatory functions in relation to the education and training of the nursing professions in Scotland.

Role

The NBS role in education in Scotland is to:
- ensure UKCC standards for education are met
- gather and disseminate information pertaining to the development of standards
- support approved institutions in the development of internal quality assurance mechanisms
- gather and disseminate information pertaining to good practice in education
- advise on changing educational needs and areas for development
- advise purchasers of education and prospective students on available courses and options for qualifying
- evaluate approved courses
- gather and disseminate statistical information relating to educational developments and resources.

The Board also provides a careers information service and is a clearing house for applications for training.

Commitments to Quality

NBS is committed to ensuring consistency, flexibility, responsiveness and speed in relation to its services to the public and the professions.

NBS is also committed to demonstrating that the regulation of professional education contributes not only to the quality of the education experienced by individual students but also to the quality of care delivered in the Scottish Health Service.

A research and developments programme underpins the Board's commitment to effective education and informs the Board's future work.

Working Together

The role of NBS is to develop and ensure professional standards of education and training in Scotland. The regulation of educational matters is closely linked to the regulation of matters concerning registration and professional conduct, which are the sole responsibility of the UKCC. While NBS and UKCC are separate corporate bodies, their functions are inter-related with regard to the regulation of professional education and they work together, in the public interest, to set and ensure standards of professional preparation for nurses, midwives and health visitors.

NBS collaborates not only with UKCC but also with purchasers and providers of education, other awarding bodies, SHEFC and HEQC and the professional organisations. NBS works in the context of health care in Scotland and is accountable to the Secretary of State for its use of public funds to ensure the protection of the public by the regulation of professional education.

Through its Professional Officer contacts, committee and task group membership and the Register of Experts, NBS maintains a wide network of people working with and for the nursing professions in Scotland.

Supplied courtesy of Lyn Mitchell, Chief Executive

FOR INFORMATION ON:

- **Requirements for Education and Practice**

- **Developing Educational Standards**

- **Professional Validation of Courses**

- **Careers and Courses Available**

- **Research and Development Projects**

- **Educational Trends and Statistics**

NBS

CONTACT US AT:

22 Queen Street, Edinburgh EH2 1NT.
Telephone: 0131 226 7371
Facsimile: 0131 225 9970

NATIONAL BOARD FOR
NURSING, MIDWIFERY
AND HEALTH VISITING
FOR SCOTLAND.

Table 4.5.2 *Levels of competence*

Level	Competence, which involves the application of:
1	Knowledge in the performance of a range of varied work activities, most of which may be routine or predictable.
2	Knowledge in a significant range of varied work activities, performed in a variety of contexts. Some of the activities are complex or non-routine and there is some individual responsibility and autonomy. Collaboration with others, perhaps through membership of a work group or team, may often be a requirement.
3	Knowledge in a broad range of varied work activities, performed in a wide variety of contexts, most of which are complex and non-routine. There is a considerable responsibility and autonomy and control or guidance of others is often required.
4	Knowledge in a broad range of complex, technical or professional work activities, performed in a wide variety of contexts and with a substantial degree of personal responsibility and autonomy. Responsibility for the work of others and the allocation of resources is often present.
5	A significant range of fundamental principles across a wide and often unpredictable variety of contexts. Very substantial personal autonomy, often significant responsibility for the work of others and for the allocation of substantial resources feature strongly, as do personal accountability for analysis and diagnosis, design, planning, execution and evaluation.

Source: NCVQ (1995)

can be undertaken by Skillscan, which is an activity checklist that helps to compare what the employee does at work with the units of competence required for a specific S/NVQ (NVQ Communications). A 'job competence model' should relate to: task performance and management, contingency management and job role environment. (NCVQ, 1995)

There may be times when it would be appropriate for an employee to attain relevant core skills before undertaking an occupational specific S/NVQ, for example, Communications, should English be a second language. Core skills are available in levels 1–5, underpinning most qualifications: Communications, Application of Number, Information Technology, Personal Skills — Working with Others, Personal Skills — Improving Own Learning and Performance, Problem Solving.

The structure of an S/NVQ consists of a number of units of competence, approximately 10–12, which describe the required competence. Some units within an award are mandatory, sometimes called core units, while others are optional and relate to specific roles. The unit is then divided up into elements, approximately 2–4, which describe the competence to be undertaken, based on an outcome specifying what the candidate can do. Each element comprises *performance criteria*, which are benchmarks against which the candidate is assessed, and a *range statement* through which the breadth or scope of an element is defined.

Methods of assessment can be dependent on the level of the S/NVQ. For instance, at level 5 there will be a need for analysis and resynthesis of knowledge requiring written questions, assignments and projects; while at lower levels naturalistic observation, direct questions, case studies and review of work, to demonstrate both performance and knowledge evidence.

On completion of all the required mandatory and optional units within an award an NVQ can be awarded to the candidate. There may be times when individual units are recorded, for example the Training and Development (TDLB) standards that are applicable to Assessors and Verifiers.

Total quality management

Quality assurance is built into the S/NVQ framework with the overall responsibility resting with the National Council for Vocational Qualifications (NCVQ) or Scottish Vocational Education Council (SCOTVEC). It ensures the quality of assessment throughout, from NCVQ to the candidate. (See Table 4.7.3.)

The focus is the National Occupational Standards, developed by specific Lead Bodies/Occupational Standards Councils, which enable a candidate to be assessed using identical criteria, whether they are in Cardiff, Bournemouth or Aberdeen. In order to prove their own competence, those involved with assessment and verification should hold one or more of the following certificates, as appropriate:

- Assessors — D32 Assess Candidate's Performance; D33 Assess Candidate Using Differing Sources of Evidence.
- Internal Verifiers — D34 Internally Verify the Assessment Process.
- External Verifiers — D35 Externally Verify the Assessment Process.

The Statutory Body in England which

- approves institutions and validates education programmes

- monitors the development and quality of the approved education programmes

- promotes educational quality and audit

- ensures the implementation of the education, training and practice implications arising from Government health care policy

- contributes to the development of national and local educational / health care policy

- undertakes educational research and development

- provides career advice and guidance

- disseminates statistical data to aid workforce planning

- facilitates the development of the professions to respond positively to changing health care demand

English National Board for Nursing, Midwifery and Health Visiting

"...ensuring that practitioners have the knowledge and skills to meet the needs of patients and clients and the skills to respond positively to change in health care demand."

English National Board for Nursing, Midwifery and Health Visiting

Chairman:
Maureen Theobald

Chief Executive:
Anthony P. Smith

Head Office
Victory House
170 Tottenham Court Road
London WIP 0HA

Telephone 0171 388 3131
Fax 0171 383 4031

English National Board for Nursing, Midwifery and Health Visiting

The key function of the Board is to approve educational institutions and to validate education programmes leading to qualifications in nursing, midwifery or health visiting. The Board ensures that the educational institutions it approves conduct programmes which equip practitioners with the skills to meet the heath care needs of patients and clients throughout England.

The Board's education staff work with each educational institution to ensure that high quality, cost effective education programmes are developed to meet the needs for skilled practitioners in a rapidly changing health service. The Board has been instrumental in influencing the development and delivery of continuing professional education for nurses, midwives and health visitors.

The most significant impact of this influence has been:

- the establishment of systems to credit prior learning, in particular that achieved through practice
- the introduction of modular patterns of education provision
- the development of core modules to increase shared learning opportunities

The introduction of these key factors has reduced overlap and duplication. This has resulted in an increase in the cost effectiveness and the value for money obtained from investments made in continuing education for nurses, midwives and health visitors.

Research and development

The Board has an active R&D programme which is responsive to central NHS initiatives. The Board's R&D function supports its educational policy development designed to improve the quality of nursing, midwifery and health visiting education.

National resources

An important part of the Board's work is to provide a range of support mechanisms for educators, practitioners and managers. Among these are:

- **Health Care Database**, a comprehensive computerised information service about nationally available learning materials.
- **ENB Campus**, an on-line computer service giving access to national databases.
- **Open learning resource**, includes available open learning materials for review and selection.
- **Conference programme**, provides a national forum for managers, educators and practitioners.
- **Publications**, relate to contemporary issues in nursing, midwifery and health visiting education as well as statutory guidance.
- **ENB NEWS**, the Board's quarterly newsletter keeping everyone up to date with the Board's activities.

Quality initiatives

The Board has produced and disseminated comprehensive guidelines for educational audit within the approved educational institutions. These guidelines include examples of good practice and advice on the development of quality frameworks. The Board has pioneered the development of a number of audit tools designed to obtain feedback regarding its own performance.

Collaborative working

The Board's national overview of education, training and practice issues place it in a unique position to contribute to and influence changes occurring within the health service and higher education. The Board contributes to national and local health care policy development and to securing the implementation of the education, training and practice implications.

Careers information

The Board provides the main source of information in England about careers in nursing, midwifery and health visiting. Extensive communication networks exist with local education careers advisers to ensure that advice is available to school leavers. Networks have been established with the employment service through the office of the Chief Nursing Consultant to ensure that information is available to potential mature entrants.

Local Offices:

BRISTOL
English National Board for Nursing, Midwifery and Health Visiting
1st Floor, Narrow Quay House
Prince Street
Bristol BS1 4PP

Tel: 01179 259143
Fax: 01179 251800

CHESTER
English National Board for Nursing, Midwifery and Health Visiting
BSP House
Station Road
Chester CH1 3DR

Tel: 01244 311393
Fax: 01244 321140

LONDON
English National Board for Nursing, Midwifery and Health Visiting
Victory House
170 Tottenham Court Road
London W1P 0HA

Tel: 0171 388 3131
Fax: 0171 383 4031

YORK
English National Board for Nursing, Midwifery and Health Visiting
East Villa
109 Heslington Road
York YO1 5BS

Tel: 01904 430505
Fax: 01904 430309

Table 4.5.3 *Total quality management*

NCVQ/ SCOTVEC	Accredits and monitors the Awarding Bodies, ensuring that they have adequate resources and systems in place to ensure quality, best practice, cost effectiveness and fitness for purpose and the support from employers and providers. Receives reports from Awarding Bodies.
Awarding Bodies	Accredits, approves and monitors Centres, ensuring sufficient and competent assessors and verifiers are available to deliver S/NVQs effectively. They ensure there are workable systems, adequate resources, quality assurance and control and equal opportunities for assessment. This is undertaken by an External Verifier appointed by the Awarding Body who reports back to them and is supported by the Awarding Body.
Centre	Set up quality assurance systems to ensure equal opportunities, administer assessment and internal verification by appointing, training and monitoring Internal Verifiers and Assessors. Records completed units with the Awarding Body and prepares an annual report.
Internal Verifier	Monitors and supports the Assessors in the workplace, samples completed units to ensure all performance and range statements are covered. Reports to Centre Co-ordinator.
Assessor	Supports the candidate, plans assessment and assesses the candidate in the workplace, ensuring all evidence is relevant, authentic, current, sufficient and of an agreed quality and variety. Reports to the Internal Verifier and Centre Co-ordinator.
Candidate	The candidate is responsible for maintaining the quality of their evidence and, so doing, working to National Occupational Standards, thus enhancing the quality of client care, at the same time developing themselves in their role and within a team.

As all those involved with the assessment and verification process are certificated, a standardised system will evolve and be maintained, thereby ensuring total quality throughout the system.

National occupational standards and the vocational qualifications they underpin are still relatively new and during the initial implementation phase they have attracted some criticism related to the resource intensive nature of criterion-referenced assessment and standardisation in terms of quality monitoring. However, as expertise in making them work has developed it has become apparent that S/NVQs make a considerable, positive and cost-effective impact on standards of care delivery. The focus for S/NVQ development to date has been, unfortunately in some respects, on the lower levels of the NCVQ framework, where an urgent need had been identified. Increasingly, however, professional organisations, higher education and occupational standards councils are beginning to turn their attention to the higher levels (4 and 5), the advent of which is seen as highly relevant with the UK's rapidly changing care system.

In 1994 the Care Sector Consortium undertook a functional analysis of the entire care sector. The functional map of health and social care will result in a set of performance outcomes which, taken together, describe performance requirements of the sector. The final report is awaited. National occupational standards for such health professionals as medical staff could not only be used to inform initial professional education but also to provide the framework for Continuing Vocational Education (CVE). An improved structure for CVE will help to ensure consistency in research-based practice across the UK within clinical specialities.

The emergence of higher level standards will present opportunities for NHS Trusts, Higher Education and Training and Enterprise Councils to work in partnership. Not only would initiatives of this kind be valuable for clinical practice but they would also provide a framework for quality monitoring and contract negotiation. Effective use of the vocational qualification framework would assist employers to develop strategies for staff development, which would enhance their care provision and maintain standards of good practice, while enabling employees to fulfil their job potential.

References

CareMatch NVQ Database, Concord Video & Film Council Ltd, 201 Felixstowe Road, Ipswich, Suffolk IP3 9BJ

HMSO (1986) *Review of Vocational Qualifications in England and Wales: A Report by the Working Group*, April, HMSO, London.

National Advisory Council for Education and Training (1995) *National Educational Targets*, Department for Education and Training, London.

NCVQ (1994–5) 'Accredited NVQs', *The NVQ Monitor*, Winter, NCVQ, London.

NCVQ (1995) *NVQ Criteria and Guidance*, NCVQ, London.

NVQ Communications, HMSO, London.

White Paper (1986) *Working Together – Education and Training*, July,

HMSO, London.

White Paper (1991) *Education and Training in the 21st Century*, May, HMSO, London.

White Paper (1994) *Competitiveness: Helping Business to Win*, HMSO, London.

4.6

The Changing Face of Management Qualifications: Choosing the Most Suitable Course

Christina Townsend

Every week, six nurses meet to review progress on their BTEC programme in a medium-sized NHS Trust. They have no tutor and no lecturer. They have each designed their own learning contracts, on topics ranging from budget control to staff management, IT to assertiveness. The members of the team monitor each other's progress. They set each other's criteria for success and challenge each other's achievements. They are each other's sternest critics and strongest supporters.

There are of course some external controls. This self-managed team has had its programme approved by experts and an external verifier makes stringent checks on standards. But at the last visit the verifier's verdict was overwhelmingly positive: 'This is what education and learning is all about.' Most significantly, however, at the very same Trust where this state-of-the-art programme is in progress, some students are still attending traditional day-release courses at the local university and others are on structured in-house programmes led by specialist tutors.

What the Trust is demonstrating is how to make full use of what has become a very wide spectrum of management training opportunities for NHS staff. It is recognising the key message of this chapter – that the right course depends entirely on the specific needs of the person, the post and the organisation as a whole. What follows is a set of key guidelines, or criteria, by which managers can find their way towards the right course for the right person at the right time.

CIPFA

THE ONLY PROFESSIONAL ACCOUNTANCY QUALIFICATION OFFERING SPECIFIC TUITION ON NHS MATTERS.

CIPFA is the respected accountancy qualification for finance staff in health care. Supported by a wide range of products and services evolved to meet the needs of the public sector it covers-

- Financial Management and commercial accounting
- Costing and resource management
- Budgeting and forecasting
- Contracting and tendering
- Tax and treasury management
- Developing purchasing policies

For more information on what CIPFA can offer you and your colleagues contact the Marketing Communicatio Unit at CIPFA, 3 Robert Street, Lond WC2N 6BH or telephone 0171 895 8823 Extension 262

The training spectrum

Today's training world is complex and challenging, but it is also full of opportunity. In fact, during the 1990s, choosing the right management course has become a skill – or a competence – in its own right.

The advent of the internal market in health care has led to the emergence of a separate training marketplace where universities, colleges, consultants, training companies and the NHS all compete keenly to meet the needs of staff. Where once there were a few relatively simple and well-understood, health-related management courses, there are now proliferating training providers and a wide range of courses and other packages. There are also many more people looking for training, especially from professional health service backgrounds.

The straightforward three-level structure of certificate, diploma and masters courses has been partly overgrown by short courses, work-based training projects and NVQs, most now available in a number of modes – full-time, part-time or open learning. But, as in any market, profusion need not mean confusion. The key to finding the right choice lies as ever in knowing precisely what you are looking for.

As most managers will have found, the classic mistakes involve sending staff on courses that cover old ground and fail to deal with their specific needs – or conversely sending them on courses that cover only part of the ground and fail to give the trainee the range of learning required. A useful rule of thumb is to apply three steps in each choice of training provision:

- defining the training need as precisely as possible;
- searching and negotiating to secure training to meet the need;
- ensuring that the training leads to a nationally recognised qualification if possible and appropriate.

Defining the need

Defining training needs requires the assessment of the needs of the individual as a person and as a postholder – as a manager who will need a range of basic and specific skills during a career, and as an operative needing particular aptitudes to carry out an assigned role in the organisation. There are also needs for succession planning, looking to the body of skills needed by an organisation and ensuring that all are accounted for. The individual's needs then need looking at in terms of the kind of experience and environment which will best enable them to learn.

When the NHS reforms first started to take effect, the instinctive response was to ensure that individual managers were ready for anything the new culture threw at them. Hence, many were sent on general management courses to ensure they had their own personal set of transferable business skills.

The NHS has proved a leader in providing generic health management courses, for example through its training scheme for initial entrants and the 'Managing Health Services' programme of basic management skills. But as the reforms have bedded down, and the initial rush to prepare people for management roles has subsided, a more considered approach has emerged.

As Dr Alison Baker of the Institute of Health Services Management observes:

> The most noticeable change has been a shift of emphasis from individual skill training to organisational development. As health service trusts have begun to formulate clearer organisational objectives and to think more strategically about organisational performance there has been a concern to link management development into these objectives.

Sometimes this will still mean sending an employee on a full length academic-based general management course – where a wide range of skills with substantial underpinning knowledge is required – but increasingly it means instead tailoring learning to specific tasks that the individual is going to fulfil. This is partly responsible for the division and sub-division of management courses into shorter programmes, the growth of NVQs and the use of individual units, modules, projects and informal activities.

The chapters of this Handbook reflect many of the new areas in which dedicated training is needed – purchasing, quality, financial information, customer care. The new reforms of 1995–6, replacing the RHAs with regional Management Executive bases and merging FHSAs with the districts, will give rise to new specific needs – business process re-engineering, career management, team building and information management among them.

A further realignment of training needs is coming about with the advent of care in the community and new ways of delivering services. The danger in this process is that of creating a compartmentalised service with consequent breakdowns in trust and understanding. Hence 'defining the need' as a concept should embrace the specific practical needs of the individual but also his or her need to understand and do business with their professional 'neighbours'.

For example the IHSM's Medicine for Managers course, or its counterpart – a broad introduction to management for clinicians – are elements of a holistic approach to training, creating mutual understanding and bridging the artificial divide between professionals in medicine and management.

These are some accepted tools for defining needs – including job descriptions, sets of competence standards from bodies like the Management Charter Initiative or the NHSTD, self-assessment guides and questionnaires. Defining needs in terms of learning modes and styles is an important concomitant of identifying the training content. Will a person work best on a full-time course? With others or alone? Based at work, or at college or university?

Finally, though it is not theoretically part of the individual's needs profile, the type of programme will also be governed by the mode of study that the employer is prepared to accept – full or part time, day release or open learning. Realistically, this will always be a consideration, but it should remain secondary to the individual's needs if training is to fulfil its main purpose. This does not mean failing to tackle the issue head-on. For example, one should look at the opportunity cost of projects not undertaken while a manager is in training as an aspect of the cost of the training itself.

These are the questions to answer before starting to look at the range of available provision – and if answered fully, they will enable the alternatives to be whittled down fairly speedily.

Securing the training

Armed with one's specification for training, the natural first ports of call remain the local or Trust NHS training manager and nearby universities and colleges. Other providers, such as consultants and independent trainers, can be contacted directly or through the training manager.

The key to a successful outcome at this point is to stick to one's specification and not be persuaded to accept more or less than you require. In other words, do not be frightened to negotiate with a training provider – the education world these days is just as much driven by the idea of customer care as that of health. And here, you are the customer.

The first priority is to match the need you have defined to the content of the programme. Does it require a full- or part-time course as traditionally envisaged, or one of the newer tailored short courses, single units, open or distance learning programmes, or projects.

For example, it may be that a manager's urgent needs will be best served by working towards one or two elements of an NVQ – rather than the whole qualification. It may be that a unit or module from one course needs to be bolted on to another in order to serve a particular individual's purposes.

It may be that formal training is not really what is needed at all. Increasingly managers are discovering that new initiatives such as mentoring, research projects, and self-help groups are very useful in some areas – even though they do not usually provide qualifications –

while other topics demand much more traditional learning approaches.

The provider should be able to offer a clear and complete statement of what the course will provide. BTEC has argued in a recent submission to the government that higher education institutions should be required to produce statements setting out the outcomes of each course – to distinguish between similar sounding courses at different centres. MBAs would be a prime example of the need for such statements.

Mode of study

Keeping the mode of study secondary to its fitness becomes crucial here. If the most suitable course is only available on a day-release basis, the manager has a simple choice between leaving the need unmet and gaining a greater quantity of work in the present, or meeting the training need and seeing a higher quality in the future.

However, having broken down the training needs into specifics, it may become apparent that they can better be met, for example, by a work-based training project, which can be fitted around existing duties – in conjunction with a distance learning course and occasional evening seminars.

Assessment

Assessment is another deciding factor. Will the individual be best served by the experience of problem-solving under pressure in an exam, or by the discipline of coursework? Or will it be helpful to make one's own work the focus of assessment in an NVQ, which demands a portfolio of evidence to demonstrate competence.

Choosing the course

Choosing between similar programmes in terms of content, mode and assessment becomes a question of looking at practical factors.

Quality
Ask to see success and drop-out rates, examples of work, schedules of lecturers, backgrounds of students. What are the entry requirements? What are the opportunities for progression? What links exist with employers? What practitioners contribute to hands-on courses? What visiting experts lend authority to academic ones? Ask to speak to former students and tutors.

Learning materials and methods
What introduction to study skills is given? How well stocked and

accessible is the library? What IT is used? How accessible are the tutors out of teaching time?

Value for money
Assess the cost in terms of replacement staff as well as fees. Take into account the opportunity cost of losing the manager if training is off-site. Then look at what the fee includes — tuition? examinations? revision classes? residential sessions?

Practical factors
Look at commonsense indicators — is clear and comprehensive information provided? Are times and places set out? Are the training staff helpful and responsive? Are transport links good?

When managers come back from courses, it is important to make sure the organisation gets the full benefit of what they have achieved. It is important to examine what has been learned, ensure that it is applied as fully as possible, and to spread the benefits by enabling those recently trained to share their new-found skills and knowledge with others.

Confirming the achievement

A separate and distinctive criterion in choosing a course is the qualification it leads to. The NHS has always prized nationally recognised qualifications — and rightly so.

Although the main value of any course is the skills and knowledge learned, the recognition of that achievement is important in a number of ways. It provides a way of demonstrating what an individual has achieved. It acts as a spur to achievement. It provides a yardstick against which managers can define needs. And it enables individuals to progress in their careers through the conferring of a set of letters and numbers which indicate that certain aptitudes have been acquired.

Such recognition comes through gaining a qualification awarded by a university, a professional body or a national awarding body such as BTEC.

The aim of bodies like BTEC is to provide qualifications that are recognised nationally and internationally — thereby setting the goals for training that enable people to reach the required levels. BTEC aims to provide a range of qualifications from the more traditional and general, like the Certificates and Diplomas in Management Studies and the HNC in Caring Services (Managing Care), to the more modern and specific, such as its diploma in total quality management. Nowadays the good news is that managers do not have to go on lengthy courses to achieve national qualifications.

NVQs, in particular, allow for the recognition of particular detailed competencies, like 'justify proposals for expenditure on projects' or 'monitor procedures for media library management'. This recognition comes irrespective of the training or experience that has led to its acquisition. This puts the emphasis on the workplace, thereby creating more flexibility and the opportunity to work towards a series of goals over time, rather than enlisting for the more traditional course.

A subsidiary but key factor in choosing a course leading to a qualification is the scope for gaining access or gaining exemptions from early stages by establishing credit for previous courses or experiences. Many courses now have credit ratings on the Credit Accumulation and Transfer System (CATS), subscribed to by most higher education institutions.

There are occasions on which a training need will not relate to a qualification, but in most cases such recognition serves the needs of the individual, in terms of personal satisfaction, and of the organisation through providing an aid to recruiting, assessing and evaluating the contribution of each employee.

Today's scope for measuring and assessing skills and knowledge makes for the development of more detailed individual profiles than ever before. Hence the process comes full circle. Training NHS managers has become more complex – but it has its rewards. As the panorama of qualifications and credit systems gradually provides a more comprehensive picture of the workforce, so training needs can be more accurately pinpointed. Then, in turn, more relevant programmes can be offered and the quality of training – and thus of management itself – can steadily improve.

PART FIVE

MANAGING INFORMATION

ITT London & Edinburgh

It's about quality of life.
It's about understanding your needs.
It's about protection and prevention...
...it's about our Commitment to Care.

Commitment
to Care

- An Insurance and Risk Management Programme
designed to help Trusts help themselves.

Ask your broker to tell you more.

**BRITISH INSURANCE INDUSTRY AWARDS
"UNDERWRITER OF THE YEAR"**
Providing innovative solutions
to customer requirements

The Battle for Better Healthcare

Your central aim as a Trust manager will be the enhancement of patient care within your hospital. Your management skills will provide many of the solutlons to the plethora of issues which face today's busy Trusts, but you may not be prepared for the enemy which lurks along every corridor and behind every ward door.

This foe can strike when you least expect it and can have a devastating potency. It is commonly known as RISK.

What can you do?

- To prepare for the onslaught of RISK you must identify all of the hazards, clinical and non-clinical, insurable and uninsurable, to which your hospital is exposed.

- You will then have to evaluate the consequences, direct and indirect, of controlling or not controlling these hazards, apply your decisions and then monitor them.

First of all however, you need to develop a strategy, for this is a war!

- You need to impose your will upon the enemy and dictate your terms.

- Be proactive rather than reactive.

- The war will not be won by the command staff alone, but only by solid input from all staff.

- Once developed, ensure that all your staff are familiar with it. Without direction their efforts can be disparate and wasted.

Follow the strategy, make available the resoures, seek expert advice to keep the enemy at bay, and you will readily limit your losses.

Ignore the hidden enemy at your peril!

CREDIT

By Terry Flaherty, Senior Risk Surveyor (Health Sector) of ITT London & Edinburgh whose 'Commitment to Care' product offers a comprehensive Insurance and Risk Management programme designed specifically for NHS Trusts.

5.1

Casemix: Where to From Here?

Alastair Lord

Introduction

This chapter contends that the initial fast pace of implementation of
casemix systems outstripped the ability of many Trusts to make the
requisite organisational changes, placed high demands on the quality
of their data and systems, and preceded the ability of suppliers to
provide stable and reliable products. Clearly, this has resulted in
widespread disappointment.

Now that the dust is settling, the challenge is to achieve the
benefits originally envisaged without throwing away the casemix
baby with the bath water. This chapter attempts to find a path for
Trusts to take, based on the author's experience of assisting several
Trusts to procure and implement casemix systems.

History: where did casemix come from?

The Resource Management Initiative (RMI) was instigated in the late
1980s, with its objectives including:

- stimulating, encouraging and developing a hospital management
  process involving doctors, nurses and other clinical and managerial
  staff in strategic and operational decision making
- ensuring that such a process is underpinned by a patient based
  information system which is timely, accessible and credible to all
  participants

The early thinking on RMI was developed further in the initial RMI
pilot sites, culminating in the production of a national core
specification for casemix management systems in acute hospitals.
Some regions then further refined the requirements and conducted
regionwide casemix system shortlisting exercises.

The national core specification defined casemix as being: 'A system to provide a common management information database to clinicians and managers as an aid to improve effective and efficient use of resources and measurable improvements in patient care'. The specification envisaged that this would require:

- Recording details of the patient (eg sex, date of birth, etc), details of their hospital stay (eg date of admission), diagnosis and operative procedures, and individual events occurring during the episode (eg date and nature of a pathology test, etc).
- Holding care profiles for groups of patients, against which actual care patterns can be compared.
- Holding standard costs for individual events, so that various analyses and projections can be undertaken.
- Providing analysis, reporting and presentation facilities, for direct use by clinicians and managers.

Experience to date: how has it worked?

Few doubt the need for systems to support management and decision-making in Trusts. However, experience from the initial RMI pilots, supported by later experience from following casemix sites, is that there have been common and substantial difficulties in implementation. Some of these are described below.

How Trusts planned and procured the system

At the time that casemix systems were being funded, many Trusts were still grappling with the implementation of clinical directorates. This left such Trusts trying to define the system requirements to support an organisational model that was not stable, and perhaps not well understood. The result was that many Trusts did not really know what they would, or could, use a casemix system for.

At the same time, the NHS 'internal market' was developing. Purchasers began to pressure Trusts to contract for patient treatment in new and sophisticated ways, gradually moving away from simple block contracts towards, for example, cost and volume contracts, compound packages of care, etc. Since most patient administration systems (PAS) at that time could support only the simplest forms of contracting (if any at all), many Trusts saw casemix systems as an opportunity to 'fill the contracting systems gap'. Therefore, for many Trusts, contract management became a (or the) prime requirement for a casemix system. And a common side effect of this was to turn clinicians away from it.

Other parts of Trusts saw different potential uses for casemix systems. For example, some clinicians saw it more as an aid to clinical audit than to clinical management. Others saw it as an opportunity to streamline the procedural duties of medical secretaries and patient administration more generally. The link between these needs and the original notion of casemix might be tenuous, but the perceived needs were strong, and casemix was often regarded as a 'free' opportunity.

This situation led to procurements where many Trusts did not have a clear corporate view on their requirements. In some cases, local 'champions' would define the requirements as they saw them (sometimes leaning towards contracting, sometimes clinical audit, sometimes something else). In others, Trusts would adopt either the national core specification or a neighbouring Trust's requirements, with little critical analysis and little resulting local ownership.

The final piece in the casemix planning puzzle was the casemix system suppliers themselves. What kind of systems did they build? Ones to meet the original vision of RMI, as set out in the national core specification? To meet regionwide specifications? To meet contracting needs? Clinical audit needs? Patient administration add-ons? All of the above? The answer is that they all tried to meet the national core specification, but then diverged, sometimes greatly, on their systems' functionality. Whatever they decided to do, they had little time to build the products, since there was typically great pressure from RHAs for Trusts to buy and implement the products quickly.

How casemix implementations fared

Casemix systems have almost always been more difficult to implement than Trusts originally envisaged. Common difficulties experienced included:

- Many PASs had trouble sending data to casemix because they were built on old, proprietary software platforms and 'closed' application architectures. This meant that many implementations stalled just trying to get basic data reliably out of PAS.
- Many were overambitious in trying to feed casemix with data from several departmental systems from day one. The difficulties in setting up so many interfaces so fast were simply beyond the resources of many projects.
- Many Trusts' departmental systems did not hold entirely accurate and common patient data. For example, the PAS would use one patient numbering scheme, and the pathology system another. This meant that the casemix system had to match up such records using 'fuzzy matching' methods, eg matching on surname, date of birth, etc. But such schemes tended to show up further inconsistencies between the data in these systems, and the results were often either unsuccessful, or required substantial ongoing manual effort to keep the links running. Another common data problem was that clinical coding in PAS was often inaccurate or incomplete.

At the same time, many Trusts realised that they had underestimated the user training and education needs, particularly for clinicians. Indeed, the cultural difficulties involved in implementing the wider RM Initiative sometimes generated a backlash against the systems from clinicians and others.

The resulting implemented casemix systems

With all the uncertainties upfront, and all the technical and data problems experienced during implementation, the resulting system was often disappointing to the intended users. Common comments from Trusts post-implementation were:

- 'None of the reports are of any use to us.'
- 'The finance department uses it for contracting, but the doctors don't use it at all.'
- 'A few doctors use it, but most directorates aren't very interested.'

- 'We spend days each month manually matching up data records from feeder systems, and trawling through exception reports.'
- 'The system always seems to be down just when I want to use it.'
- 'My data are hopelessly incomplete.'

On top of this, another key shortcoming was observed in many systems: a lack of flexibility. Since Trusts had a relatively poor grasp of their needs during the procurement, they tended to learn very fast post-implementation. This led to a great demand for new reports, changes to existing reports, different types of inquiries, etc. And many casemix systems did not easily lend themselves to such user-driven modifications. Rather, the Trust had a choice: either to pay the supplier to make the changes, or to abandon the changes (and perhaps the system) altogether.

This lack contrasted with the needs of many Trusts, noting that these needs were often only discovered after implementation. In effect, what many Trusts ended up looking for was either:

- the equivalent of advanced spreadsheet functionality, such as scenario definition and exploration, multi-dimensional data analysis, list manipulation and filtering, etc;
- an Executive Information System (EIS) which would (among other things) take all the raw data and convert them into the Trust's key performance indicators, for review, 'drill-down analysis', graphical presentation, etc.

The result of all these experiences was that many Trusts simply stopped using their casemix systems altogether. Others narrowed the use of the system to the Finance and Contracting Department.

The future: where to for casemix from here?

Despite the difficulties experienced in the past, the outlook for casemix is not all bleak. There are several things that Trusts could consider doing to improve matters and to provide benefit for themselves in so doing.

What are your needs?

Since many of the problems involved in casemix implementations are actually rooted in a lack of clarity on the requirements, then it may be helpful to review the original definition of requirements. Figure 5.1.1 illustrates the sort of process that a Trust might undertake, which suggests that a review of casemix requirements is linked with a review of the overall information needs of the Trust.

Such an exercise may well not result in any formal procurements,

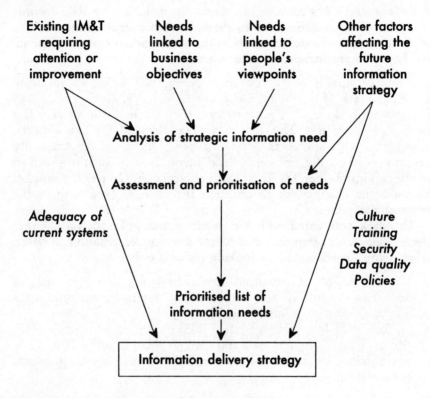

Figure 5.1.1 *Information delivery strategy*

and may not require any additional expenditure. But it should clarify corporately the role of casemix in the overall systems architecture and strategy of the Trust. And it should provide a plan for making real improvements.

Learning lessons from the past, such an exercise should involve the whole organisation in the thinking and decision-making. In this way, not only would the resulting answers be more likely to be correct, but it would also allow a relaunch or reshaping of the perception and profile of casemix around the Trust.

How should those needs be supported?

Broadly speaking, for any given need, the next step would be to decide whether to redouble efforts to use current systems, or to use a different and more appropriate system for the purpose. The suggestions below are some specific examples of what other Trusts have done in this situation.

Make better use of casemix
One of the major difficulties in taking casemix forward is that the original implementation may have given it a poor reputation around the Trust. So, for example, when some Trusts are forced to provide more activity or cost information for GP fundholders, they resort immediately to developing manually prepared spreadsheets without considering whether casemix might provide the answer with little or no effort. Therefore, it is worth trying to match casemix to the Trust's emerging needs, while avoiding reinventing the wheel.

It can also be helpful to revisit the major concepts of RMI and how casemix supports them, and then mould them to how the Trust works. For example:

- Regarding the use of care profiles: if the organisation feels uncomfortable with these as a concept, then it is probably futile to try to use casemix to support them. A more fruitful approach would be to rethink the potential uses of care profiles, and then use casemix to support whatever is decided should be the way forward.
- Regarding the application of standard and actual costing within casemix: whereas many initially tried to cost items down to the individual activity level (eg with different costs per pathology test type, and 'charged' per test done), this has proved difficult to implement in practice.

Make use of other systems
Many functions that were traditionally thought to be within the remit of casemix may now be able to be supported as well – or better – by other systems. Some examples are provided below:

- If casemix is being used merely as a substitute for poor PAS reporting abilities, then it might be that PAS has since improved. Some major suppliers have developed their PASs substantially over the past couple of years so that reporting is now much more powerful and flexible. It might be that such improved products would prove better and cheaper than retaining a poor, expensive casemix implementation.
- A reporting or EIS tool might be able to be fitted 'on top of' casemix. For example, some Trusts use products such as Business Objects to provide flexible reporting on their casemix database. Others feed casemix data into a separate EIS for management reporting and analysis.
- Other core systems might be able to provide casemix-like information. For example, integrated HISS products may now offer a casemix-like product at little or no extra charge. If the Trust is soon to make such an investment, then it may not be cost effective to continue improving casemix in the short term.

In closing, experience from Trusts that have already taken such measures suggests that the concepts and principles behind RMI and casemix can indeed be beneficial, and that difficult implementations can be saved given enough time and effort.

What can HISS Mean for Me?

Matthew Robins

Introduction

Publicity regarding Hospital Information Support Systems (HISS) can tend to be confused. Some tell stories of HISS disasters while others report astounding success. Faced with this conflicting situation, what should a trust do? Perhaps a reasonable conclusion to draw is that the HISS path may offer lots of potential but that it is very easy to get things wrong on the way.

This chapter seeks to review the current status regarding HISS by looking at its potential, how hospitals are responding, and some of the lessons being learnt. It draws on experience of working with a wide range of acute providers who have been involved in HISS, from those who are seeking to define the role of HISS in their strategic planning to those who have implemented it. A key question frequently asked is: 'Can HISS be implemented incrementally or do we have to go for a big bang?' However, focusing on this question misses the fundamental issue of what HISS actually is and what it is not.

What HISS is not

To illustrate what HISS is not, here is a description of a typical trust which has not implemented any of the components of HISS:

- Individual computer systems are used to support specific functional areas, often providing valuable support to that specific area, but increasingly becoming 'islands of information' inaccessible to the wider organisation.
- The task of keeping these 'islands' in step grows as the systems develop in number and scope. Typically, there is considerable

duplication in the data being used and, therefore, in the resource needed to keep the systems up to date.

- Clinical and business pressures are difficult to satisfy as the information needed to complete tasks such as audit or costing is fragmented across many 'islands'. Clinicians and patients may get the least direct benefit from the existing investment.

From this point, the question is: how can/should we move forward towards HISS?

What HISS is: the core elements

There is no single agreed definition of HISS. There is, however, a common denominator: the integration of operational patient-based information. In practice, this means linking together the basic information relating to any individual patient, keeping it in step and making it available to those who need it.

Taking this forward, a number of potential levels of ambition emerge – each with increasing complexity and, in theory, increasing potential benefit:

- **Level 1: sharing basic demographic information between operational systems.** For example, the radiology department and the patient administration system using the same patient identifiers and demographics. This can reduce duplication, errors and enable management systems to 'link' patient events across departments.
- **Level 2: delivery of diagnostic information from support departments to wards and clinics.** Using electronic communication rather than paper information, known as 'results reporting', can speed up the flow and accuracy of information in support of patient care. Time and effort in chasing information at both ends of the process can also be substantially reduced.
- **Level 3: two-way communication between wards and support departments.** Known as an order communications system (OCS), enables orders for services and tests to be placed electronically. This represents a major change in the working practice, particularly for junior doctors and nursing staff.
- **Level 4: the electronic patient record (EPR).** A computer system becomes the primary source of patient information replacing the paper medical record. This would include images as well as textual information and clearly represents fundamental change in working practice for the majority of staff groups.

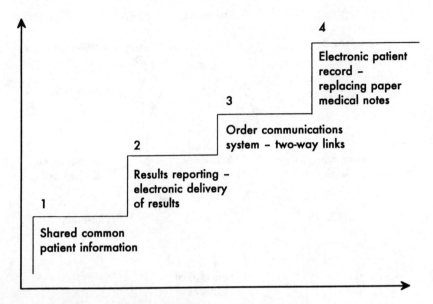

Figure 5.2.1 Levels of ambition

What HISS is: exciting opportunities

In addressing these core elements, there are a variety of opportunities to be unlocked, for example:

1. As patient events become linked across multiple departments, a repository of detailed patient information can become available, for example to support:

   - staff being able to access all the information about a patient;
   - more timely and comprehensive discharge information;
   - clinical audit based on more comprehensive clinical data.

2. As facilities are provided at the ward to order services and tests, they can be further developed to provide direct support to patient care, for example the management of protocol based care.
3. As activity data are linked at the patient level, they can be used increasingly for management purposes, for example resource management and service costing.

Perhaps the greatest potential of truly integrated information is that of enabling organisational change. As integrated information becomes available, the barriers to change, created by isolated pools of information, break down. This raises the potential to move from working practices and processes which fit round the current

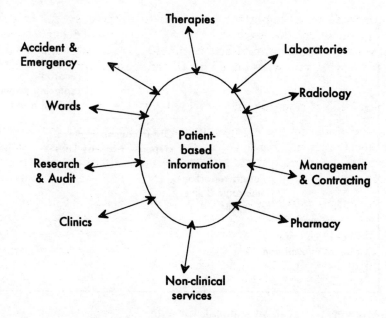

Figure 5.2.2 Integrated information

information systems to those designed to optimise the effectiveness of patient care.

Clinical and business pressures for HISS

Alongside these opportunities, most trusts have to contend with some significant issues and problems that tend to drive them down a HISS route. These include clinical and business pressures.

- External demands from purchasers and fund-holding GPs are putting more pressure on the delivery of management information and on improving the quality and timeliness of patient information.
- The ability to satisfy internal demands for effective management information is largely dependent on the quality and relevance of basic operational data. Specific pressures include the need for costing, activity management, service planning and quality management.
- The development of clinical audit is dependent on access to a base of detailed and accurate patient-based data. In the face of difficulties encountered with 'stand alone' audit systems, there is increasing pressure to take a corporate and integrated approach to audit information.

While these are all important areas to address, there is a risk that they are pursued to the exclusion of all the patient-related benefits discussed earlier. The message is simple: take a clear and balanced view on what you want, based on all the reasons why you want it.

Which HISS is right for us?

When considering the opportunities above, most trusts conclude that the question is not HISS: yes or no? but rather HISS: which aspects, when and how? Here are some rules of thumb that have served many trusts well:

- **Electronic patient record (EPR)** (level 4) is still in its infancy and represents too much for many trusts to take on immediately. So it might be a long-term goal but perhaps not for the next few years.
- **Order communication system (OCS)** (level 3) provides great potential benefit, but is relatively expensive and requires substantial organisational change. This is often the eventual strategic goal of trusts, but only those trusts which are 'OCS believers', from management through to clinicians, may wish to tackle this immediately.
- **Results reporting** (level 2) provides many benefits with less expense than OCS and does not require such a great organisational upheaval. For this reason, it is the immediate goal of many trusts.
- **Basic integration** (level 1) is beneficial to all trusts and may be the short-term stopping-point for those which have little money to invest, or have little current capacity for organisational change.

An added complication is that many of these goals can be regarded either as stepping-stones to other levels, or as end points in themselves. Some more rules of thumb, which hold true in many circumstances, include the following.

- For many reasons, basic integration (level 1) might be a cul-de-sac. For example, it may be cheap and simple to shore up old systems to this level, but improving them any further may not be feasible. Rather, whole new systems may need to be procured to improve past this point.
- Results reporting (level 2) can be a natural stepping-stone to OCS (level 3). For this reason, many trusts aim to implement results reporting first, and then move on to OCS if and when the time feels right.
- It is not clear which approach is best to take when trying to set up EPR (level 4). There are some suppliers that offer a path, but NHS experience of this is very limited. An EPR project involving pilot sites is currently trying to take thinking forward on this issue.

How should we go about it?

A number of valuable lessons are coming from the experience of early HISS sites, the most important of these being that HISS is far more about organisational issues than technical ones. When planning your local response to HISS, key messages to take on board are:

- Ownership and understanding throughout the organisation is essential for success. Developing and maintaining ownership must be managed carefully, especially where the need for a long-term corporate view is at odds with a culture of devolved management responsibility and greater autonomy.
- HISS cannot be delegated to or solely pushed by the Information Management & Technology department. In several sites this approach has foundered at the implementation phase or, when operational, has failed to deliver long-term benefits on the scale envisaged. In particular, it has led to worse rather than better data quality, usually linked with inappropriate working practices. In such circumstances, paper and electronic systems run in parallel and the staff feel burdened rather than supported by HISS.
- Moving to real time information systems on wards and clinics is a complex task. There are cultural and skills issues in moving from paper records to real time operational systems. Developing these skills and managing quality becomes more difficult when responsibility is moved from centralised departments. A key lesson here is the importance of education to address why as well as training to address how.

The above issues or pitfalls may seem daunting but there are success stories. A number of hospitals have shown that organisational issues can be managed effectively. In these, and in future sites, the real measure of success will be whether the envisaged goals and benefits are realised in practice. Again lessons can be learnt:

- Benefits do not just happen. A vital element, before any systems are procured, is identifying and planning for the realisation of benefits. This is a major project in its own right, usually undertaken in conjunction with the preparation of the business case. Planning for organisational changes must be included and be closely linked with the trust's organisational development and human resource strategies.
- Organisation-wide involvement is essential, including staff from all areas and all levels in the hospital. In particular, HISS sites have found a multi-disciplinary view of the impacts and opportunities to be very valuable. Those with the authority to ensure delivery of the benefits should be signed up to the process and to the resulting plans.

It would be helpful to know how accurate benefits realisation plans have proved to be. Unfortunately there is little hard evidence currently available from HISS sites that enables a direct comparison of the benefits planned 'before' with those realised 'after'. However, the general view emerging is that staff time savings are real but prove difficult to realise in cash terms. Rather, HISS sites are finding many of the benefits emerge as genuine quality improvements, often supported by the planned reinvestment of time savings.

The final lesson to bear in mind is the need to 'do it properly'. HISS has such an impact on the organisation that any attempts to cut corners, either on the organisational work or on the systems themselves, have led to problems out of all proportion to the savings sought.

5.3

A Basic Introduction to Computer Software for Healthcare Managers

Philip Burnard

All healthcare managers have to use computers. The computer industry is expanding constantly as technology advances and as prices for components drop. The Internet — a vast, international computerised network of computers — also means that managers can obtain information about almost any topic from any part of the world in seconds. It is thought, by many, that the Internet will revolutionise the way we work with information in the future. Whether or not this really is the case remains to be seen.

There are two types of personal computer in common business use — the IBM compatible computer and the Apple Macintosh®. Both types run different sorts of software and it is not, generally, possible to transfer information from one sort directly to the other. This has changed, in recent months, with the introduction of the PowerMac™ computer — one that combines features of both the IBM compatible and the Apple Macintosh® and which will run programs designed for either machine.

Given the wider range of software available for the IBM compatible computer, this chapter identifies the sort of software that is available for this type of computer. The reader is referred directly to the Apple Macintosh® company for details of software for that company's machines.

Software

First, the question of the word software. While hardware refers to the physical components of the computer (the keyboard, the mouse, the computer box and the monitor), software refers to the programs that are run on the computer. Thus a word-processing program is software. No computer will run without the appropriate software and, usually, software is bought in addition to the computer itself. Some computer companies offer package deals in which they sell their computers with a range of software programs. Many, however, do not and simply sell the computer itself. Software to run on that computer can almost double the original outlay. If a computer costs around £1000, it is quite possible that a range of programs suitable for use by a manager will cost another £800. All of this should be borne in mind when budgeting for computing equipment.

The range of available software

Computer programs are produced by a range of different companies and are produced for various different uses. The following list illustrates the broad range of categories of programs that will be of use to the manager:

- wordprocessors;
- spreadsheets;
- databases;
- graphics packages;
- suites of programs;
- specialised healthcare programs.

It should be noted that, currently, most new programs are produced to run under the *Windows*™ operating system. This system allows the user to work with a graphical interface and use the 'push-button' facilities of a mouse. Generally, *Windows*™ programs are the easiest to use.

Wordprocessors

Word-processing programs are the most commonly used of all computing programs. They can be used for day-to-day correspondence, the production of papers and reports and the development of much larger projects such as theses and books. The choice of a word-processing program is influenced by the following factors:

- the organisation's policy about word-processing;
- the user's personal and prior experience of word-processing;
- the intended use of the program.

Reasonably, many organisations buy one type of wordprocessor for all their employees to work with. If documents are to be transferred between computers and if a corporate image is to be portrayed, this makes good sense. Training costs are limited if a single type of wordprocessor is used throughout an organisation and the cost of buying copies of the programs – in bulk – is reduced.

Currently, there are three market leaders in the field of word-processing: *Word for Windows*®, *WordPerfect for Windows*® and *Word Pro*®. All have similar features but all three 'feel' very different to use. If managers do have a choice in what wordprocessor is used, they should try each of these.

There are certain key features in word-processing programs that vary from program to program and, again, the potential user should check to see whether or not features that are needed are included in the package. A shortlist of word-processing features includes the following:

- on-screen editing of words, phrases, sentences and paragraphs;
- spell checking;
- grammar checking;
- ability to work with figures, pictures and diagrams;
- ability to handle large documents easily;
- ability to manage desktop publishing projects.

Spreadsheets

A spreadsheet offers the facility of working with rows and columns of figures or words. Most commonly, spreadsheets will be used to handle numerical data of various sorts. Typically, they are used to prepare accounts and to forecast financial positions. Currently, most of the major spreadsheet programs work in very similar ways and the two market leaders are *Excel*® and *Quattro*®. Features to look for in a spreadsheet program include:

- the ability to read in data from other programs;
- the ability to work with multiple sheets;
- a range of accounting or statistical functions;
- the ability to represent figures graphically in the form of charts and graphs.

Databases

Database programs store information – usually in a highly structured format. Managers, for instance, who need to keep detailed staff records or records of companies with whom they deal, will find a database program invaluable.

The database program, unlike other sorts of programs described in this chapter, is not the most easy to set up and use. While a user can quickly learn how to use a wordprocessor or spreadsheet, the database program takes a little setting up in order to use it. Many companies buy in the expertise of others in order to set up a database. There are three main features to almost all database programs:

- The table, in which all data are stored in a structured way;
- The form, or the means by which data are entered into the table or viewed on the screen;
- The report, or the print-out from a database.

In a well set up database, the end user rarely needs to refer to the table. Instead, information is put into the database and viewed on the screen by using forms. Printed information from the database is outputted as a report.

Examples of top-selling database programs include *Access*® and *Paradox*®. Both are well suited to beginners and 'power users' although the absolute beginner is probably best advised to get some help in setting up a new database.

Graphics packages

Graphics packages allow the user to draw graphs, charts, slides and a whole range of pictures. Most of the top-level word-processing programs already contain reasonable graphics facilities and many users may find that these are enough in themselves. However, the manager who draws many charts or who prepares overhead transparencies for presentations may find the ease of use and comprehensive nature of the dedicated graphics package useful. *PowerPoint*® and *Harvard Graphics*® are two best-selling packages and both are fairly easy to use.

Suites of programs

The alternative to buying a range of programs is to buy a suite. A suite of programs is a package produced by a single software manufacturer which contains, for example, a wordprocessor, database program, graphics package and spreadsheet. The advantage of buying in this way is clear: all of the programs come from one manufacturer and usually work in similar sorts of ways. Once you have learned to use the suite's wordprocessor, you can usually learn to use the spreadsheet fairly quickly. The disadvantage of buying a suite of programs is that you may be buying programs that you rarely – if ever – use. If, for example, your management role never requires you to work with large sets of figures, then you may never need a spreadsheet.

On the other hand, buying a suite of programs usually represents a considerable financial saving over buying individual programs. Site licences (which enable a number of people in an organisation to use the programs) are also available and these can enable further savings. Examples of popular suites of programs are *Microsoft Office*™ and *Novell's PerfectOffice*™.

Summary

All managers need to get to grips with computers and their software. This chapter has considered some of the more commonly used computer programs. In working out a budget for setting up a new single-user computer, the manager needs to consider the following issues:

- the cost of the hardware (computer, screen, keyboard and any 'add ons');
- the cost of the software (the programs that run on the computer);
- the cost of training staff in using the programs;
- the time taken by staff to become skilled in using the programs.

It is a common experience for managers to find that staff are using their computers like glorified typewriters. Computers and computer software really can save time and effort at all levels of management. Commitment to the right software and thorough training in its use is vital.

Further reading

Burnard, P (1995) *Health Care Computing*, Chapman and Hall, London.
Chellen, S S (1995) *Information Technology for the Caring Professions*, Cassell, London.
Peckitt, R (1989) *Computers in General Practice*, Sigma, Wilmslow.

PART SIX

MANAGING THE ESTATE

6.1

Estates: A Strategic Approach

Gordon Massey

Introduction

The need for trusts to adopt a strategic approach to estates management is vital because, as one of the four fundamental trust resources, it forms an integral part of trust corporate planning. Chairmen and chief executives should, therefore, take a keen interest in estate management since they are ultimately responsible for ensuring that the trust has the necessary quality and quantity of buildings to allow it to carry out its functions effectively and efficiently. In support of this, NHS Estates have published five important documents: the *Capital Investment Manual; Estatecode; Concode; Firecode* and *Better by Design*, which are referred to in this chapter.

The need for an estates strategy

In order to make best use of the estate, trusts should develop an estates strategy that is fully integrated into their strategic business planning. The role that chairmen and chief executives adopt in the development of an estates strategy is particularly important today because:

- increased customer focus has drawn attention to the need for better surroundings and how they may contribute to the more effective treatment of patients as well as to the well-being of staff;
- removal of Crown immunity has highlighted the need to attain statutory standards and the responsibility of managers for this;
- improved estate is a way of achieving competitive advantage;

- the introduction of capital charges means that inadequate or inefficiently used assets will be adding to the cost of patient services with no commensurate benefits.

Developing the estates strategy

Strategic management of a trust involves blending four major resources within known constraints in order to achieve corporate objectives. The resources are:

- people: their energy, skills and dedication;
- finance: revenue and capital, recurring and non-recurring;
- assets: land, buildings, plant and equipment;
- information: hard and soft data and their analysis.

Strategic asset management forms an integral part of this corporate resource planning process and will lead to decisions affecting estate acquisition, refurbishment and disposal in accordance with trust corporate objectives. The chief executive has two specific responsibilities:

1. The strategic management of assets involving regular review of productivity, cost and fitness for service need and any resultant rationalisation or investment plan.
2. The operational maintenance of assets ensuring that they are up to the required quality and meet all the necessary Health and Safety regulations.

In order that the chief executive can carry out this role, a structure should be introduced which integrates the technical management of the estate with the general management of the trust. Advice on appropriate structures can be found in the 'Project Organisation' document within the *Capital Investment Manual* and 'Strategic Asset Management' in *Estatecode*, Volume 1. *Estatecode* is for all managers in trusts and health authorities who have responsibility for the estate at a strategic or operational level. It aims to make all Health Service managers appreciate the cost of owning and running the estate (land, buildings and equipment) and provides guidance on mechanisms for achieving efficient and effective management.

An estate action plan should be developed as an integral part of the total business planning activity. This is explained in *Estatecode*, Volume 1. It is ideally suited to establishing the role of the estate within strategic planning because it allows objective assessment within a structured framework of:

- the inappropriate location of services in terms of buildings;
- the underuse or overprovision of space;

- the planning and development potential of land and property;
- the need for capital resources to generate change.

A significant part of this strategic business planning process will involve the identification and appraisal of options. This is the estate investment programme, an interactive process that aims to utilise the estate to attain the healthcare service policy objectives within financial constraints. It will indicate:

- the existing estate to be retained;
- the degree of modification envisaged;
- the need for additional land and building;
- the availability for disposal of unwanted land and buildings;
- the potential for asset reuse;
- timescale for any proposals;
- the resources to sustain the resultant estate.

Managers should use this process to formulate alternative proposals that will satisfy the approved option. For example, careful consideration should be given to maximising the use of the trust's lowest value land so that, perhaps, the highest value land can be sold for development or other appropriate use. This also highlights the point that trusts should seek to develop their estate in such a way as to ensure that high value land could be sold off, should it become surplus to requirements.

Implementing the estates strategy

Any proposed major changes to the estate involving major capital investment should be supported by the development of a formal business case. This will need regional office approval for any projects with a cost over the trust's delegated limits.

The Capital Investment Manual

The *Capital Investment Manual* provides guidance on the management considerations and technical requirements of the capital appraisal process, together with a framework for establishing management arrangements to ensure that the benefits of every investment are identified, realised and evaluated (HSG (94)31).

There are three main stages to the development of a business case:

The strategic context
This establishes the case for capital investment and should be largely derived from the activity described in the previous section.

The outline business case
The outline business case evaluates the various options (using economic appraisal) and identifies the preferred one in terms of meeting the trust's strategic objectives. At this stage, there should be consideration of private finance opportunities.

The full business case
This includes testing the best privately financed option against the publicly funded alternative, making a decision on funding and then working up the full business case. In particular, this process should be used to re-examine the following points:

- customer requirements;
- competitive position;
- service facilities;
- affordability.

Once this process has been completed and a project has been authorised, strict management is vital. The *Capital Investment Manual* contains the required guidance on the subsequent processes for managing the delivery of the approved scheme, aimed at providing the healthcare facilities specified in the full business case, obtaining best value for money and maintaining probity.

A good understanding of the process of managing the delivery of a capital construction scheme is important. Senior managers will be held responsible for the performance of the trust in implementing construction projects. Good use should be made of other relevant guidance such as *Concode*, which advises on the contracting aspects of health building projects, including the implementation of policy and EU directives. *Concode* can help trusts in the appointment of works contractors and consultants and the use of various forms of contract.

Designing for quality

The NHS should be commissioning health buildings of quality, durability and style as they provide an improved environment for patient satisfaction and recovery, as well as increased staff and visitor contentment. Good quality buildings will also be of interest to purchasers who look to buy services from trusts which can provide such benefits.

If quality is seen as an integral part of the construction process, then the chance of procuring fine, economical buildings tailored to the needs of present and future users will be greatly increased and value for money should be achieved.

Chairmen and chief executives are obliged to create fine buildings. As patrons, they should ensure that both high quality architecture and the vision and values of the trust are fundamental to the design process. Further details on these issues can be found in *Better by Design*, which is aimed at assisting chairmen, chief executives and general managers in considering quality in healthcare building.

Private finance – its value to the estates strategy

The Private Finance Initiative (PFI) gives the NHS access to private sector skills and expertise as well as a new source of finance for capital infrastructure investment. The NHS Executive has been promoting PFI in order to secure:

- value for money;
- transfer of risk from the NHS to the private sector.

Value for money

Value for money has been improved through PFI in a range of diverse areas such as magnetic resonance imaging (MRI) and clinical waste incineration. This is being achieved through:

- new sources of income from extra sales to wider markets (eg MRI units serving both public and private sectors)
- building bigger to gain economies of scale with shared use of capital assets (eg clinical waste incinerators);
- increases in operational effectiveness and efficiency by using existing private sector expertise (eg low dependency accommodation and services);
- scope for companies to recover costs of facilities through user charges (eg restaurants and car parks);
- short leases, after which other users can reuse assets (eg offices).

Generating savings or more income in these ways means that NHS money can buy more patient care.

Transfer of risk

This is a fundamental principle of PFI. Where the private sector is well placed to manage the risks, a trust should transfer many of the risks which it would run if it were to construct and manage the new facilities. For example:

- construction costs overrunning;
- losses through completion delay;
- quality standards of facilities failing to meet performance targets;
- poor design which hinders effective delivery of services;
- problems through facilities failing to keep up with new technology.

When such risks occur they impede a trust's ability to provide the highest quality and quantity of healthcare. In PFI contracts, therefore, such risks should be transferred to the private sector. There are a number of steps to be followed in attempting to obtain a privately financed capital scheme. These are outlined in HSG(95)15 and must be observed when developing a business case.

Each regional office has a PFI specialist and this should be the first point of contact. They are supported by the Private Finance Unit at the headquarters of the NHS Executive.

Health and Safety issues

The evolution of an estates strategy is not just about new developments or improvements to existing buildings to enhance patient care. Tighter legislation and the removal of Crown immunity means that trust managers need to pay careful attention to Health and Safety issues such as fire. This can involve considerable financial investment.

Firecode

Firecode comprises a set of documents dealing with all aspects of fire safety in healthcare premises, defining policy and giving practical guidance.

NHS Estates

NHS Estates is an Executive Agency of the Department of Health, addressing all aspects of health estate management, development and maintenance. The Agency produces definitive health estates technical guidance and provides other services including consultancy and training on the areas outlined.

Setting standards

Five of the major NHS Estates publications have already been referred to. They are the *Capital Investment Manual, Estatecode, Concode, Firecode* and *Better by Design*.

NHS Estates also provides guidance covering space requirements, safety, the internal environment and costs which assist healthcare organisations to maintain the required standards. The guidance includes:

- *Health Building Notes* which give advice on briefing and design, whether procuring new buildings or adapting/extending existing ones.

- *Quarterly Briefing* which gives statistical data and advice on trends in the building industry and the likely effect on building in the healthcare sector.
- *Activity Database* which is a computerised design tool to assist in the design and equipment of rooms and spaces in health buildings.
- *Health Technical Memoranda* which cover a range of subjects including emergency electrical supply systems, steriliser technology and equipment, medical gas pipeline systems and the control of legionella.
- *Encode*, a publication supported by a software package, which shows how to plan and implement a policy of energy efficiency in existing health buildings. NHS Estates offers a consultancy on the design of energy efficient hospitals and alternative site energy strategies.

Johnson & Johnson

MEDICAL COMPANIES

Introduction

Walk into any hospital in the UK – and in most countries of the world – and you will be in an environment where Johnson & Johnson is known and respected.

Johnson & Johnson

MEDICAL

Johnson & Johnson Medical provides a wide range of essential products for the operating theatre, intensive care, medical and nursing staff. Its products embrace wound management, infectiion prevention, surgical specialities, patient monitoring equipment and vascular access products.

Johnson & Johnson

INTERVENTIONAL SYSTEMS

Johnson & Johnson Interventional Systems provides interventional cardiologists, interventional radiologists and vascular surgeons with devices used in the treatment of cardiovascular disease.

We are the leading suppliers of stents – scaffolding devices designed to restore blood flow through otherwise occluded vessels.

Johnson & Johnson

FINANCE LIMITED

Johnson & Johnson Finance Limited offer financing alternative which address the unique capital requirements of our health care customers, including the NHS under the Private Finance Initiative, for the acquisition of capital equipment, medical products and services.

Johnson & Johnson

PROFESSIONAL

Johnson & Johnson Professional provides advanced quality, cost-effective devices and services to orthopaedic specialists, spinal surgeons and neurosurgeons. Products supplied include precision surgical instruments, orthopaedic, spinal and neurosurgical implants, and innovative fracture repair products and braces.

Our innovative product range also includes specialised neurosurgical equipment used for neuroendoscopy and electrosurgery, disposables, hand-held micro surgical instruments, implants for the treatment of hydrocephalus, intracranial aneurysms and spinal instability and single-use products used in neurosurgical and spinal surgical procedures.

THERAKOS

Therakos specialises in innovative advances in extracorporeal disease management through photomedical therapy.

Johnson & Johnson Medical
Customer Service, The Braccans, London Road,
Bracknell, Berks. RG12 2AT
Tel: 01344 864000   Fax: 01344 864001

Patient-focused Facilities Management (FM) at South Tees

Andrew Collingwood

This new NHS Acute Hospitals Trust has enjoyed a powerful facilities management (FM) presence from its inception, partly due to the way in which it was set up and partly due to the belief that FM would be a key element in the delivery of healthcare under the trust banner of 'putting people first'. The benefits of this central position, in terms of improved quality, reduced costs and better use of resources, are clear to see.

We have three main sites: South Cleveland, which has been operational since 1981, with some 625 beds; Middlesbrough General, originally opened in Victorian times with various additions, with a bed complement of 344; North Riding Infirmary, another Victorian building, with 58 beds. We also have a presence at two other hospitals, giving a total bed complement of approximately 1050. We employ some 4000 staff and have an income in excess of £100 million. We are also in the position of having most of the key clinical specialities within our Trust.

We became a Trust in April 1992 primarily through an amalgamation of two separate acute units within the then South Tees District Health Authority.

Setting up the Trust

To facilitate the change process a Trust Steering Group was formed which placed firm emphasis on clinician involvement to generate a sense of ownership. As a member of this Steering Group I was given responsibility for feeding back the responses of the non-clinical support staff to the idea of the two organisations joining together to become one Trust.

The process was undertaken by briefing senior non-clinical support staff, then cascading within the organisation a series of briefings with feedback sessions. It is fair to say that the majority of staff were quite vociferous in their views, some of which were extreme. But in general the vast majority were concerned about the perception of the general public that 'doctors and nurses are wonderful but the rest of health service staff are ****'! To put it mildly, they had low self-esteem. They had been fragmented into rigid groups and were often used as a management training route for administrators. I do not believe that we were so different from many other units at this time.

As this information was fed back to the Steering Group, we decided to form a facilities management division within the Trust. We were fortunate in being able to develop at the same time as the rest of the organisation, not as an afterthought but deemed to be a key element in the delivery of healthcare. Like other divisions, we used some external facilitation to help to develop the concept. We made contact with Keith Alexander, Director of the Centre for Facilities Management at the University of Strathclyde, whom we met on several occasions to consider the merits of FM. He interviewed a number of the existing functional and service managers and two internal seminars were held with a larger representative group from the 'estates' and 'hotels' functions.

The focus of these sessions was on the customer service required to support the prime objectives of the clinical divisions. The working definitions adopted for the study suggested that FM was: 'the process by which an organisation delivers and sustains agreed support service levels within a quality environment to provide full value in use to meet strategic objectives'. Facilities Management currently employs some 700 staff and has a budget of approximately £13 million.

Philosophy of service

We like to consider the Trust as a 'hotel' for healthcare with FM making significant contributions to patient care and therapy. This 'hotel' service starts with the initial contact made between the Trust and the patient. For example, is the invitation to attend an outpatients clinic clear and precise? Does the patient know which entrance to use, where the nearest bus stop is, where to park his car and whether change is needed for the parking meter? Do the grounds and gardens look tidy? Does the entrance foyer look welcoming? Is the reception counter easily located and are the faces behind it smiling and keen to help?

At the end of the visit do patients feel they have been well treated?

If a patient is admitted to a bed, why (within the obvious limits of cash resources) should he not feel as though he is in a hotel? We already know that the doctors and nurses are wonderful but why shouldn't the ward look clean and tidy? Why shouldn't the linen be crisp and clean and, perhaps more importantly, why shouldn't the food and beverages be of a reasonable standard and quality?

Front of house/back of house

This is a steal from Disney World – we are quite prepared to steal good ideas. As part of the 'hotel' concept everything the customer sees should look 'perfect'. Emphasis must be on the visible patient areas. In going through the change process and learning new skills everyone has to question their traditional priorities. We experienced reluctance at first from FM colleagues who were deemed to be backroom boys; initially they felt their efforts were not being acknowledged. In fact, even though we try and concentrate on the front of the house, in my book the back-of-house staff are perhaps more important. We must beware of the 'out of sight/out of mind' syndrome – always a difficult balance.

The NHS Estates publication *Better by Design* sums up the situation:

First impressions tend to stick. Negative first impressions will perhaps damage patient confidence. Good experience will help the caring process and make the job of other colleagues down the line easier and more effective. How often do we see quality clinical treatments being compromised by drab, inappropriate physical surrounds?

So how do we attempt to provide this 'hotel' standard of service?

We believe that FM is a partnership between Trust staff and the 100 or more contractors who work with us on a daily basis. This figure does not include the contractors, subcontractors and designers who work for us to achieve capital developments. This partnership can be thought of as a form of mixed economy.

We regard ourselves as a business within healthcare. Although I am an Associate Director of the Trust Board and report directly to the Chief Executive my main responsibility is to run FM as the managing director of a business. The FM Board is a partnership of myself and four senior managers responsible for the main function strands and one representative from each of finance and personnel. In addition, one of the non-executive directors of the Trust Board takes a full and active part. Commercial organisations would have non-executive directors – why not FM in healthcare?

Structure and communications

This present format/structure of FM is different from what we started with around three years ago. The change has been gradual but in net terms we have two fewer Board members. These changes have been subject to consultation/discussion and hence acceptance and have achieved our target of improving quality and reducing costs.

We also try hard not to be rigid in reporting requirements – staff are encouraged to communicate horizontally at all levels and also diagonally. We try to prevent the vertical communication up one leg of FM, across the Board level and down another leg. This helps to achieve empowerment of staff, or to use a word I prefer, 'ownership'.

One point of contact/seamless service

This has been an attempt to break down traditional barriers: no more being fobbed off by someone on the telephone. FM staff are encouraged to 'own' the problem. We would suggest that it is each person's responsibility to report a broken door hinge, not to leave it to 'works' – it will get fixed quicker that way. If you call FM it will be actioned and not passed on to another department.

Generic workers

To help achieve a seamless service, we have considered the use of generic workers: this is not a commodity sitting on the shelf, nor can it be introduced overnight. Over the last two years we have been developing and training staff from various parts of FM, to interact, to understand and to share each other's duties. This is leading to a seamless service delivery.

Quality assurance

The key to our Trust's success is quality. The Trust mission statement is: 'Striving for the best in health care'. Facility Management's mission statement, as one would expect, mirrors the Trust's: 'To provide a continually improving quality and commercially oriented cost effective service to our customers', but acknowledges the commercial field in which FM works.

We are, of course, challenged by our clients, the clinical divisions, on issues of quality, cost and volume. To meet these challenges we have embarked on a number of quality initiatives.

The NHS Executive's Information Management Technology (IM&T) Strategy for the NHS in England

"Getting better with information" is the national Strategy launched in December 1992 to enable the NHS to safely share information across departments, organisations and the NHS as a whole. It encompasses key principles which need to be adopted if the NHS is to change the way in which it values and views IM&T:

• information will be person-based and focus on the common denominator, the patient or client
• information should focus on health to provide better information for the benefit of the population as a whole
• information systems should be integrated, each piece of information needs to be entered once only
• information will be shared across the NHS to provide a better quality service to the patient
• information will be confidential and secure, patients must be confident that the information they provide is recorded correctly, properly protected and available only to those who need to know and are authorised to know

Taken together these principles aim to turn the concept of seamless care into a reality and achieve the undoubted potential for improving the delivery of healthcare. They will also support improved communications, performance management and the diverse demands of the new NHS.

A national IM&T infrastructure

The practical framework for turning principles and local plans into reality is provided by the IM&T infrastructure. National projects are addressing the technical standards, a common language, a shared network and above all confidentiality and security. The infrastructure projects are so named because they provide a common basis for the whole of the NHS where national consistency and uniformity are vital. The approach is one commonly adopted by large banks and corporations to reduce the costs of sharing information. Taken together national initiatives on information sharing will provide a catalyst for new ways of working in the NHS.

For more information about the IM&T Strategy projects and initiatives, please contact:
Joy Reardon,
NHS Executive Headquarters, Information Management Group
Information Point/NHS Register of Computer Applications
c/o Cambridge and Huntingdon Health Commission
Primrose Lane, Huntingdon Cambridgeshire PE18 6SE
Telephone (++)44 1480 415118   Fax (++)44 1480 415160

Achievement of BS5750 accreditation

We have achieved BS5750 (now ISO9002) accreditation for all of FM; I proudly display the six certificates on my office wall. We have six because this allowed us to manage the process in reasonable chunks – we will rationalise this over time. We also used this process as a form of change agent uniting elements of FM from the two, previously separate, units. It also allowed us to be subjected to external assessment – never easy, but we did it and now we have got it, we are determined to retain it.

Total Quality Initiative (TQI)

A criticism of BS5750 is that it does not sufficiently involve the customer. We attempted to put this right by embarking on the TQI experience for all of our full-time staff. This has shown tangible improvements as staff come through the two-day sessions with an action plan either individually or as teams. Barriers have been broken down, better understanding of others' problems achieved, service improvement groups have been set up and existing ones expanded. We have held reviews of the process and for 1995 we are considering extending them to include more of the contractors who make up the FM partnership.

We have learned a lot from this process but to highlight an example, I would pick on the managers within FM, below Board level. They went through the process first so that they would be 'on receive' when staff came back from their sessions. Perhaps not all of them were receptive and this was relayed back by staff. We therefore held an additional management session to allow them to look into the mirror, accept criticism and recognise that we all have a job to do, either manager or member of staff, we help each other and should be prepared to discuss issues and not just resort to giving instructions. I am pleased to say that this criticism was not widespread and I believe a lesson was learned.

Investors in people

The Trust's personnel department has achieved this standard and the remainder of the Trust has agreed to follow them. We will do this in time – perhaps next year.

BS7750

We might call this the green or environmental British Standard. We have investigated the application to our Trust and recommended that it is considered as part of the brief for the rationalisation on to one site. In overall terms we like to summarise our quality thus simply, we provide a safe, clean, warm and attractive environment for our customers.

Benchmarking

Standards continually need to improve, but first we need to undertake some benchmarking. We have been fortunate to be involved in the voluntary EIC (Estates Information Consortium) benchmarking initiative, which is being supported by NHS Estates. Already this voluntary initiative has attracted some one hundred Trusts and membership is growing.

We are also encouraging development of 'quality' standards of benchmarking. At the moment the majority of information relates to estates issues and we are developing benchmarking information on catering, laundry, etc. – any help would be appreciated.

Successful initiatives

We regard the Trust as being the property owner and hence landlord – FM is the agent of the landlord. We are working with clinical divisions, the Trust's tenants, to develop a better understanding of the cost of occupancy. This has been a slower process than we had hoped, perhaps due to the need to improve our information system, but will lead to better utilisation of space.

Ward hostesses/hosts

When we were setting up FM, a major issue was control of the food chain. We have a cook–chill system and the arrangements for delivery of food to patients was such that the catering department seemed to feed the food trolley and someone else fed the patient. The same food had a higher reputation in the restaurant than it did with the patients on the wards. Improvement to the delivery system became a *cause célèbre*.

Credit must go to the staff who pioneered the ward hostess system which was implemented in April 1994. This was achieved as part of the retendering process for the domestic contract. We have employed nearly 250 part-time staff in a form of reverse privatisation and also produced a saving. The personal profile of the hostesses/hosts is that they should be optimistic, caring, courteous and well presented. Their duties include the following:

- Check that patients have enjoyed their meal and if not do something about it.

- If a patient does not like anything on the day's menu they may change it, and they do. No more getting a meal ordered by someone who was occupying that particular bed the day before.
- If patients are intimidated by doctors or nursing sisters – hard to accept, perhaps, but by no means impossible – they often find the hostess easier to talk to and she can explain things to them as part of the ward team.
- Be proactive and seek out patients' needs, offering, for example, a cup of tea and a sympathetic ear.
- Offer patients a cooked or 'prepared to order' breakfast and choice of beverages.
- They have been trained to change light bulbs – and do.

In short, they deliver a far more personal service than had previously been the case. The project has been a success and the catering staff no longer feel they are feeding the food trolly. A patient recently described his stay in hospital as 'like being in a five-star hotel'.

Staffing issues

Therefore having developed a competent team, the question arises as to who is the quality co-ordinator in a hotel? Not the engineer: more likely the cleaner who ensures that everything in the bedroom functions correctly before the next client arrives. To demonstrate this we targeted the employment of a customer-orientated restaurant manager. The person who is in post used to work for a local country house hotel of high repute. This was perhaps the demonstrable start of the customer-orientated culture.

Positive Performance Management (PPM)

There is a need for staff at every level in the Trust to have assistance to realise their potential and perform to the best of their ability in their chosen jobs. Under the banner of PPM we will provide managers with clear expectations of what is required of them at work and give feedback as to how they measure up to those requirements. It will involve:

- clarifying the role;
- setting goals;
- planning personal development;
- reviewing regularly and annually.

Each manager has now prepared an action plan indicating how they will implement PPM within their area, objectives have been shared and we are constantly learning and co-operating.

Performance agreements

These agreements have three elements: quality, productivity and attendance. Staff are only paid their full allowance when all elements of the agreement are met. These agreements have replaced traditional incentive bonus schemes.

Our Trust also benefits from its own pay and conditions package, which was introduced as an alternative to Whitley Council in January 1994. To date some 33 per cent of non-medical staff are on Trust conditions of pay.

No automatic replacement of staff

Perhaps there is nothing new in this but we operate a 'star chamber' to ensure that when a member of staff leaves there is no automatic replacement but an opportunity for change. Before any recruitment takes place three FM Board members must have agreed to the appointment.

Further initiatives

The front-of-the-house model will be extended to the portering service in October 1995. This will allow front-of-house staff to concentrate on patient/customer contact whereas the back-of-house porters will be involved with issues such as site tidiness, rubbish collection, stores distribution, etc. This model will allow us to have a hall porter on duty, like a hotel.

Forming strategic alliances

We are also working actively with neighbouring Trusts to share opportunities. The climate seems to have changed over recent years with Trusts no longer believing that 'glorious isolation' is the best solution. In FM we are looking at consortium opportunities for clinical waste, laundry, catering, etc.

We believe that it is important that the Health Service retains expertise inhouse, providing, of course, that it remains cost effective. However we must rationalise so that consortium arrangements may be the best way forward. We believe that we should consider long-term strategy and not rely on short-termism which may be expedient but of questionable value. Apart from all this activity the Trust has submitted an outline business case for the rationalisation of all our services on to the South Cleveland Site.

The benefits

So, having given a brief appraisal of FM in South Tees, what have been the benefits to the Trust? We like to consider ourselves as providing corporate benefits by releasing resources. For example, in three full years the Trust has been able to:

- treat 21 per cent more patients;
- employ over 250 more front-line staff: nurses, clinicians, paramedics or similar;

with

- no additional overhead costs;
- no increase in FM budget.

Therefore resources are going into the right place and FM intends to continue to improve quality and reduce costs. We have not completed our FM journey at South Tees — perhaps we never will. But through a form of mixed economy/partnership we are making a major impact on improved patient care and the more patients say that our hospitals are like a five-star hotel, the happier we shall be.

This article is a revision of one which first appears in *Facilities Management*, (Blenheim Publications, 1995).

6.3

Security

Jean Trainor

Responsibility and accountability

The NHS reforms mean that responsibility and accountability for management, including security, has moved away from a centralised system to one where control now rests with local management within NHS Trusts and primary care organisations. Security in the NHS depends on all staff being aware of their responsibility to be observant and to record all incidents. Staff should perform their daily activities in accordance with local procedures and accept the element of personal responsibility for security and crime prevention.

Security within NHS Trusts is a prime responsibility of the chief executive, it being the board of the Trust's duty to consider security strategies on a regular basis. The legal responsibilities outlined below emphasise the need to take this issue very seriously at the highest possible level. Trust Boards have been asked by the NHS Executive to appoint one member to have particular responsibility for security. The Board has two key responsibilities:

- to define the objectives and formulate policy for security which will be delegated to operational managers;
- to monitor that security and crime prevention outcomes meet the corporate objectives.

The responsibility of operational managers is to ensure that procedures within their domain take account of security issues and that their own staff have appropriate training. A clear reporting mechanism which includes the regular review of managerial procedure also needs to be developed so that an overall picture of the security of the Trust is maintained by the chief executive.

In most Trusts there will be an operational services security department with professional security managers and staff with whom the day-to-day running of security matters will rest. They should act in an advisory capacity to senior managers and ultimately to the board. Security staff should support managers in discharging their responsibilities rather than reducing senior management's ultimate responsibility.

Legal responsibilities

NHS managers must be aware of the law, and their own liability, pertaining to security.

The criminal responsibility for failure of security

A hospital or other NHS body is criminally liable under the Health and Safety at Work Act 1974 if lapses of security lead to incidents which could be described as failing to provide a safe system of work. By law, a written policy is required, pointing out areas of risk and the safe procedure for dealing with them. It establishes that an organisation must provide:

- a safe system of work;
- a safe working environment;
- safe premises;
- adequate training and instruction;
- information which allows employees to ensure their safety at work.

An employer is required to assess risks within the workplace and document what those risks are. The policy should be communicated to all staff who must be properly trained and sufficiently informed to ensure effective reaction to incidents as they arise.

The civil responsibility for failure of security

Under the Occupiers Liability Act 1984 an occupier owes a 'common duty of care' to visitors, and a duty to take care to ensure that they are reasonably safe. This may extend to criminal acts by third parties if sufficient action is not taken to safeguard against them. Failure to take due care can lead to substantial damage awards.

The concept which governs both the duties is foreseeability. As violence and crime are foreseeable occurrences it is therefore the duty of authorities and Trusts to employ all reasonable security measures to reduce the risk. Warnings must be in a form to enable a visitor to avoid danger. If the danger cannot be avoided, warnings are insufficient. Exclusion of liability notices are ineffective in cases of personal injury and in other cases must be reasonable.

213

Criminal acts by staff

An NHS employer is directly liable if it fails sufficiently to protect patients and other members of staff from the possibility of criminal acts by its employees. This is not to say that healthcare bodies are responsible for all criminal acts performed by staff while they are on the premises. In order for a victim to have a case against an authority or Trust it is for them to prove that:

- the NHS institution had a duty of care, a duty to attempt to prevent the criminal act occurring;
- it did not perform that duty at all or to the requisite standard;
- the victim has suffered some loss or damage;
- this loss or damage was as a foreseeable result of the failure.

The thorough vetting of staff is something done increasingly by private industry, and failure to do so by NHS bodies at best might lead to criticism and at worst huge compensation bills. Access to criminal and medical records may help to identify those who pose a potential risk and allow for closer supervision if they are employed. Under the Children Act staff working with children should undergo specific vetting at selection stage in regard to past records of child abuse or other offences against children.

Action that can be taken

Members of the public, like members of staff, cannot be searched without their prior consent. Members of a security team have the right to arrest in certain situations so it is essential that all security staff are fully aware of, and properly trained in, the powers of arrest, the best procedures and acceptable methods to be used. Arrestable offences are defined within the Police and Criminal Evidence Act 1984. If the powers of arrest are exceeded or ignored, civil actions for assault and false imprisonment may follow.

A strategy for security

Given the responsibilities outlined above, each NHS body will need to set its own strategy for security. This needs to be set by senior management in discussion with the full Board, line managers, operational security professional, staff side organisations and the whole staff. It must be seen to be part of the organisation's health and safety and fire management procedures. According to the nature of the NHS organisation the strategy should cover the security of the following:

- patients and their visitors;
- staff;
- patient and staff property;
- the property of the organisation;
- information pertaining to patients and staff;
- the probity of the organisation.

It should outline how the following will be managed and clearly lay down the allocation of responsibilities:

- risk management;
- reporting and recording;
- access controls;
- designing out dangers;
- identification;
- financial controls;
- training.

Training

Training provision for NHS staff (with the possible exception of security officers) is patchy, with little systematic provision which covers all groups at all levels. Security awareness needs to be part of the training regime for all levels of NHS staff.

Board members are key people in the implementation of the security strategy. Their training needs are mainly in developing an awareness of their responsibilities at a level commensurate with their position and assistance in overseeing security and crime prevention strategies. Security awareness should form part of Board directors' induction training.

Line managers also need awareness-raising training, but those with explicit responsibility for security need to have access to specialist guidance in implementing security and crime prevention strategies.

All staff need training in general awareness and induction into safety procedures. Specific topics could include personal safety awareness and dealing with conflict as well as preventing and reporting crime in the workplace. Staff should be given regular feedback on the results of security initiatives.

Professional security staff need detailed training in all aspects of security and crime prevention such as:

- the legal powers of security staff;
- risk identification;
- security technology.

Such training could be linked to a formal qualification in order to ensure consistent standards throughout the NHS and in order to recognise the contribution made by security staff.

For managers and directors the NAHAT *Security Manual* provides a comprehensive review of their responsibilities. Supporting this are the NAHAT *Security Video* and the NHS Training Division's video *Dealing with Aggression – Management Responsibility*. For this group there are occasional conferences with a security and crime prevention focus. Additionally the National Association for Healthcare Security provides support to security managers through publications, meetings and conferences. NAHAT's Centre for NHS Board Development also runs courses for Board directors.

For operational staff there is little training provision beyond the NHS Training Division's video *Dealing with Aggression – Staff Responsibility* and any locally developed security training. Most locally developed training is in response to local incidents and commonly deals with topics such as self-defence.

Reporting and recording crime

The development of appropriate reporting and recording procedures is vital in all NHS institutions. Up-to-date information is essential to know the extent of crime, as well as contributing to a clear strategy in order to reduce crime-related incidents. All healthcare organisations should compile an inventory of their assets, not just those above asset register minimum values. This will facilitate the tracking of any losses.

A culture needs to be developed and continually reinforced within NHS bodies to ensure that staff and patients not only report all crime but also near misses.

- Systems should be set up effectively to manage stock/assets control in all areas, so that any discrepancies can be investigated.
- Crime reporting should be included in managers' and supervisors' job descriptions.
- Reporting should be made simple.
- Regular security awareness initiatives should be made.
- An effective feedback system is paramount.

Trusts

All crimes which occur in an NHS Trust should, as appropriate, be reported to the police, the Health and Safety Executive, the local Fire Officer or other statutory bodies. NHS staff (usually security staff) should carry out a basic investigation, if appropriate, pass the results to the local police crime desk and remain responsible for all follow-up action. Crimes against staff should be reported to the police only if the victim has requested this. Should the crimes follow a pattern or be linked with crimes against the organisation, this should be reported to the police and the victim informed.

Monitoring of crime

Crime recorded data should be provided for line managers, senior managers and security user groups on a quarterly basis.

There should also be a requirement that within a Trust or other NHS organisation, Boards receive a yearly report covering security issues including data on crime. This can then be matched against targets set for crime reduction.

Identification

Identification badge systems are a key element of a comprehensive security regime. It is vital to be able to identify and recognise fellow staff and people with a *bona fide* reason for being on the premises. It is important that all personnel including the most senior managers and clinical staff wear identity badges at all times and that all staff and indeed patients are empowered and encouraged to challenge anyone not wearing a badge.

Ownership by staff and management is key to the success of any ID badge policy. Complex systems where the badge is used as an access tool to the building will possibly promote a higher ownership pattern by the occupants.

Before selecting an ID system certain questions should be asked:

- Who is to be issued with the badge?
- How are non-staff to be treated?
- Is a 'pass system' necessary?
- How is the system to be controlled and administered?
- What features should the badge have?
- What will the badge design be?

Pass system

These are provided to authorise temporary access to official visitors and other individuals whose work placement or visit is of short duration. The need for local control of pass systems means that section heads and department managers should control the issue of passes in their own premises, either by the use of sequentially numbered passes, which can be controlled via a local register, or a time-expired disposable pass to cover the duration of the visit.

All contracts with contractors should contain a clause which stipulates the ID badge policy on sites as well as the action taken for breach of policy. Short-stay locum doctors should be treated in a similar manner. Their agency, as their employer, should be required to provide the personal ID badge. On arrival at the hospital, locum doctors should then be issued with an additional 'doctor's pass'. Since doctors have relatively unrestricted access to patients security must be tightly controlled for this group. Doctors on temporary contracts of longer duration should be provided with the general staff ID badge.

After deciding on the type of system and its administration, there are two main problems to solve. First, how to badge effectively an existing staff population without disrupting services. Second, what arrangements should be put in place to receive badges from leavers and to issue new badges to starters.

Badging existing staff
Existing staff will require briefing on the process to be followed for issue of ID badges. The logistical problems that are to be solved are the requirements to photograph, authorise and centrally record all details for a large population.

Arrangements for new employees
If the integrity of the system is to be maintained, new employees must be badged on their first day of work. Where badges are processed by a central bureau, it will be necessary for the local manager to issue a temporary badge to cover the intervening period until the new badge arrives.

ID badge policy and procedures document

The importance of a policy
The mainstay of any ID badge system is that it must be underpinned by a policy document. The document must be fully consulted on and involve both managers and staff side representatives to ensure that the arrangements are owned by the NHS body and its staff. It must spell out the procedures and policy areas that are to form part of the local ID badge system. In particular, it must identify the manager's responsibility.

Enforcement
Healthcare premises should publicise and signpost the fact that an ID badge system is in use and that visitors can expect to be challenged. Enforcement is possibly the most controversial area of any ID badge policy. Generally it could be said that if an ID policy is adopted, then it would naturally follow that breaches of such a document would promote disciplinary action.

Staff responsibilities

Contracts of employment should be amended to bring to the employee's attention the arrangements that are in place for the ID badge system. In particular, points which should be amplified are:

- badge to be worn at all times, clearly visible;
- lost badges must be reported immediately to the staff member's manager;
- when not being worn, the ID badge must be locked away securely;
- security staff will, from time to time, check the ID badge.

Access controls

Clearly the use of access controls to NHS premises will be key to keeping intruders and unwanted visitors at bay. Where NHS premises have multiple access points, consideration should be given to restricting access via certain points at certain times without creating a hostile fortress atmosphere. Access points can be classified in terms of:

- essential for access at all times;
- necessary between certain hours;
- open for convenience only.

The locking of doors except those designated as essential between 6 pm and 7 am should be considered. Security professionals should always be consulted on the design of new NHS buildings in order to avoid the inclusion of security risk zones. Expert advice on reusing space and the use of improved lighting can be used to 'design out' vulnerable areas and senior managers should encourage the use of imaginative alternative designs where problems occur.

PART SEVEN

MANAGING RELATIONSHIPS

7.1

Managing Relationships With Purchasers

Barrie Fisher

Introduction

In a speech given at the Royal College of Physicians on 19 May 1993 Dr Brian Mawhinney, then Minister for Health, said:

> The purchaser–provider relationship cannot be restricted to formal negotiations – the cat-and-mouse game of bid and counterbid, taking a piece here, knocking a percentage off there. It has to be constant and ongoing. Both must realize that it is not a contest about who wins and loses in the contracting negotiation process. A dialogue needs to be developed in which purchasers and providers jointly work to achieve their objectives.

Similarly, *Progress through Partnership*, a document which brought together four speeches made by the Secretary of State for Health, Mrs Virginia Bottomley, between June 1994 and January 1995, stressed that:

> Partnership is the key to further progress based on values and aspirations which all those involved with the NHS should share. Health professionals and managers must work together, each realising the vital contribution that the other group has to make to providing services which are effective, responsive to need, and which make the best use of the resources available.

It is, therefore, clear that a mature partnership and a continuous dialogue is essential to the development of effective purchaser–provider relationships – but how is this happy state to be achieved?

Key features of a successful purchaser-provider relationship

Given that a successful dialogue between purchaser–provider is of such prime importance it is helpful to analyse how this is characterised. Again, some of the key elements emphasised by Dr Mawhinney in his 1993 speech are instructive:

- Dialogue should involve openness and explicitness about the service and financial context in which contracts operate and an agreed approach to risk sharing.
- Joint working should take place in common areas of interest, for example, consumer consultation or dialogue with GPs on care in the community.
- There should be an agreed approach to information sharing.
- A shared understanding is required of who does what in each organisation and who are the key contacts on particular issues.
- Flexibility to adapt relationships to changing circumstances should be retained.

Mature purchaser–provider relationships are also likely to be characterised by:

- longer agreements and lower transactions costs and a drive for greater cost effectiveness;
- GP involvement;
- general debate about, and a clear process for, determining priorities and values;
- agreed strategic and policy frameworks with an emphasis on evidence-based medicine.

In addition, a clear understanding of the purchaser role and functions is fundamental to the provider in deciding how and when to engage and influence purchaser thinking and in developing the relationship that is a feature of successful purchaser–provider partnerships.

This chapter concentrates on the relationship with health authority purchasers, although clearly there are several models of shared purchasing such as:

- general practice fundholding in which GPs purchase certain services for their patients;
- total purchasing in which the authority's whole budget for a given population is delegated to a GP practice or group of practices;
- locality commissioning whereby the health authority and GPs and local agencies seek to develop a common approach to purchasing for a defined locality.

Understanding the role of the new health authority

The three key roles of the new health authority are set out in the NHS Executive letter 'Developing NHS purchasing and GP fundholding' (NHSE, 1994).

1. Strategy: Health authorities are charged with developing a strategy in collaboration with GPs, local people and other agencies (particularly local authorities) to meet national and local priorities. They remain responsible for discharging public health functions and for establishing a local population perspective of health and health care needs, working with others to ensure this influences local health strategy. Health authorities are expected to involve the public in developing local strategy and to increase public understanding about health and the changing nature of health services.

2. Monitoring: Within the national framework health authorities will advise on budget allocations to GP fundholders and ensure that the way in which GPs fulfil their providing and purchasing role is in the interest of patients and local people. They will be responsible for ensuring that national policy and local strategy are implemented effectively.

3. Support: Health authorities will provide support to GPs in both their primary care provision and fundholding capacities through the provision of advice, investment and training. They will purchase directly those services which require a broad population base. They will also provide information to practices to support GP purchasing decisions.

Health authorities continue to have a major role as direct purchasers of hospital and community health services – for instance those services requiring a broader population base and services currently outwith the fundholding scheme. At present DHAs purchase some 90 per cent of such services and will continue to have a direct purchasing role for some time – including, of course, the negotiation and monitoring of contracts with providers.

The key elements of the process by which the health authority undertakes this role are:

- needs assessment: to identify the health needs of the local population;
- strategy development: to develop strategies aimed at meeting identified needs;
- priority setting: debating and determining priorities for local service provision in the context of needs and available resources;
- service specification: developing and agreeing specifications for the services to be delivered by providers;

- contracting: negotiating contracts with providers to deliver an agreed range and quality of services at a given price;
- monitoring: monitoring the services provided to ensure that they meet standards of quality and efficiency;
- review: reviewing the services provided against specifications and perceived needs and adjusting as necessary.

This is the theory, but how do these roles and processes work in practice and how can providers influence the thinking and work of health authorities?

Influencing health authorities/purchaser thinking

For providers to influence the work of health authorities it is vital to establish clear lines of communication and not just at chairman and chief executive level. On all aspects of the health authorities' role, providers need to know how what they are doing relates to, say, key Health of the Nation targets. They should therefore be involved throughout the cycle of health authority work.

It is particularly important for professionals to become involved in this process, especially consultants and other clinicians. The importance of this factor has recently been highlighted in guidance on *Professional Involvement in Health Authority Work* (NHSE, EL(95)6 and HSE(95)H). There are many health authority functions where appropriate professional advice is an essential component of fulfilling responsibilities – for example, all clinical staff have a role to play and many have advice to give on improving clinical effectiveness. The initiatives involved include clinical audit, clinical guidelines, service specifications and clinical outcome measurement.

Reviews of specific services and the subsequent purchasing of most services should involve provider clinicians and may require specialist knowledge about aspects of service delivery which the new health authorities are unlikely to possess (in entirety) themselves.

A recent review of emergency healthcare services undertaken by North Yorkshire Health Authority presents a case study of the involvement of local clinicians in the strategy review process. This review was undertaken with the intention of determining the future location and role of the main hospital providers in the county and of creating a high degree of certainty for major providers about their role in emergency care for a generation. This should enable the development of longer term contracts and enable the more rapid review and restructuring of other specialties. The review process involved the active participation of a wide variety of local groups, but professional advice from leading specialists outside the county was also sought in order to ensure that the Authority's recommendations were made, and seen to be made, on the firmest foundation possible.

An important component of the Authority's approach has been to appoint a medical director, one of whose key roles is to relate to provider medical directors on clinical issues. Trust medical directors therefore have a clear route of communication with the health authority on matters of clinical policy and can readily put forward their viewpoint on these issues to the purchaser and help co-ordinate work on clinical standards setting.

In conclusion, it is evident that genuine dialogue, partnership and mutual understanding are the critical issues to address in managing the purchaser–provider relationship. This requires openness and explicitness on both sides, particularly about the service and financial context in which contracts operate; joint working in areas of common interest; a good understanding of who does what in each organisation and retaining the flexibility to adapt relationships to changing circumstances.

References

NHSE (1993) *Purchasing for Health – A framework for action*, speeches by Dr Brian Mawhinney and Sir Duncan Nichol, NHSE, London.

NHSE (1994) *Developing NHS Purchasing and Prescribing*, EL(94)79, NHSE, London.

NHSE (1995) *Progress through Partnership – four speeches given by Secretary of State for Health, Virginia Bottomley*, NHSE, London.

NHSE (1995) *Professional Involvement in Health Authority Work*, EL(95)6, NHSE, London.

NHSE (1995) *Professional Involvement in Health Authority Work*, HSG(95)11, NHSE, London.

Managing Relationships – Trust-to-Trust

Louise Adams

Introduction

Five years from the establishment of the first 57 there are now 528 Trusts in the UK ranging in income from £2.6 million to £264 million.[1] In the design stages no one envisaged so many, so soon, nor that trust status would be adapted to suit such a variety of healthcare providers. Attempts at grouping them produce 12–13 variations, ranging from 'all district' services to single specialties. Little wonder then that government and external audiences have difficulty identifying meaningful comparisons between Trusts or that Trusts themselves have had to develop whole new mechanisms for talking to and working with each other.

So how do service providers make sense of this diversity in their own relationships? The purchaser–provider split with funding following contracts of an increasingly detailed nature, engineered and encouraged a level of competitive isolation that inspired the individual Trust board to approach their position in the NHS market with a big business aggression previously foreign to the NHS. Today's more experienced and knowledgable boards have clearer strategic objectives, participate in a more mature market moving to longer term contracting arrangements, and are realistic about the political environment in which they are providing health care services. Once fashionable adjectives, such as 'independent' and 'self-governing', perpetuating images of splendid isolation, soon fell out of use.

In 1995, most Trusts prefer the benefits of collaborative relationships, but the extent of collaboration varies. All in all perhaps a collaborative ethos has grown up because NHS management teams see greater benefit and opportunity in effective cooperation with regards resources, than in the investment required to truly compete. The key is to secure the income stream and the methods are many. This chapter looks at the benefits of collaboration over competition in the NHS market in the late 1990s and specifically at how Trusts are working together to achieve changes in service to benefit patients and improve services.

Mergers and finding a law of configuration

Periodic reviews over the last 2–3 years suggest there is no constant law of configuration – what works well in some areas cannot automatically be replicated elsewhere.[2] At the design stage there appears to have been almost no prescribed pattern to configuration: Trusts were set up based on the assessment of financial soundness of their originating application. Now they are judged annually on attaining their financial targets, meeting Health of the Nation targets and Patients Charter standards. In such an age of continuous improvement and with increasing mechanisms by which to measure it, prescription over size, shape or components is unnecessary.

The trend to merge seems so far to have been inspired by consolidation through Trusts seeking to achieve economies of scale and/or best use of their inherited assets, as suggested by the Audit Commission.[3] Some acute and community Trusts are also looking to come together to help integration of services.[2] Yet no one pattern has emerged; instead Trusts have taken on board the logic of regular review and the need to stay abreast of innovation and good practice. Currently, trends suggest a gradual increase in Trust mergers.

Evidence on the operation of the internal market from the NHS Executive issued in December 1994, indicates that they will support mergers and joint ventures between NHS providers, where such projects do *not* lead to the acquisition and abuse of monopoly power with subsequent detrimental effects on patients' welfare. Where mergers between acute and community Trusts are proposed, the safeguarding of the full range of services is crucial.

Collusion

Quality and the effectiveness and efficiency of care are the drivers for more co-operative relationships, although without competition or contestability some would suggest the NHS is losing out on innovation and choice. Such non-competitive behaviour is subject to rules. The NHS Executive describes collusion as follows:

- keeping prices significantly above cost but agreeing not to compete;

- agreeing not to compete in certain localities or in certain services;
- agreeing not to bid against each other when purchasers put contracts out to tender.

Co-operation undertaken in the interest of patients is distinguished from action serving to protect the interests of purchasers and providers. As the market continues to mature, Trusts have found a variety of formal and informal mechanisms by which to engage in collaborative activity, whilst public scrutiny over accountability of Trusts has left them all too aware of the risks of accusation of collusion.[4]

Working together for better services and meeting contracts

The NHS continues to strive for a more responsive service sensitive to patients' needs. Upon GP referral, patients fast encounter packages of care that may be provided by 2–3 different agencies within the NHS alone. The patient's experience is then influenced by the extent to which the boundaries between organisations interfere with their perception of continuity of care. More complex still, some staff are employed by one organisation but work consistently in the culture and environment of another, eg mental health nurses working in acute general hospitals. Care provided by a mix of organisations has formalised trust-to-trust relationships that begin at working level and may not have been originally rooted in strategy but practicalities. The challenge of 'care packages', 'care pathways' and 'seamless care', is in not being able to see the join.

Purchasers too, frustrated by inefficient and undesirable patterns of care have built expectations of joint working into the contracting relationships. 'Preferred provider' mechanisms or tenders for clinical services are examples. Elderly care, for example, may conceivably involve three Trusts; purchasers may decide to allot contract responsibility to one Trust leaving it to sub-contract for components not currently within its capability. Such relationships ensure informed decisions about purchasing and make best use of the high quality of professional advice available in the preferred provider. 'Lead' provider is another such term, although the provider taking the lead need not be the one providing the largest component of the relevant service. Indeed more leverage may be secured by the purchasing authority where they are not. For example, community Trusts may thus look to sub-contract for the tangible acute episode component of care for stroke whilst looking to provide the community and rehabilitation components themselves. As Trusts become more aware of their own strengths and weaknesses so they are better able to develop services that transcend organisational boundaries.

Tertiary referrals will continue to require good trust-to-trust relationships, many of which have long existed on consultant referral routes. Such mechanisms are becoming formalised to meet contract specifications; this cuts down on the high transaction costs of ECRs. This satisfies the purchaser, but in practice clinicians may feel it restricts their freedom of choice of service for the individual patient. So whilst the introduction of the market is synonymous with increased choice, the clinician feels his/her clinical decision is increasingly in the shadow of contractual relationships. Almost inevitably there is a sense in which this results in reduced competition.

Some services have been subject to national advice, where variations in service quality and identification of better/more effective models have resulted in central planning. Where there is national advice but no extra funding, local providers are likely to collaborate to identify the way forward. Purchasers will also be involved and the health authority has a significant role to play as referee.

Trust-to-Trust relationships for education, training, manpower and substitution

Educational and training links also transcend organisational boundaries with staffing rotations that may involve staff gaining experience in a number of organisations. Such rotations between hospitals are well established and much is made of historic links between teaching and non-teaching hospitals. NHS education and training has new challenges to face. New skills are needed as caring responsibility transfers to nurse practitioners or midwives serving as lead professionals in childbirth and other new staff roles in the community. New expertise needs to be developed – nurses trained to work in institutions need to be reskilled and retrained to work outside of them too. Such trends in staff moving across boundaries are set to continue. Medical staff trained and experienced in working in hospital environments are rarely experienced in working from the GP's surgery or the patient's home and yet increasing amounts of care will be delivered there. From such changes the NHS is facing new relationships between professionals as well as organisations.

Manpower planning needs to precede service planning in such circumstances. The advent of new education consortia in each region to manage training needs will encourage Trusts to work together to develop the workforce for the future. Some Trusts are already exploring their boundaries: in Yorkshire, paramedics from the local ambulance service are working on hospital wards to relieve pressure on junior doctors, whilst gaining valuable experience themselves.[5] Trusts with long-standing responsibility to train post-registration professionals, are working with Royal Colleges to agree training and placement packages that transcend the boundaries created by natural competition.

The introduction of local pay in the Health Service has also acted as a lever. Whilst enabling Trusts to set their own pay rates for new staff and establish pay and reward systems that match local needs, they also enable Trusts to work together to recruit and retain staff in 'difficult to recruit' groups. Such working relationships are vital where shortages in specialties would otherwise mean the rate for the job could progressively spiral. The majority of Trusts only began to embark on meaningful local pay schemes this year. A clear understanding of local markets is necessary and such 'cartel' arrangements, although anti-competitive, can be justified in that whilst pay is reasonable, the services gain little from increased spiralling, poaching, or an unnecessarily high turnover. Indeed, the degree to which unofficial 'cartel' arrangements become more necessary with the move to local pay will be the subject of some interest when Trusts embark on local pay for a second year.

Conclusion

In an environment that is actively pro-competition, Trusts seem to be increasingly seeking to collaborate, not because the market is 'lazy' or nominal, but because resources are sufficiently tight that energy spent in competitive activity, instead of strategic collaborative activity, may not be in the interests of patients and the service. The foreseeable benefits of working together for patient care standards are persuasive, as Séan Boyle and Anthony Harrison have said, 'reliance on an old organisational structure is inhibiting the development of new ways of delivering health service'[6] or, at least, it could if Trusts were not recognising that the future lies in strategic relationships that enable services to develop in spite of organisational boundaries.

References

1 NAHAT (1995) *1995-6 NHS Handbook (10th Edition)*, NAHAT, Birmingham.
2 NAHAT (1994) *The future of provider services in the NHS – Trust mergers and demergers*, NAHAT, Birmingham.
3 Audit Commission (1995) *A price on their heads: measuring management costs in NHS trusts*, HMSO, London.
4 *The operation of the internal market: local freedoms, national responsibilities*, NAHAT Briefing No: 77.
5 *The Independent* 30 August 1995.
6 Boyle, S and Harrison, A (1995) *The Health Service Journal*, 30 March.

Managing the Relationship between Doctors and Managers

Jenny Simpson

Much has been written about the rhetoric of the doctor's role in management, but little about the realities. The experience of members of the British Association of Medical Managers (BAMM) and, more specifically, research conducted by the Association, has identified factors critical to the success of devolved management structures.

In the Management Enquiry, which Sir Roy Griffiths undertook for the Secretary of State in 1983, he states that 'The nearer the management process gets to the patient, the more important it becomes for the doctors to be looked upon as the natural managers'. Since then there have been a number of initiatives aimed at involving doctors more fully in the management of health care during a period of gradual change in attitude among the medical profession. Ten years ago, a doctor who expressed an interest in management was, at best, suspected of eccentricity, but more often accused of a lack of clinical commitment. Now, however, a move into management, especially on a part-time basis, is widely regarded as a healthy and interesting development in a clinical career. This has been reinforced by a well-established trend in the USA, Canada and Australia, where doctors with specific talents in management progress to senior positions in the management of their organisations.

Key principles

The research already mentioned identified a number of key principles for the effective involvement of clinical staff in management:

KEY PRINCIPLES

- Hospitals exist to care for sick and injured people – core of management process.
- The driving force of the hospital is its clinical teams – devolved management.
- Services are designed around patients.
- Decisions are taken openly and rationally.
- All decisions are taken with consideration of the clinical perspective.

First, there must be a shared belief that the hospital exists to care for sick and injured people. All other activities, whatever they may be, are secondary to this and each and every management process must have the patient at its heart.

Second, the driving force in the hospital must be multi-disciplinary clinical teams, assisted and supported by management, financial and personnel expertise. The service of the organisation is delivered by clinicians – nurses, doctors and other clinical professionals. They hold the intimate knowledge of patient needs, and it is vital that this unique knowledge is harnessed in the effective management of the service. To do this clinicians must be helped and genuinely supported by administrative staff.

The third component focuses on the design of clinical services, which must be geared to the needs of the patient rather than those of the staff. Clinical services, just as any other service, must be designed around the needs of the 'customer'. In many instances the 'customers' of the health service are ill, distressed and vulnerable, and there is no justification for designing the service in terms of, for example, appointment systems, facilities or access, merely to meet the needs of the hospital staff.

The fourth factor concerns the way decisions are made. In the ideal scenario, decisions are taken on the basis of hard fact and expert knowledge by all stakeholders, rather than on the basis of politics or convenience. We are all familiar with the way in which apparently straightforward decisions sometimes result in a completely unpredictable outcome simply because of political interference – either within the organisation or by external forces which have some vested interest.

Finally, there is the ideal of decisions at every level of the organisation being taken in the light of a clinical perspective.

How principles are compromised

In reality clinical management places considerable demands both on clinicians and on managers. It is not by any means easy to lead an organisation when much of the power and authority has been devolved to teams of professionals, particularly when those teams may have little management expertise and almost certainly have varying degrees of skill and aptitude for management.

The general manager and the corporate team must strike a balance between retaining central control and a gradual letting go of the reins in parallel with development and education of clinical management teams. Many managers do not get this balance right, and far fewer hit upon a formula that works for an entire hospital. Some do however, and it is to these Trusts that we must look for guidance. It is a mistake to believe that decentralisation of management is a structural issue involving merely the drawing up of a new set of organisational charts. In reality, it means a true devolution of management power. Some chief executives and indeed executive teams find it extremely difficult to relinquish central control. Equally, some clinicians are reluctant to take on the power and the responsibility of a managerial role.

The effect of these changes is far more wide-reaching than those doctors and managers involved. In reality, the entire organisation is affected. In particular the 'tribal hierarchies' which for decades have formed a major part of the lives of clinicians are no longer appropriate. The introduction of a directorate system of devolved management, in which all staff are accountable to the clinical director, leaves the director of nursing services without a direct managerial line to the nursing staff. The excellent directors talk of 'managing nursing not nurses'. This type of change has led to some tension and indeed in some organisations to outright war. It takes considerable skill and a thorough understanding of the principles of change management to bring about major organisational change effectively and with the minimum of pain.

The false front

In a small number of hospitals the antithesis of the ideal scenario is developing. Clinical managers may be in place on paper – indeed the organisational chart may well be extremely detailed and technically devolved. On analysis, however, there is no real devolution of management authority. This can be extremely confusing for the key organisational players. While they may have the title and other evidence of the status of clinical director, such as an extra secretary or a management office, they may nevertheless be completely excluded from the decision-making process. Worse, they may realise that this is so, or remain unaware of the true nature of the organisation.

There are Trusts in which clinical directors spend considerable amounts of time and energy attending meetings, preparing papers and making an active contribution in a variety of ways. However, these contributions are never acted upon and strategies greeted with enthusiasm are never implemented, even when a full agreement is reached at meetings. Another symptom of this particular and confusing organisational pathology, is the existence of a parallel decision-making body in addition to that of the clinical management board. The chief executive will meet with a group of non-medical managers on a regular basis who will, in fact, be making the decisions that run the hospital. Meanwhile, the clinical directors are meeting in the belief that their decision-making is the driving force. A common but less extreme variant of this syndrome is one in which clinicians are involved in the decision-making process, but only ever at an operational level. In this situation the clinicians are allowed to make decisions within their own directorate or affecting the whole hospital – such as whether the car park gates should lift up and down or swing out and in. However, they are excluded from the long-term decision-making for the strategic direction of the hospital, which takes place in some inner cabal and is delivered as a *fait accompli* to the clinical directors.

A further problem encountered in some Trusts is continuing resistance by long-established tribal middle managers, who have effectively been relieved of their traditional powerbase. If mishandled, they may feel extremely threatened by devolved management and are capable of using complex damaging tactics to undermine every aspect of the directorate structure. For example, they will be reluctant to relinquish meetings with directorate staff of their own discipline, even though this is no longer appropriate in the new structure, and will make strenuous efforts to maintain the old relationships and the status quo.

There may also be a lack of understanding on the part of management that clinical staff involved in the management process need appropriate information, time and support. There may be a grudging attitude towards the involvement of clinical staff in management, and little enthusiasm for providing administrative or clerical support, or even investing in further clinical help to free up the clinical director for the role.

Organisations with these characteristics are understandably populated by a cynical and demoralised clinical staff, who quickly reach the conclusion that an involvement in management leads rapidly to taking the blame for the hospital's overspend without any authority to do anything about it.

THE FALSE FRONT

- Clinical managers in place on paper only; clinicians get the blame for overspend but have no authority.
- Undermining of the devolved structure by tribal middle/senior managers.
- Expectation that clinical managers should be effective without information, time or managerial support.
- Demoralised and cynical clinical staff.

Challenges for medical managers

For the doctor in management, whether as a clinical director with a two to three sessional commitment, or as a medical director with a part-time or even a full-time managerial post, there are a number of challenges and usually very little time to achieve them.

First, doctors in management must learn to direct their peers. Doctors are generally used to being single players, leading their clinical team. They are unused to being responsible for the actions of their colleagues and to any form of hierarchy at consultant level other than seniority. They must also learn to be directed, as they learn to be managerially accountable for their actions – a new concept for most consultants.

Second, doctors must learn to contribute to the management decision process. Traditionally, doctors have influenced decision-making in an advisory capacity, often using their professional powerbase to achieve whatever outcome they wished to see. This has frequently led to accusations of shroud waving on the part of managers. In a decentralised management structure, medical professionals must learn to play a very different role, engaging in rational debate to achieve outcomes that will benefit the hospital as a whole, working as a team whether it be at directorate or at hospital board level. They must learn to allocate resources effectively to ensure the future well-being of the organisation and its patients, not merely concentrating on their own particular speciality or service.

Finally, there is a full range of expertise that must be acquired. Finance, business planning, personnel management, marketing and strategy formulation are new areas of study for most clinicians, all of which are needed to some extent in the role of clinical or medical director. They need to be able to understand and evaluate the specialist advice of management accounts, personnel specialists and others. The busy clinician must also master perhaps the most difficult and trying challenge of all, the management of time. For a clinician all management activities inevitably represent a conflict with clinical or personal time.

ISSUES FOR DOCTORS
- Learning to be directors and directed.
- Learning to contribute to management decision-making.
- New areas of expertise and technical skills.

The keys to success

Devolved management structures appear to work very much better in some organisations than others. The BAMM survey was designed to identify the characteristics of those which were functioning well from the perspectives of patients, clinicians and management. Eight fundamental success factors were identified by the study, and the following list gives some indication of the types of environment in which decentralised clinical management will thrive, and therefore the conditions those contemplating a move into management should seek to identify in their own organisations.

Trust, respect and openness on both sides between doctors and managers

In any organisation there are tensions, and this is even more the case in complex organisations such as hospitals. There must be a fundamental trust and respect on both sides if clinical management is to survive. Essentially there needs to be a recognition of the differences between the managerial cultures of power and role and the professional cultures which are task and person oriented. Both clinicians and managers must then concentrate on shared values, shared goals and objectives and an open dialogue aimed at establishing a shared view of what the organisation exists to do. This requires flexibility, trust and time for all parties.

Debate and dialogue based on appropriate, accurate and timely information

The quest for achieving high quality, accurate information upon which doctors in management may base their decision-making has dogged the health service for decades. Indeed, Florence Nightingale wrote in 1863, 'In attempting to arrive at the truth, I have applied everywhere for information but in scarcely an instance have I been able to obtain hospital records fit for any purpose of comparison. If they could be obtained ... they should show what amount of good has really been done with it and whether the money was not doing mischief rather than good'.

An appropriate level of consistent administrative support for clinical directors

Clinicians cannot simply take on additional, complex work without administrative help. The supportive organisation will make strenuous efforts to relieve doctors from clinical duties by bringing in some form of additional clinical back-up. It should ensure that clinical directors are supported by business managers, finance and personnel expertise. It will tolerate the learning stages through which a clinician new to the world of management must pass and will make every effort to assist him or her.

Development of strong, powerful teams within directorates

Teams within directorates must be allowed to flourish and thrive. They will meet many challenges and pressures. Their survival will be dependent upon excellent communication and a determination to work together to deliver an excellent clinical service.

Development of a single management board comprising clinical and non-clinical managers

The entire Trust must be governed by a single decision-making body. The development of a second executive or 'administrative body', or, worse still, of a plethora of small committees with a bewildering array of three-letter titles is a bad sign.

Agreement on the role and job descriptions of the directorate members

There must be clarity as to what is expected of those who venture into management. Job descriptions should be made explicit and the objectives to which clinical directors and directorate team members are working should be made public and circulated throughout the directorate. Similarly, clinical directors should be aware of the objectives to which the chief executive and executive team are working.

Open and explicit processes for election or appointment of clinical directors

Whatever the approach to appointment of clinical managers taken by a hospital, it must be open and explicit. The process must be fair with open access to all those interested in taking on a management role. Given that the clinical director must in the end be in a position to lead his colleagues, many chief executives involve the consultant staff in the process of appointment of clinical directors.

Formal contracts and an appropriate, agreed and explicit reward scheme for clinical directors

If the integrity of the new system is to be maintained, it is essential that clinical directors are rewarded in a consistent and open fashion. The mechanism of reward varies from hospital to hospital and ranges from financial incentive to clinical support, to an increase in paid leave. Whatever the reward scheme chosen, it should be perceived as appropriate and should be explicit.

The absolute requirement

A number of factors recur consistently throughout both the BAMM survey and subsequent studies. From this body of research, the following minimum requirements for successful implementation of developed management structures are drawn:

- **Chief Executive** A strong, highly skilled general manager who is capable of, and totally committed to, relinquishing the existing powerbase and leading a fully devolved organisation. This commitment must be visible in every single decision taken within the Trust.
- **Doctors** A sufficient number of senior medical staff members with the enthusiasm, stamina and determination to take on a management role, to accept the constraints that this places on clinical work and to take on the challenge of learning how to do it effectively and efficiently.
- **Information** Recognisably accurate, timely and appropriately presented information detailing the clinical activity taking place within a directorate.
- **Investment** In support and education for clinical directors and their teams, on the part of corporate management.

The benefits

It is clear from the experience of those who have been deeply involved in medical management that it is by no means an easy task. Some doctors have become bitter and cynical as a result of tangling with management – usually those in organisations which have been less than supportive of the idea of clinical management. On the other hand there are many doctors who, after their term of office has ended, have wished to stay on in their management roles, finding it difficult to step back from the more strategic perspective. Such doctors generally acknowledge the complexities of the task, but do in fact find the management role extremely stimulating, enjoyable and, above all, interesting. Many are now questioning whether it is sensible to adhere to a time-limited term of office as clinical director, or whether the system should be changed to allow those who have a particular interest or talent in management to train and take on a long-term position. Some are looking to move into a medical director role in due course.

Those chief executives and medical directors who can create a culture in which doctors take on a variety of management roles and begin to build bridges between doctors and managers will find in the long run that the organisation becomes proactive, flexible and self-developing in ways which are hard to imagine.

References and bibliography

BAMM, BMA, IHSM, RCN (1993) *Managing Clinical Services*, IHSM, London.

Griffiths, E R (1983) *Management Inquiry for Department of Health and Social Security*, HMSO, London.

Handy, C (1976) *Understanding Organisations*, Penguin Education Series, Harmondsworth, p 177.

Harrison, R (1972) 'How to describe your organisation', *Harvard Business Review*.

Kakabadse, A, Ludlow, R and Vinnicombe, S (1987) *Working in Organisations*, Gower, London, pp 214–25.

Mintzberg, *et al.* (1987) 'The structure of unstructured decision process', *Administrative Seminar Quarterly*, pp 250–51.

Mintzberg, H (1983) *Structure in Fives: Designing Effective Organisations*, Prentice-Hall, New York, Chapter 10.

Mintzberg, H (1988) *The Professional Organisation, Mintzberg on Management*, Free Press, New York, pp 180–81.

Peters, T J, Phillips, J R and Waterman, R H (1980) 'Structure is not organisation', *Business Horizons*.

Simpson, J (1993) 'BAMM clinical directorate survey', *Clinician in Management*, vol 2, no 4, p 13–15.

Waterman, R H, Peters, T J, Phillips, J R (1988) 'The 7-S framework in the strategy process', in Quinn, Mintzberg and James, *Concepts, Contexts and Cases*, Prentice-Hall International, New York, pp 271–2.

PART EIGHT

APPENDICES

Appendix I

Health Service Guidelines

HSG(94)1   General ophthalmic services: Increases in NHS domiciliary sight test fees and domiciliary visiting fees
HSG(94)2   Decision of the NHS Tribunal
HSG(94)3   Health Service use of ionising radiation
HSG(94)4   Developing NHS purchasing and GP fundholding
HSG(94)5   Abortion Act 1967 – Guidance on the provision of treatment for termination of pregnancy
HSG(94)6   People with a mental illness: Local authority specific grant for 1995–6
HSG(94)7   The pay and conditions of service for general and senior managers
HSG(94)8   NHS responsibilities for meeting continuing healthcare needs
HSG(94)9   People with a mental illness supplementary credit approval for capital funding in 1994–5
HSG(94)10   Hospital infection control
HSG(94)11   Professional involvement in HA work
HSG(94)12   Decisions of the Professional Conduct Committee of the General Medical Council
HSG(94)13   Revised and expanded Patient's Charter: Implementation
HSG(94)14   General ophthalmic services: Increases in spectacle voucher values
HSG(94)15   Private finance and capital investment projects
HSG(94)16   Confidential enquiry into stillbirths and deaths in infancy
HSG(94)17   Increased NHS prescription charges: Revised prescription forms
HSG(94)18   Conditions of service for general and senior managers
HSG(94)19   Information to support the Health of the Nation
HSG(94)20   Taxation of staff benefits and allowances – Crown cars and mileage allowances
HSG(94)21   Clinical audit of suicides and other unexplained deaths
HSG(94)22   The new regional health authorities/regional offices
HSG(94)23   Charges for drugs and appliances
HSG(94)24   The education of sick children

HSG(94)25 GP fundholding: List of goods and services
HSG(94)26 GP fundholding: The National Health Service (Fundholding Practices) Amendment Regulations 1994
HSG(94)27 Guidance on the discharge of mentally disordered people and their continuing care in the community
HSG(94)28 Priority treatment for war pensioners
HSG(94)29 General medical services GP practice vacancies: Revised selection procedures
HSG(94)30 Decisions of the General Medical Council's Professional Conduct Committee
HSG(94)31 Capital investment in the NHS: The Capital Investment Manual
HSG(94)32 Decisions of the Professional Conduct Committee of the General Medical Council
HSG(94)33 Dental advice to family health services authorities
HSG(94)34 Changes to the welfare foods scheme
HSG(94)35 Secretary of State's list for dental prescribing
HSG(94)36 Distinction awards: Nominal roll of consultants
HSG(94)37 Mutual recognition of qualifications for the provision of hearing aids in the private and public sectors
HSG(94)38 Dental advice for RHAs, DHAs and FHSAs
HSG(94)39 Appointment of doctors to hospital posts: Termination of pregnancy
HSG(94)40 General ophthalmic services: Increase to the NHS sight test fees for optometrists
HSG(94)41 Interventional ventilation and organ transplant
HSG(94)42 Decision of the NHS Tribunal
HSG(94)43 Protection of children: Disclosure to NHS employers of criminal background of those with access to children
HSG(94)44 Decisions of the Professional Conduct Committee of the GMC
HSG(94)45 Abortion notification envelopes – HSA4 ENV
HSG(94)46 Removal and associated expenses – payments to staff for loss of equity and additional housing costs
HSG(94)47 Framework for local community care charters in England
HSG(94)48 NHS low income scheme. NHS optical voucher scheme. Extension of automatic entitlement to help with health costs to recipients of DWA whose capital is £8000 or less
HSG(94)49 Disciplinary procedures for hospital and community medical and hospital dental staff
HSG(94)50 Clinical waste management
HSG(94)51 Occupational Health Service for NHS Staff
HSG(94)52 Emergency planning in the NHS: Health Services arrangements for dealing with major incidents – protective clothing
HSG(94)53 Regional health authorities/regional offices: Further guidance for RHA/RO staff on the division of functions
HSG(94)54 NHS trading agencies: Future arrangements
HSG(94)55 The operation of the NHS internal market
HSG(94)56 GP fundholding management allowance
HSG(95)1   General ophthalmic services: Increases in NHS domiciliary sight fees and domiciliary visiting fees

HSG(95)2   Decision of the NHS Tribunal
HSG(95)3   Health service use of ionising radiations
HSG(95)4   Developing NHS purchasing and GP fundholding
HSG(95)5   Abortion Act 1967 – Guidance on the provision of treatment for termination of pregnancy
HSG(95)6   People with mental illness: Local authority specific grant for 1995–6
HSG(95)7   The pay and conditions of service for general and senior managers
HSG(95)8   NHS responsibilities for meeting continuing healthcare needs
HSG(95)9   People with a mental illness: Supplementary credit approval for Capital Funding in 1994–5
HSG(95)10   Hospital infection control
HSG(95)11   Ensuring the effective involvement of professionals in health authority work
HSG(95)12   Decisions of the Professional Conduct Committee of the General Medical Council
HSG(95)13   Revised and expanded Patient's Charter
HSG(95)14   General ophthalmic services: Increases in spectacle voucher values
HSG(95)15   Private finance and capital investment projects
HSG(95)16   Confidential enquiry into stillbirths and deaths in infancy
HSG(95)17   Increased NHS prescription charges: Revised prescription forms
HSG(95)18   Hospital laundry arrangements for used and infected linen
HSG(95)19   GP fundholding: List of goods and services
HSG(95)20   Guidance on the revised operation of notification arrangements for tertiary extra contractual referrals
HSG(95)21   Professions supplementary to medicine issue of directions in relation to the staff of NHS contractors
HSG(95)22   Decisions of the Professional Conduct Committee of the General Medical Council
HSG(95)23   Hepatitis and blood transfusion look back
HSG(95)24   Road Traffic Act charges
HSG(95)25   NHS early retirement arrangements
HSG(95)26   Health authority drug misuse services 1995–6
HSG(95)27   Changes to the Welfare Food Scheme

Appendix II

Executive Letters

EL(95)1   Patient perception booklets
EL(95)2   Report of the Working Party on the Unified Training Grade
EL(95)3   Working together to achieve the New Deal
EL(95)4   Health of the nation: Assessing the options in the CHD and stroke key area
EL(95)5   Purchasing high-tech health care for patients at home
EL(95)6   Health authority; professional involvement
EL(95)7   Quality in the NHS breast screening programme
EL(95)8   Prescribing expenditure: Guidance on allocation and budget setting for 1995–6
EL(95)9   Service increment for teaching
EL(95)10   The Patient's Charter: GP Practice Charters
EL(95)11   Day hospitals for elderly people
EL(95)12   Improvements to the operation of the cervical screening programme
EL(95)13   'Vision for the Future': Implementation and evaluation 1995 and beyond
EL(95)14   HIV/AIDS funding
EL(95)15   Public health laboratory service
EL(95)16   Strategic planning for Information Management and Technology
EL(95)17   Reduction in junior doctors' hours in Trent region: The nursing contribution
EL(95)18   Public health in England: Dental aspects
EL(95)19   Not issued
EL(95)20   Annual Report of the Advisory Committee on Distinction Awards
EL(95)21   Doctors and their careers: A new generation
EL(95)22   Specialist palliative care services including the Drugs for Hospices Scheme
EL(95)23   Changing childbirth: Invitation to bid for development funds
EL(95)24   The creation of the new health authorities
EL(95)25   1995 Departmental Report for Department of Health and OPCS

EL(95)26	Revised and expanded Patient's Charter: Implementation
EL(95)27	Education and training in the new NHS
EL(95)28	Not issued
EL(95)29	Market testing in the NHS: Update and future plans
EL(95)30	Applying NHS standards when procuring computer standards
EL(95)31	Future regional public health role
EL(95)32	Special constabulary: Medical and nursing staff
EL(95)33	Interim NHS support for MRC-funded clinical research
EL(95)34	Local pay: Guidance for purchasers
EL(95)35	Management of construction projects: Revised monitoring arrangements
EL(95)36	PREP
EL(95)37	Acting on complaints
EL(95)38	Family Health Services Appeal Authority
EL(95)39	Community care monitoring: Report of 1994 national resources
EL(95)40	Clinical negligence scheme for Trusts
EL(95)41	Community health councils
EL(95)42	Not issued
EL(95)43	Health and well-being: A guide for older people
EL(95)44	Review of ambulance training
EL(95)45	The Human Fertilisation and Embryology Act 1990: Storage of sperm (or eggs) for cancer patients
EL(95)46	Supporting R&D in the NHS: Implementation plan
EL(95)47	Review of primary care projects for homeless people
EL(95)48	Funding of hospital and dental training grade posts
EL(95)49	Local pay
EL(95)50	Hospital doctors: Training for the future – proposals for implementing legislation: The specialist medical order
EL(95)51	Strategic policy framework for cancer services
EL(95)52	Review of central requirements for information: Uses made of information collected from the NHS
EL(95)53	Local elections
EL(95)54	An accountability framework for GP fundholding
EL(95)55	Cervical cytology
EL(95)56	Tackling drugs together
EL(95)57	The transfer of patients to shorter waiting lists
EL(95)58	Making it happen: Public Health – the contribution, role and development of nurses, midwives and health visitors
EL(95)59	(a) NHS Performance Tables 1994–5 (b) 'Charter Week'
EL(95)60	Code of practice on openness in the NHS: Guidance on implementation
EL(95)61	New NHS number
EL(95)62	Hospital doctors: Training for the future – supplementary reports on general practice, overseas doctors and academic and research medicine
EL(95)63	Undergraduate medical and dental education
EL(95)64	Outturn 1994–5 (non-financial information)
EL(95)65	Not known
EL(95)66	Managing in the NHS: A study of senior executives

EL(95)67	Contract energy management
EL(95)68	Priorities and planning guidance for the NHS: 1996–7
EL(95)69	Overseas work experience and professional development of NHS staff
EL(95)70	Not issued
EL(95)71	Second Report of the Medical Workforce Standing Committee (MWSAC)
EL(95)72	The New Deal
EL(95)73	Employee assistance for health authority staff affected by organisational change
EL(95)74	The Quality Register
EL(95)75	Handling confidential patient information on contract minimum data sets: Guidance for purchasers undertaking a review of compliance with data protection principles
EL(95)76	Code of conduct for community health council members
EL(95)77	Changing patterns of maternity care: Implications for pay and grading for midwives and midwifery senior management
EL(95)78	Accountability framework for GP fundholding
EL(95)79	The use of costed HRGs in the 1996–7 contracting cycle
EL(95)80	Student bursaries
EL(95)81	Health service commissioner's annual report
EL(95)82	Monitoring local pay
EL(95)83	'Maintaining medical excellence' – the review of guidance on doctor's performance
EL(95)84	Building on the benefits of occupational standards and National Vocational Qualifications in the NHS
EL(95)85	Publication of health authority costs
EL(95)86	Nursing, midwifery and PAMs – contracts for education and training with institutions of higher education – a joint declaration of principles
EL(95)87	Costing for contracting themes and issues in the community, mental health and learning disability services
EL(95)88	NHS responsibilities for meeting continuing health care needs – NHS Executive/SSI Monitoring
EL(95)89	Health at work in the NHS
EL(95)90	Consultation document: Patient's Charter and services for children and young people
EL(95)91	Costed HRG 1995–6 evaluation summary report
EL(95)92	Joint medical capital projects: Guide to university/NHS capital planning interactions
EL(95)93	Revised arrangements for B, A and A+ distinction awards
EL(95)94	Supra regional services: Applications for designation
EL(95)95	Supra-regional services: Dedesignation of the fulminant hepatic failure
EL(95)96	Non-medical education and training – planning guidance for 1996–7 education commissioning
EL(95)97	New drugs for multiple sclerosis – issue delayed
EL(95)98	The SCHARR report: Catching the tide: New voyages in nursing
EL(95)99	Strategic review of pathology services

Appendix III
NHS Trusts

Aberdeen Royal Hospitals NHS Trust
Aberdeen Royal Infirmary
Foresterhill
Aberdeen
AB9 2ZB
TEL: 01224 681818
FAX: 01224 685307

Addenbrookes NHS Trust
Addenbrookes Hospital
PO Box 146
Hills Road
Cambridge
CB2 2QQ
TEL: 01223 245151
FAX: 01223 216520

Aintree Hospitals NHS Trust
Fazakerley Hospital
Longmoor Lane
Liverpool
L9 7Al
TEL: 0151 525 3622
FAX: 0151 525 6086

Airedale NHS Trust
Airedale General Hospital
Skipton Road
Steeton
West Yorkshire
BD20 6TD
TEL: 01535 651511
FAX: 01535 655129

Alexandra NHS Trust
Alexandra Hospital
Woodrow Drive
Redditch
B98 7UH
TEL: 01527 503030
FAX: 01527 517432

Allington NHS Trust
Allington Clinic
Woodbridge Road
Ipswich
IP4 4ER
TEL: 01473 275200
FAX: 01473 275275

Anglian Harbours NHS
  Trust
Northgate Hospital
Northgate Street
Great Yarmouth
NR30 1BU
TEL: 01493 337646
FAX: 01493 337648

Angus NHS Trust
Whitehills Hospital
Forfar
Angus
Scotland
DD8 3DY
TEL: 01307 464551
FAX: 01307 465129

251

Argyll & Clyde NHS Trust
Unit Office
Aros
Lochgilphead
Argyll
Scotland
PA31 8LB
TEL: 01546 606600
FAX: 01546 606622

Ashford Hospital NHS Trust
London Road
Ashford
Middlesex
TW15 3AA
TEL: 01784 884488
FAX: 01784 884017

Avalon Somerset NHS Trust
Avalon House
Broadway Park
Barclay Street
Bridgwater
Somerset
TA6 5YA
TEL: 01278 446151
FAX: 01278 446147

Avon Ambulance Service Trust
Central Ambulance Station
Tower Hill
Bristol
BS2 0JA
TEL: 0117 927 7046
FAX: 0117 925 1419

Aylesbury Vale Community
    Healthcare NHS Trust
Manor House
Bierton Road
Aylesbury
HP20 1EG
TEL: 01296 393363
FAX: 01296 392606

Ayrshire & Arran Community
    Healthcare NHS Trust
1a Hunters Avenue
Ayr

Scotland
KA8 9DW
TEL: 01292 281821
FAX: 01292 610213

Barnet Healthcare NHS Trust
Napsbury Hospital
Nr St Albans
Hertfordshire
AL2 1AA
TEL: 0181 200 1555
FAX: 0181 200 9499

Barnsley Community & Priority
    Services NHS Trust
Unit 11 HQ Kendray
    Hospital
Doncaster Road
Barnsley
S70 3RD
TEL: 01226 730000
FAX: 01226 296782

Barnsley District General Hospital
    NHS Trust
Gawber Road
Barnsley
S75 2EP
TEL: 01226 730000
FAX: 01226 202859

Basildon & Thurrock General
    Hospitals NHS Trust
Basildon Hospital
Nethermayne
Basildon
Essex
SS16 5NL
TEL: 01268 533911
FAX: 01268 593757

Bassetlaw Hospital & Community
    Services NHS Trust
Barrowby House
Hyland Grove
Worksop
S81 0JF
TEL: 01909 500990
FAX: 01909 480879

Bath Mental Healthcare Trust
St Martins Hospital
Midford Road
Bath
BA2 5RP
TEL: 01225 832255
FAX: 01225 835940

Bath & West Community
    Trust
Avon & Somerset House
St Martins Hospital
Midford Road
Bath
BA2 5RP
TEL: 01225 840055
FAX: 01225 840407

Bedford Hospitals NHS Trust
Kempston Road
Bedford
MK42 9DJ
TEL: 01234 355122
FAX: 01234 218106

Bedford & Shires Health & Care
    NHS Trust
40 Kimbolton Road
Bedford
MK40 2NR
TEL: 01234 267444
FAX: 01234 342463

Bedfordshire & Herts Ambulance
    NHS Trust
Hammond Road
Bedford
MK41 0RD
TEL: 01234 270099
FAX: 01234 215399

Belfast City Hospital Trust
51 Lisburn Road
Belfast
N Ireland
BT9 7AB
TEL: 01232 329241
FAX: 01232 326614

Bethlem & Maudsley NHS Trust
Monks Orchard Road
Beckenham, Kent
BR3 3BX
TEL: 0181 777 6611
FAX: 0181 777 6039

Bexley Community Health Trust
Bexley Hospital
Old Bexley Road
Bexley
Kent
DA5 2BW
TEL: 01322 526282
FAX: 01322 555491

BHB Community Healthcare Trust
The Willows
117 Suttons Lane
Hornchurch, Essex
RM12 6RS
TEL: 01708 465000
FAX: 01708 441049

Birmingham Childrens Hospital
Ladywood Middleway
Ladywood
Birmingham
B16 8ET
TEL: 0121 454 4851
FAX: 0121 456 4697

Birmingham Heartlands Hospital
    NHS Trust
45 Bordesley Green East
Birmingham
B9 5ST
TEL: 0121 766 6611
FAX: 0121 773 6897

Birmingham Womens HC Trust
Birmingham Maternity Hospital
Q E Medical Centre
Edgbaston
Birmingham
B15 2TG
TEL: 0121 472 1377
FAX: 0121 627 2602

Bishop Auckland Hospitals NHS Trust
Bishop Auckland Gen Hospital
Co Durham
DL14 6AD
TEL: 01388 604040
FAX: 01388 604040 x 2237

Black Country Mental Health
48 Lodge Road
West Bromwich
West Midlands
B70 8NY
TEL: 0121 553 7676
FAX: 0121 607 3579

Blackpool Victoria Hospital NHS
    Trust
Whinney Heys Road
Blackpool
Lancashire
FY3 8NR
TEL: 01253 300000
FAX: 01253 303528

Blackpool W & F Community NHS
    Trust
Devonshire Road Hospital
Blackpool
FY3 8AZ
TEL: 01253 303254
FAX: 01253 303250

Blackburn, H & RV Healthcare NHS
    Trust
Queens Park Hospital
Haslingdon Road
Blackburn
BB2 3HH
TEL: 01254 263555
FAX: 01254 293803

Bolton Community Healthcare NHS
    Trust
St Peters House
Silverwell Street
Bolton
BL1 1PP
TEL: 01204 377000
FAX: 01204 377004

Bolton Hospitals NHS Trust
Bolton Gen Hospital
Minerva Road
Bolton
BL4 0JR
TEL: 01204 390390
FAX: 01204 390794

Borders Community NHS
    Trust
Huntlyburn House
Melrose
Scotland
TD6 9BP
TEL: 01896 662300
FAX: 01896 822887

Borders General Hospital Trust
Borders Gen Hospital
Melrose
Scotland
TD6 9BS
TEL: 01896 754333
FAX: 01896 823476

Bournewood NHS Trust
St Peters Hospital
Guildford Road
Chertsey
Surrey
KT16 0PZ
TEL: 01932 872010
FAX: 01932 875346

Bradford Community Health NHS
    Trust
Leeds Road Hospital
Maudsley Street
Bradford
BD3 9LH
TEL: 01274 494194
FAX: 01274 725652

Bradford Hospitals NHS Trust
Duckworth Lane
Bradford
BD9 6RJ
TEL: 01274 364787
FAX: 01274 364786

Bridgend & District NHS Trust
Quarella Road
Bridgend
Mid Glamorgan
TEL: 01656 752752
FAX: 01656 665377

Brighton Healthcare NHS Trust
Royal Sussex County Hospital
Eastern Road
BN2 5BE
TEL: 01273 696955
FAX: 01273 626653

Bromley Hospitals NHS Trust
Farnborough Hospital
Orpington
Kent
BR6 8ND
TEL: 01689 814100
FAX: 01689 862423

Burnley Healthcare NHS Trust
Burnley General Hospital
Casterton Avenue
Burnley
BB10 2PQ
TEL: 01282 472 5071
FAX: 01282 474 4444

Burton Hospitals NHS Trust
Belvedere Road
Burton On Trent
Staffordshire
DE13 0RB
TEL: 01283 566333
FAX: 01283 568091

Bury Healthcare NHS Trust
Fairfield General Hospital
Rochdale Old Road
Bury
BL9 7TD
TEL: 0161 764 6081
FAX: 0161 705 3602

Caithness & Sutherland Trust
Caithness Gen Hospital

Wick
Caithness
KW1 5LA
TEL: 01955 605050
FAX: 01955 604606

Calderdale Healthcare Trust
Royal Halifax Infirmary
Free School Lane
Halifax
HX1 2YP
TEL: 01422 357222
FAX: 01422 342581

Calderstones NHS Trust
Mitton Road
Whalley
Blackburn
BB61 9PE
TEL: 01254 822121
FAX: 01254 823023

Camden & Islington Community
    Health Services NHS Trust
National Temperance Hospital
112 Hampstead Road
London
NW1 2LT
TEL: 0171 380 0717
FAX: 0171 383 5579

Canterbury & Thanet Community
    Healthcare NHS Trust
Littlebourne Road
Canterbury
CT1 1AZ
TEL: 01227 459371
FAX: 01227 812268

Cardiff Community Healthcare
    NHS Trust
Trenenydd
Fairwater Road
Llandaff
Cardiff
CF5 2LD
TEL: 01222 5522112
FAX: 01222 578032

Cardiothoracic Centre
Liverpool NHS Trust
Broadgreen Hospital
Thomas Drive
Liverpool
L14 3LB
TEL: 0151 228 1616
FAX: 0151 220 8573

Carlisle Hospitals NHS Trust
Cumberland Infirmary
Newtown Road
Carlisle
CA2 7HY
TEL: 01228 23444
FAX: 01228 591889

Carmarthen & District Trust
West Wales Gen Hospital
Glangwili
Carmarthen
Dyfed
SA31 2AF
TEL: 01267 235151
FAX: 01267 237662

Causeway HSS Trust
8E Coleraine Road
Ballymoney
Northern Ireland
BT53 6BP
TEL: 012656 66600
FAX: 012656 61201

Ceredigon & Mid Wales Trust
Bronglais Hospital
Aberystwyth
Dyfed
SY23 1ER
TEL: 01970 623131
FAX: 01970 635923

Chase Farm Hospitals NHS Trust
Chase Hospital
The Ridgeway
Enfield, Middlesex
EN2 8JL
TEL: 0181 366 6600
FAX: 0181 366 1361

Chelsea & Westminster Healthcare
  NHS Trust
The Hospital
Fulham Road
London
SE10 9NH
TEL: 0181 746 8000
FAX: 0181 846 1111

Cheshire Community Healthcare
  NHS Trust
B Block, Barony Hospital
Nantwich
Cheshire
CW5 5QU
TEL: 01270 610000
FAX: 01270 627469

Chesterfield & N Derby Royal
  Hospital NHS Trust
Derbyshire Royal Hospital
Calow
Chesterfield
S44 5BL
TEL: 01246 277271
FAX: 01246 276955

Chester & Halton Community
Countess of Chester Hospital
Liverpool Road
Chester
CH2 1UL
TEL: 01928 790404
FAX: 01928 591153

Cheviot & Wansbeck NHS Trust
Ashington Hospital
West View
Ashington
Northumberland
NE63 0SA
TEL: 01670 521212
FAX. 01670 520034

Chichester Priority Care Services
  NHS Trust
9 College Lane
Chichester
West Sussex

PO19 4FX
TEL: 01243 787970
FAX: 01243 530767

Chorley & South Ribble Trust
Chorley District Hospital
Preston Road
Chorley
PR7 1PP
TEL: 01257 261222
FAX: 01257 245309

Christie Hospital NHS Trust
Wilmslow Road
Withington
Manchester
M20 9BX
TEL: 0161 446 3000
FAX: 0161 446 3977

City & Hackney Community
   Services NHS Trust
St Leonards, Nuttal Street
London
N1 5LZ
TEL: 0171 739 8484

City Hospital NHS Trust
Dudley Road Hospital
Birmingham B18 7QH
TEL: 0121 554 3801
FAX: 0121 523 0951

City Hospital Sunderland NHS
   Trust
Chester Road
Sunderland
SR2 0NB
TEL: 0191 565 6256
FAX: 0191 514 0220

Clatterbridge Centre for Oncology
   NHS Trust
Clatterbridge Hospital
Bebbington
Wirral
L63 4JY
TEL: 0151 334 1155
FAX: 0151 334 0882

Cleveland Ambulance NHS Trust
Venture House
Marton Road
Middlesborough
TS4 3TL
TEL: 01642 850888
FAX: 01642 855007

Clwyd Community & Mental Health
   NHS Trust
Catherine Gladstone House
Howarden Way
Mancot Deeside
CH5 2EP
TEL: 01244 538883
FAX: 01244 538884

Central Manchester NHS Trust
Cobbett House
Manchester Royal Infirmary
Oxford Road
Manchester
M13 9WL
TEL: 0161 276 1234
FAX: 0161 273 6211

Central Middlesex NHS Trust
Acton Lane
London
NW10 7NS
TEL: 0181 965 5733
FAX: 0181 961 0012

C Nottinghamshire Healthcare NHS
   Trust
Southwell Road
Mansfield
Nottinghamshire
NG18 4HH
TEL: 01623 785050
FAX: 01623 634126

Communicare NHS Trust
Queens Park Hospital
Haslingden
Blackburn
BB2 3HH
TEL: 01254 263555
FAX: 01254 687161

✓ Cornwall Healthcare NHS Trust
Porthpean Road
St Austell
Cornwall
PL26 6AD
TEL: 01254 263555
FAX: 01254 687162

Cornwall & Isles of Scilly Learning
  Disabilities NHS Trust
4 St Clement Vean
Truro
Cornwall
TR1 1NR
TEL: 01872 72494
FAX: 01872 260081

Countess of Chester NHS Trust
Liverpool Road
Chester
CH2 1BQ
TEL: 01244 365000
FAX: 01244 365112

Coventry Healthcare NHS Trust
Parkside House
Quinton Road
Coventry
CV1 2NJ
TEL: 01203 553344
FAX: 01203 526800

Craigavon & Banbridge Comm NHS
  Trust
Bannvale House
Moyallen Road
Gilford, Belfast
BT63 5JX
TEL: 01762 831983
FAX: 01762 831993

Craigavon Area Hospital Group
  NHS Trust
68 Lurgan Road
Portadown
Craigavon
BT63 5QQ
TEL: 01762 334444
FAX: 01762 350068

Crawley Horsham Health Service
  NHS Trust
Crawley Hospital
Crawley
West Sussex
RH11 7DH
TEL: 01293 600300
FAX: 01293 500360

Croydon Community NHS Trust
12–18 Lennard Street
Croydon
CR9 2RS
TEL: 0181 680 2008
FAX: 0181 666 0495

Central Scotland Healthcare NHS
  Trust
Old Denny Road
Larbert
Scotland
FK5 4SD
TEL: 01324 570700
FAX: 01324 562367

Central Sheffield University
  Hospitals Trust
Royal Hallamshire Hospital
Glossop Road
Sheffield
S10 2JF
TEL: 0114 2766222
FAX: 0114 2713646

Cumbria Ambulance Service NHS
  Trust
Salkeld Hall
Infirmary Street
Carlisle
Cumbria
CA2 7AN
TEL: 01228 596909
FAX: 01228 514350

Darlington Memorial Hospital NHS
  Trust
Hollyhurst Road
Darlington
Co Durham

DL3 6HX
TEL: 01325 380100
FAX: 01325 743622

Dartford & Gravesend Acute NHS
    Trust
Joyce Green Hospital
Dartford, Kent
DA1 5PL
TEL: 01322 227242
FAX: 01322 283496

Darwen NHS Trust
St Davids Hospital
Carmarthen
Dyfed, Wales
SA31 3HB
TEL: 01267 237481
FAX: 01267 221895

Derbyshire Ambulance Service
    NHS Trust
Ambulance HQ
Kingsway
Derby
DE22 3XB
TEL: 01332 372441
FAX: 01332 3466824

Derby City General Hospital NHS ✓
    Trust
Uttoxeter Road
Derby
DE22 3NE
TEL:01332 340131
FAX: 01332 290559

Derbyshire Royal Infirmary NHS
    Trust
London Road
Derby
DE1 2QY
TEL: 01332 347141
FAX: 01332 295652

Dewsbury Healthcare NHS Trust
Woodkirk House
Healds Road
Dewsbury

West Yorkshire
WF13 4HS
TEL: 01924 465105
FAX: 01924 816912

Doncaster Royal & Montagu NHS
    Trust
Doncaster Royal Infirmary
Doncaster
DN2 5LT
TEL: 01302 366666
FAX: 01302 320098

Doncaster Healthcare Trust
St Catherines Hospital
Tickhill Road
Doncaster
CN4 8QN
TEL: 01302 796000
FAX: 01302 796066

Dorset Ambulance NHS Trust
Ringwood Road
St Leonards
Ringwood
BH24 2SP
TEL: 01202 896111
FAX: 01202 891978

Dorset Community Healthcare NHS
    Trust
Grove House
Millers Close
Dorchester
DR1 1SS
TEL: 01305 264479
FAX: 01305 264474

✓ Dorset Healthcare NHS Trust
11 Shelley Road
Boscombe
Bournemouth
BH1 4JQ
TEL: 01202 303400
FAX: 01202 301798

Down Lisburn HSS Trust
Lisburn Health Centre
Linenhall Street

Lisburn
Co Antrim
BT28 1LU
TEL: 01846 665181
FAX: 01846 665179

Dudley Group of Hospitals NHS
Trust
Wordsley Hospital
Stourbridge
West Midlands
DY8 5QX
TEL: 01384 401401
FAX: 01384 244395

Dudley Priority Healthcare NHS
Trust
Ridge Hall
Brierley Hill Road
Stourbridge
West Midlands
DY8 5ST
TEL: 01384 457373
FAX: 01384 400217

Dumfries & Galloway Acute Royal
Infirmary NHS Trust
Bankend Road
Dumfries
Scotland
DG1 4AP
TEL: 01387 246246
FAX: 01387 241639

Dumfries Community Trust
Campbell House
Crichton Royal Hospital
Glencaple Road
Dumfries
DG1 4TG
TEL: 01387 255301
FAX: 01387 244086

Dundee Healthcare NHS Trust
Royal Dundee Liff Hospital
Monifieth
Dundee
Scotland
DD2 5NE

TEL: 01382 580441
FAX: -1382 580004

Dundee Teaching Hospitals NHS
Trust
Ninewells Hospital
Dundee
Scotland
DD1 9SY
TEL: 01382 660111
FAX: 01382 660445

Durham County Ambulance Service
NHS Trust
Finchdale Road
Framwellgate Moor
Durham
DH1 5JS
TEL: 0191 386448
FAX: 0191 3831207

Ealing Hospital NHS Trust
Uxbridge Road
Southall
Middlesex
UB1 3EU
TEL: 0181 574 2444
FAX: 0181 967 5630

East Anglian Ambulance Trust
Hospital Lane
Hellesden
Norwich
NR6 5NA
TEL: 01603 424255
FAX: 01603 418667

Eastbourne & County Healthcare
NHS Trust
Bowhill, The Drive, Hellingly
Hailsham
East Sussex
BN27 4EP
TEL: 01323 330022
FAX: 01323 842868

Eastbourne Hospitals NHS Trust
Kings Drive
Eastbourne

East Sussex
BN21 2UD
TEL: 01323 417400
FAX: 01323 414966

Eastman Dental Hospital
    Trust
256 Grays Inn Road
London
WC1X 8LD
TEL: 0171 915 1000
FAX: 0171 915 1012

East Berkshire Community Health
    NHS Trust
Frances House
81 Frances road
Windsor
Berks
SL4 3AW
TEL: 01753 860441
FAX: 01753 636107

East Berkshire NHS Trust
Church Hill House
Easthampstead
Bracknell
Berkshire
TEL: 01344 422722
FAX: 01344 867990

East Cheshire NHS Trust
Westpark Branch
Prestbury Road
Macclesfield
SK10 3BL
TEL: 01625 421000
FAX: 01625 661644

Edinburgh Child Health Trust
Royal Hospital For Sick
    Children
9 Sciennes Road
Edinburgh
Scotland
EH9 1LF
TEL: 0131 536 0000
FAX: 0131 536 0001

Edinburgh Healthcare Trust
Carlton House
Carlton Terrace
Edinburgh
EH7 5DG
TEL: 0131 537 9000
FAX: 0131 537 9500

East Glamorgan NHS Trust
Church Village
Pontypridd
Mid Glamorgan
Wales
CF38 1AB
TEL: 01443 218218
FAX: 01443 217213

East Gloucestershire NHS Trust
Burlington House
Lypiatt Road
Cheltenham
GL50 2QN
TEL: 01242 221188
FAX: 01242 221214

East Hertfordshire NHS Trust
Queen Elizabeth Hospital
Howlands
Welwyn Garden City
Hertfordshire, AL7 4HQ
TEL: 01707 328111
FAX: 01707 353379

East & Midlothian NHS Trust
Edenhall Hospital
Pinkie Burn
Musselboro
Scotland
TEL: 0131 536 8000
FAX: 0131 536 8152

Enfield Community Care Trust
Highlands Hospital
Worlds End Lane
London
N21 1PN
TEL: 0181 366 6600
FAX: 0181 366 9166

Epsom Healthcare NHS Trust
Dorking Road
Epsom
Surrey
KT18 7EG
TEL: 01372 735735
FAX: 01372 746856

✓ East Somerset NHS Trust
Yeovil District Hospital
Higher Kingston
Yeovil
Somerset
BA21 4AT
TEL: 01935 75122
FAX: 01935 26850

Essex Ambulance Service Trust
Court Road
Broomfield
Essex
CM1 5EP
TEL: 01245 443344
FAX: 01245 443619

Essex & Herts Community Services
Rutherford House
Haymeads Lane
Bishops Stortford
CM23 5JH
TEL: 01279 444455
FAX: 01279 465873

Essex Rivers Healthcare Trust
Colchester Gen Hospital
Turner Road
Colchester
CO4 5JL
TEL: 01206 853535
FAX: 01206 854877

East Suffolk Local Health Trust HQ
Anglesea Heights
1 Ivy Street
Ipswich
Suffolk
IP1 3QW
TEL: 01473 286940
FAX: 01474 286892

East Surrey Hospital & Community
   Healthcare NHS Trust
East Surrey Hospital
Three Arch Road
Redhill
RH1 5RH
TEL: 01737 768511
FAX: 01737 778535

East Surrey Learning Disabilities
   NHS Trust
Royal Earlswood
Brighton Road
Redhill
Surrey
RH1 5RH
TEL: 01737 763591
FAX: 01737 779106

✓ East Wiltshire Healthcare NHS Trust
PO Box 415
St Margarets Hospital
Highworth Road
Swindon
SN3 4GB
TEL: 01793 425000
FAX: 01793 425005

✓ Exeter & District Community Health
   Service NHS Trust
Newcourt House
Old Rydon Lane
Exeter
EX2 7JU
TEL: 01392 449700
FAX: 01392 445435

East Yorkshire Community
   Healthcare NHS Trust
Westwood Hospital
Beverley
N Humberside
HU17 8BU
TEL: 01482 886600
FAX: 01482 886541

East Yorkshire Hospitals Trust
Castle Hill Hospital
Castle Road

Cottingham
North Humberside
HU16 5JQ
TEL: 01482 875875
FAX: 01482 876331

Falkirk & District Royal Infirmary
1 Majors Loan
Falkirk
Scotland
FK1 5QE
TEL: 01324 624000
FAX: 01324 612340

Fife Community Healthcare NHS
   Trust
Cameron Hospital
Cameron Bridge
Leven
Scotland
KY8 5RG
TEL: 01592 712812
FAX: 01592 712762

Forest Healthcare NHS Trust
PO Box 12, Claybury Hall
Woodford Green
Essex
IG8 1BB
TEL: 0181 504 4411
FAX: 0181 505 6756

Fosse Health Community
   Trust
Gipsy Lane
Humberston
Leicester
LE5 0TD
TEL: 0116 246 0100
FAX: 0116 246 1222

Foundation NHS Trust
Mellor House
Corporation Street
Stafford
ST16 3SR
TEL: 01785 57888
FAX: 01785 58969

Freeman Group of Hospitals
Freeman Road
Newcastle Upon Tyne
NE7 7DN
TEL: 0191 284 3111
FAX: 0191 213 1968

Frenchay Healthcare NHS
   Trust HQ
Beckspool Road
Frenchay
Bristol
BS16 1ND
TEL: 0117 970 1070

Frimley Park Hospital Trust
Portsmouth Road
Frimley
Camberley
Surrey
GU16 5UJ
TEL: 01276 692777
FAX: 01276 61453

Furness General Hospital NHS Trust
Dalton Lane
Barrow in Furness
Cumbria
LA14 4LF
TEL: 01229 870870
FAX: 01229 871182

Gateshead Hospitals NHS Trust
Sherrif Hill
Gateshead
Tyne & Wear
NE9 6SX
TEL: 0191 487 8989
FAX: 0191 491 1823

Gateshead Healthcare NHS Trust
Whinney House
Tynegate Precinct
Sunderland Road
Gateshead
NE8 3EP
TEL: 0191 402 6000
FAX: 0191 402 6001

George Eliot Hospital Trust
College Street
Nuneaton
Warwickshire
CV10 7DJ
TEL: 01203 351351
FAX: 01203 865058

Greater Glasgow Community &
   Mental Health NHS Trust
Gartnavel Royal Hospital
1055 Gt Western Road
Glasgow
G12 0XH
TEL: 0141 334 4416
FAX: 0141 334 0875

Glan Clywd General Hospital NHS
   Trust
Ysbyty Glan Clwyd
Bodelwyddan
Rhyl, Clwyd
LL18 5UJ
TEL: 01745 583910
FAX: 01745 583143

Glan Hafren NHS Trust
Maple Centre
St Woolos
Stow Hill, Newport
Gwent
NP9 4SZ
TEL: 01633 234234
FAX: 01633 221217

Glan-Y-Mor NHS Trust
Trinity Building
21 Orchard Street
Swansea
SA1 5BE
TEL: 01792 651501
FAX: 01792 458730

Glasgow Dental Hospital
378 Sauchiehall Street
Glasgow
Scotland
G2 3JZ

Glasgow Royal Infirmary Trust
84 Castle Street
Glasgow
Scotland
G4 0SF
TEL: 0141 552 3535
FAX: 0141 304 4889

Glenfield Hospitals NHS Trust
Glenfield Gen Hospital
Groby Road
Leicester
LE3 9QF
TEL: 0116 287 1471
FAX: 0116 258 3950

Gloucestershire Ambulance Service
   NHS Trust
Horton Road
Gloucester
GL1 3PX
TEL: 01452 395050
FAX: 01452 383331

Gloucester Royal NHS Trust
Gloucester Royal Hospital
Great Western Road
Gloucester
GL1 3NN
TEL: 01452 528555
FAX: 01452 394737

Greater Manchester Ambulance
   Service NHS Trust
Bury Old Road
Whitefield
Manchester
M45 6AQ
TEL: 0161 231 7921
FAX: 0161 223 1351

Good Hope Hospital NHS Trust
Rectory Road
Sutton Coldfield
West Midlands
B75 7RR
TEL: 0121 378 2211
FAX: 0121 311 1074

Grampian Healthcare NHS Trust
East Bank
Woodend Gen Hospital
Aberdeen
AB2 9LR
TEL: 01224 663131
FAX: 01224 840790

Grantham & Kesteven NHS
    Trust
Grantham & Kesteven Hospital
101 Manthorpe Road
Grantham
Lincolnshire
NG31 8DG
TEL: 01476 65232
FAX: 01476 590441

Great Ormond St Hospital for Sick
    Children NHS Trust
Great Ormond Street
London
WC1N 3JH
TEL: 0171 405 9200
FAX: 0171 829 8643

Green Park HSS Trust
Musgrave Park Hospital
Stockmans Lane
Belfast
BT9 7JB
TEL: 01232 669501
FAX: 01232 382008

Greenwich Healthcare NHS Trust
Memorial Hospital
Shooters Hill
London
SE18 3RZ
TEL: 0181 856 5511
FAX: 0181 856 8712

Grimsby Health NHS Trust
District Gen Hospital
Scartho Road
Grimsby
DN33 2BA
TEL: 01472 874111
FAX: 01472 875328

Guild Community Healthcare NHS
    Trust
Whittingham Hospital
Preston, Lancashire
PR3 2JH
TEL: 01772 562656
FAX: 01772 200220

Guys & St Thomas's NHS Trust
St Thomas Hospital
Lambeth Palace Road
London
SE1 7EH
TEL: 0171 928 9292
FAX: 0171 922 8079

Gwent Community NHS Trust
Llanfrechfa Grange
Llanfrechfa
Cumbran
Gwent
NP44 8YN
TEL: 01633 838521
FAX: 01633 643864

Gwynedd Community Healthcare
    NHS Trust
Bryn-Y-Neuadd Hospital
Llanfairfechan
Gwynedd
LL33 0HH
TEL: 01248 682682
FAX: 01248 681832

Gwynedd Hospitals NHS Trust
Ysbyty Gwynedd
Bangor
Gwynedd
LL57 2PW
TEL: 01248 384384
FAX: 01248 370629

Hairmyres & Stonehouse Trust
Hairmyres Hospital
East Kilbride
Lanarkshire
G75 8RG
TEL: 01355 220292
FAX: 01355 234064

Halton Gen Hospital Trust
Hospital Way
Runcorn
Cheshire
WA7 2DA
TEL: 01928 714567
FAX: 01928 790951

Hammersmith Hospitals NHS
Trust
150 Du Cane Road
London
W12 0HS
TEL: 0181 743 2030
FAX: 0181 740 3169

Hampshire Ambulance Service NHS
Trust
Highcroft
Romsey Road
Winchester
Hampshire
SO22 5DH
TEL: 01962 860421
FAX: 01962 842156

Harefield Hospital NHS Trust
Harefield
Middlesex
UB9 6JH
TEL: 01895 823737
FAX: 01895 822870

Haringey Healthcare NHS Trust
St Anns Hospital
St Anns Road
South Tottenham
London
N15 3TH
TEL: 0181 442 6000
FAX: 0181 442 6567

Harrogate Healthcare NHS Trust
Ebor Rise
Cornwall Road
Harrogate
HG1 2PU
TEL: 01423 885959
FAX: 01423 501391

Harrow & Hillingdon Healthcare
NHS Trust
Siddons House
Roxeth Hill
Harrow
HA2 0JX
TEL: 0181 864 5432
FAX: 0181 422 3118

Hartlepool Community Care NHS
Trust
Child Health Care
Caroline Street
Hartlepool
TS26 9LE
TEL: 01429 267901
FAX: 01429 261744

Hartlepool & Peterlee Hospital NHS
Trust
The General Hospital
Holdforth Road
Hartlepool
TS24 9AH
TEL: 01429 266654
FAX: 01429 235389

Hastings & Rother NHS Trust
St Annes House
729 The Ridge
St Leonards on Sea
East Sussex
TN37 7PT
TEL: 01424 754488
FAX: 01424 754263

Havering Hospitals NHS Trust
Harold Wood Hospital
Gubbins Lane
Romford
Essex
RM3 0BE
TEL: 01708 345533
FAX: 01708 384730

Heatherwood & Wexham Park
Hospitals NHS Trust
Wexham Park Hospital
Wexham

Slough
SL2 4HL
TEL: 01753 633000
FAX: 01753 691343

Heathlands Mental Health Services
  NHS Trust
Ridgewood Centre,
Old Bisley Road
Frimley
Surrey
GU16 5QE
TEL: 01276 692919
FAX: 01276 678174

Hereford & Worcester Ambulance
  NHS Trust
Bransford
Worcester
WR6 5JD
TEL: 01886 834200
FAX: 01886 834210

Herefordshire Community Health
  NHS Trust
Belmont Abbey
Belmont
Hereford
HR2 9RP
TEL: 01432 344344
FAX: 01432 363900

Hereford Hospitals NHS Trust
County Hospital
Hereford
HR1 2ER
TEL: 01432 355444
FAX: 01432 354310

Highland Community NHS
  Trust
Royal Northern Infirmary
Ness Walk
Inverness
Scotland
IV3 5SF
TEL: 01463 704000
FAX: 01463 713844

Hillingdon Hospital NHS Trust
Pield Road
Hillingdon
Middlesex
UN8 3NN
TEL: 01895 238282
FAX: 01895 811687

Hinchingbrooke Healthcare NHS
  Trust
Hinchingbrooke Hospital
Huntingdon
Cambridgeshire
PE18 8NT
TEL: 01480 416416
FAX: 01480 416561

Homerton Hospital
Homerton Row
London
E9 6SR
TEL: 0181 919 5555
FAX: 0181 985 6376

Horizon NHS Trust
Harperbury Hospital
Harper Lane
Shenley, Hertfordshire
WD7 2BB
TEL: 01923 855912
FAX: 01923 855909

Horton General Hospital
Oxford Road
Banbury
Oxfordshire
OX16 9AZ
TEL: 01295 275500
FAX: 01295 229055

Hounslow & Spelthorne Community
  & Mental Health NHS Trust
Phoenix Court
531 Staines road
Hounslow
TW4 5DP
TEL: 0181 565 2211
FAX: 0181 565 2249

Huddersfield NHS Trust HQ
The Royal Infirmary
Huddersfield
HD3 3EA
TEL: 01484 422191
FAX: 01484 482493

Hull & Holderness Community NHS
   Trust
Victoria House
Park Street
Hull
HU2 8TD
TEL: 01482 223191
FAX: 01482 229668

Humberside Ambulance NHS Trust
Springfield House
Springfield Way
Anlaby
North Humberside
HU10 6RZ
TEL: 01482 54277
FAX: 01482 658770

Inverclyde Royal NHS Trust
Inverclyde Royal Hospital
Larkfield Road
Greenock
Scotland
PA16 9ER
TEL: 01475 633777
FAX: 01475 636753

Ipswich Hospital NHS Trust
Heath Road Wing
Ipswich
IP4 5PD
TEL: 01473 712233
FAX: 01473 703400

✓ Isle of Wight Community Health
   Services NHS Trust
Whitecroft, Sandy Lane
Newport
Isle of Wight
PO30 3EB
TEL: 01983 526011
FAX: 01983 822456

James Paget Hospital NHS Trust
Lowestoft Road
Gorleston
Great Yarmouth
NR31 6LA
TEL: 01493 452452
FAX: 01493 452819

Kent Ambulance NHS Trust
Heath Road
Coxheath
Maidstone, Kent
ME17 4BG
TEL: 01622 747010
FAX: 01622 743565

Kent & Canterbury Hospitals NHS
   Trust
Kent & Canterbury Hospital
Canterbury
CT1 3NG
TEL: 01227 766877
FAX: 01227 783017

Kent & Sussex Weald NHS Trust
Sherwood Park
Pembury Road
Tunbridge Wells
Kent
TN2 3QE
TEL: 01892 823535
FAX: 01892 824267

Kettering General Hospital NHS Trust
Rothwell Road
Kettering
Northamptonshire
NN16 8UZ
TEL: 01536 492000
FAX: 01536 493767

Kidderminster Healthcare Trust
Kidderminster Gen Hospital
Bewdley Road
Kidderminster
Worcestershire
DY11 6RJ
TEL: 01562 823424
FAX: 01562 674125

Kings Healthcare NHS Trust
Kings College Hospital
Denmark Hill
London
SE5 9RS
TEL: 0171 737 4000
FAX: 0171 346 3445

Kings Lynn & Wisbech Hospitals
    NHS Trust
Queen Elizabeth Hospital
Gayton Road
Kings Lynn
PE30 4ET
TEL: 01553 766266
FAX: 01553 770154

Kingsmill Hospital NHS Trust
Mansfield Road
Sutton In Ashfield
Nottinghamshire
NG17 4JL
TEL: 01623 22515
FAX: 01623 21770

Kingston Hospital NHS Trust
Galsworthy Road
Kingston upon Thames
KT2 7QB
TEL: 0181 546 7711
FAX: 0181 547 2182

Kingston & District Community
    NHS Trust
Claremont, 60 St James Road
Surbiton
Surrey
KT6 4QL
TEL: 0181 390 4511
FAX: 0181 390 5049

Kirkcaldy Acute NHS Trust
Victoria Hospital
Hayfield Road, Kirkcaldy
Fife
Scotland
KY2 5AH
TEL: 01592 643355
FAX: 01592 647041

Lanarkshire Community Unit
Strathclyde Hospital
Airbles Road
Motherwell
Scotland
ML1 3BW
TEL: 01698 230500
FAX: 01698 267403

Lancaster Acute Hospitals NHS
    Trust
Springfield House
Royal Lancaster Infirmary
Ashton Road
Lancaster
LA1 4RP
TEL: 01524 583561
FAX: 01524 583581

Lancaster Priority Service Trust
Royal Albert Hospital
Ashton Road
Lancaster
LA1 5AJ
TEL: 01524 65241
FAX: 01524 846855

Lancashire Ambulance Service NHS
    Trust HQ
449–451 Garstang Road
Broughton
Preston
PR3 5LN
TEL: 01772 862666
FAX: 01772 861003

Law Hospital NHS Trust
Carluke
Lanarkshire
Scotland
ML8 5ER
TEL: 01698 361100
FAX: 01698 376671

Leeds Community & Mental Health
    Services Teaching NHS Trust
Park House
Meanwood Park Hospital
Leeds

LS9 4QB
TEL: 0113 275 8721
FAX: 0113 274 5172

Leicestershire Ambulance NHS Trust
The Roslings, Forest Road
Narborough, Leicester
LE9 5EQ
TEL: 0116 275 0700
FAX: 0116 775 1311

Leicester General Hospital NHS
  Trust
Gwendolen Road
Leicester
LE5 4PW
TEL: 0116 249 0490
FAX: 0116 258 4666

Leicester Mental Health Trust
674 Melton Road
Thurmaston
Leicester
LE4 8BA
TEL: 0116 269 3666
FAX: 0116 269 3953

Leicester Royal Infirmary NHS Trust
Firmary Close
Leicester
LE1 5WW
TEL: 0116 254 1414
FAX: 0116 258 5631

Lewisham Hospital NHS Trust
Waterloo Block
Lewisham Hospital
London
SE13 6LH
TEL: 0181 333 3000
FAX: 0181 333 3333

Lifecare NHS Trust
St Lawrences Hospital
Coulsdon Road
Caterham on Thames
KT2 7QB
TEL: 01883 346411
FAX: 01883 330309

Lifespan Healthcare NHS Trust
Ida Darwin
Fulbourn
Cambridge
CB1 5EE
TEL: 01223 884043
FAX: 01223 884038

Lincoln District Healthcare NHS
  Trust
Gervas House
Long Leys Road
Lincoln
LN1 1EJ
TEL: 01522 546546
FAX: 01522 514920

Lincoln Hospitals NHS Trust
County Hospital
Greetwell Road
Lincoln
LN2 5QY
TEL: 01522 512512
FAX: 01522 573419

Lincolnshire Ambulance & Health
  Transport NHS Trust
Cross O Cliff Court
Bracebridge Heath
Lincoln
LN4 2HL
TEL: 01522 545171
FAX: 01522 534611

Liverpool Womens Hospital NHS
  Trust
Womens Hospital
Catherine Street
Liverpool
L8 7NJ
TEL: 0151 708 9988
FAX: 0151 709 5196

Llandough Hospital NHS Trust
Llandough Hospital
Penarth
South Glamorgan
TEL: 01222 711711
FAX: 01222 708973

Llanelli Dinefwr NHS Trust
Prince Philip Hospital
Bryngwynmewr, Dafen
Llanelli
Dyfed
TEL: 01554 756567
FAX: 01554 772271

Loddon North Hampshire
    Community NHS Trust
Clock Tower House
Park Prewett
Basingstoke
RG24 9LZ
TEL: 01256 817718
FAX: 01256 56275

Lomond Healthcare
Vale of Leven Gen Hospital
Alexandria
Dunbartonshire
Scotland
G83 0UA
TEL: 01389 754121
FAX: 01389 755948

Louth & District Healthcare NHS
    Trust
Louth County Hospital
High Holme Road
Louth
Lincolnshire
LN11 0EU
TEL: 01507 600100
FAX: 01507 609 290

Luton & Dunstable Hospital NHS
    Trust
Lewsey Road
Luton
LU4 0DT
TEL: 01582 491122
FAX: 01582 492130

Maidstone Priority Care Trust
The Pagoda
Hermitage Lane
Maidstone

Kent
ME16 9PD
TEL: 01622 721818
FAX: 01622 721919

Manchester Children's Hospital
Trust Project Office
Hospital Road
Pendlebury
Manchester
M27 1HA
TEL: 0161 794 4696
FAX: 0161 794 5929

Mancunian Community Health
    NHS Trust
Mauldeth House
Mauldeth Road
Manchester
M21 2RL
TEL: 0161 958 400
FAX: 0161 881 9366

Mater Hospital NHS Trust
Mater Inforum Hospital
Crumlin Road
Belfast
BT14 6AB
TEL: 01232 741211
FAX: 01232 741342

Mid Anglia Community Health
    NHS Trust
Child Health Centre
Hospital Road
Bury St Edmunds
Suffolk
TEL: 01284 775055
FAX: 01284 750280

Mayday Healthcare NHS Trust
Mayday Hospital
Mayday Road
Croydon
CR7 7YE
TEL: 0181 401 3000
FAX: 0181 401 3396

Medway NHS Trust
Medway Hospital
Windmill Road
Gillingham
Kent
ME7 5NY
TEL: 01634 830000
FAX: 01634 829470

Mersey Regional Ambulance NHS
  Trust
Elm House
Belmont Road
Liverpool
L6 4EG
TEL: 0151 260 5220
FAX: 0151 260 7441

Merton & Sutton Community NHS
  Trust
Orchard Hill, Queens Marys Avenue
Carshalton
Surrey
SM5 4NR
TEL: 0181 770 8000
FAX: 0181 643 5807

Mid Essex Hospital Services NHS
  Trust
Broomfield Court
Pudding Wood Lane
Chelmsford
CM1 5ET
TEL: 01245 440761
FAX: 01245 514675

Mid Cheshire Hospitals Trust
Leighton Hospital
Leighton
Nr Crewe
CW1 4QJ
TEL: 01270 255141
FAX: 01270 587696

Mid Essex Community & Mental
  Health Services NHS Trust
Collingwood Road
Witham
Essex

CM8 2TT
TEL: 01376 502941
FAX: 01376 512936

Mid Glamorgan Ambulance Trust
Church Village
Pontypridd, Wales
CF37 1LA
TEL: 01443 217005
FAX: 01443 218062

Mid Kent Healthcare NHS Trust
Maidstone Hospital
Hermitage Lane
Maidstone
ME16 9QQ
TEL: 01622 729000
FAX: 01622 721511

Mid Sussex Healthcare NHS Trust
Princess Royal Hospital
Downsmere, Lewes Road
West Sussex
RH16 4EX
TEL: 01444 441881
FAX: 01444 414174

Milton Keynes Community Trust
Standing Way
Eaglestone
Milton Keynes
MK6 5ED
TEL: 01908 660033
FAX: 01908 694919

Milton Keynes General Trust
Milton Keynes Hospital
Standing Way
Eaglestone
Milton Keynes
MK6 5ED
TEL: 01908 660033
FAX: 01908 669348

Monklands & Bellshill Hospital NHS
  Trust
Monklands Gen Hospital
Airdrie, Scotland
ML6 0JS

Moorfields Eye Hospital Trust
City Road
London
EC1V 2PD
TEL: 0171 253 3411
FAX: 0171 253 4696

Moray Health Services Trust
Maryhill House
317 High Street
Elgin, Moray
Scotland
IV30 1AJ
TEL: 01343 543131
FAX: 01343 540834

Morriston North Unit NHS Trust
Morriston Hospital
Morriston, Swansea
SA6 6NL
TEL: 01792 702222
FAX: 01792 703632

Mid Staffs Gen Hospitals NHS Trust
Stafford Gen Hospital
Weston Road
Stafford
ST16 3SA
TEL: 01785 57731
FAX: 01785 45211

Mount Vernon & Watford General
    Hospital NHS Trust
Vicarage Road
Watford
Hertfordshire
WD1 8HB
TEL: 01923 244366
FAX: 01923 217440

Mulberry NHS Trust
County Offices
Eastgate
Sleaford
Lincolnshire
NG34 7DP
TEL: 01529 415960
FAX: 01529 415991

National Hospital for Neurology &
    Neurosurgery
Queen Square
London
WC1N 3BG
TEL: 0171 837 3611
FAX: 0171 813 1611

North Ayrshire & Arran Trust
Cross House Hospital
Kilmarnock
Scotland
KA2 0BE
TEL: 01563 521133
FAX: 01563 539789

Northern Birmingham Community
    Healthcare NHS Trust
Carnegie Centre, Hunters Road
Hockley
Birmingham
B19 1DR
TEL: 0121 359 5566
FAX: 0121 603 5567

Northern Birmingham Mental Health
    Trust
71 Fentham Road
Erdington, Birmingham
B23 6AL
TEL: 0121 623 5500
FAX: 0121 772 2979

North Derbyshire Community
    Healthcare NHS Trust
The Shrubberies
46 Newbold Road
Chesterfield
S41 7PL
TEL: 01246 200131
FAX: 01246 551323

North Devon Healthcare Trust
Riversvale
Litchdon Street
Barnstaple
Devon
TEL: 01271 75851
FAX: 01271 25564

North Down and Ards NHS Trust
Regent Street
Newtownards, Nr Belfast
BT23
TEL: 01247 818518
FAX: 01247 820140

North Downs Healthcare Trust
Farnham Hospital
Hale Road
Farnham, Surrey
GU9 9QL
TEL: 01252 726666
FAX: 01252 717952

North Durham Acute Hospitals
    NHS Trust
Dryburn Hospital
North Road
Durham
DH1 5TW
TEL: 0191 386 4911
FAX: 0191 383 1731

North Durham Community
    Healthcare NHS Trust
Earls House Hospital
Lanchester Road
Durham
DH1 3RE
TEL: 0191 333 6262
FAX: 0191 333 6263

North East Essex Mental Health
    NHS Trust
Severalls Hospital
Boxted Road
Colchester, Essex
CO4 5HG
TEL: 01206 852271
FAX: 01206 844435

Nevill Hall & District Trust
Nevill Hall Hospital
Brecon Road
Abergavenny, Wales
NP7 7EG
TEL: 01873 852091
FAX: 01873 859168

Newcastle City Health NHS Trust
Milvain Building
Newcastle Gen Hospital
Newcastle upon Tyne
NE4 6BE
TEL: 0191 273 6666
FAX: 0191 273 2340

Newham Community NHS
    Trust
Sydenham Building
Plaistow Hospital
Samson Street
London
E13 9EH
TEL: 0181 471 5125

Newham Healthcare NHS Trust
1 Helena Road
Plaistow
London
E13 0DZ
TEL: 0181 472 1444
FAX: 0181 552 0848

N E Worcestershire Community
    Healthcare NHS Trust
Smallwood Health Centre
Church Green West
Redditch
B97 4DJ
TEL: 01527 60121
FAX: 01527 64764

New Possibilities NHS Trust
New Possibilities House
Turner Road
Colchester
CO4 5JP
TEL: 01206 844840
FAX: 01206 842301

Newry & Mourne NHS Trust
5 Downshire Place
Newry
Co Down, N Ireland
BT34 1DZ
TEL: 01693 60505
FAX: 01693 69064

North Hampshire Hospitals NHS
 Trust
Basingstoke District Hospital
Aldermaston Road
Basingstoke
RG24 9NA
TEL: 01256 473202
FAX: 01256 313098

North Hertfordshire NHS Trust
Lister Hospital
Coreys Mill Lane
Stevenage, Hertfordshire
SG1 4AB
TEL: 01438 314333
FAX: 01438 781146

N Ireland Ambulance Service
12–22 Linenhall Street
Belfast
BT2 8BS
TEL: 01232 321313
FAX: 01232 333090

North Kent Healthcare Trust
Central Avenue
Sittingbourne
Kent
ME10 4NS
TEL: 01795 411411
FAX: 01795 478191

North Lakeland Healthcare NHS
 Trust
The Coppice
Garlands Estate
Carlisle, Cumbria
CA1 3SX
TEL: 01228 31081
FAX: 01228 5122 40

North Manchester Healthcare NHS
 Trust
North Manchester Gen Hospital
Delauneys Road
Manchester
M8 6RB
TEL: 0161 795 4567
FAX: 0161 740 4450

North Mersey Community Trust
Rathbone Hospital
Mill Lane
Liverpool
L13 4AW
TEL: 0151 250 3000
FAX: 0151 228 0486

North Middlesex NHS Trust
Sterling Way
Edmonton
London
N18 1QX
TEL: 0181 887 2000
FAX: 0181 887 4219

Norfolk & Norwich Healthcare
 NHS Trust
Brunswick Road
Norwich
NR7 0SS
TEL: 01603 421421
FAX: 01603 421118

Northallerton Health Service NHS
 Trust
Friarage Hospital
Northallerton
N Yorkshire
DL6 1JG
TEL: 01609 779911
FAX: 01609 777144

Northampton Community
 Healthcare NHS Trust
Clare House
St Edmunds Hospital
Wellingboro Road
Northampton
NN1 4DS
TEL: 01604 37221
FAX: 01604 602413

Northampton Hospital NHS Trust
Billing Road
Northampton
NN1 5Bd
TEL: 01604 34700
FAX: 01604 235457

Northern Gen Hospital Trust
Herries Road
Sheffield
S5 7AU
TEL: 0114 243 4343
FAX: 0114 256 0472

Northgate & Prudoe NHS
  Trust
Northgate Hospital
Morpeth
Northumberland
NE61 3BP
TEL: 01670 512281
FAX: 01670 510120

Northumberland Mental Health
  NHS Trust
St Georges Hospital
Morpeth
Northumberland
NE61 2NU
TEL: 01670 512121
FAX: 01670 511637

Northumbria Ambulance Trust
Inter Link House
Scotwood Road
Newcastle upon Tyne
NE4 7BJ
TEL: 0191 273 1212
FAX: 0191 273 7070

Northumberland Community Health
  NHS Trust
St Georges Hospital
Morpeth
Northumberland
NE61 2NH
TEL: 01670 517006
FAX: 01670 510416

Northwick & St Marks NHS
  Trust
Watford Road
Harrow
Middlesex
HA1 3UJ
TEL: 0181 864 3232

Norwich Community Health
  Partnership NHS Trust
Little Plumstead Centre
Little Plumstead
Norwich
NR13 5EW
TEL: 01603 711227
FAX: 01603 711460

Nottingham City Hospital Trust
Hucknall Road
Nottingham
NG5 1PB
TEL: 0115 9691169
FAX: 0115 9627788

Nottinghamshire Ambulance Service
  NHS Trust
Beechdale Road
Nottingham
NG8 3LL
TEL: 0115 9296151
FAX: 0115 9299415

Nottingham Community Health
  NHS Trust
Linden House
261 Beechdale Road
Aspley, Nottingham
NG8 3EY
TEL: 0115 942 6000
FAX: 0115 942 8606

Nottingham Healthcare NHS Trust
Mapperley Hospital
Porchester Road
Nottingham
NG3 6AA
TEL: 0115 969 1300
FAX: 0115 924 5486

North Staffs Combined Healthcare
  NHS Trust
Bucknall Hospital
Eaves Lane
Bucknall, Stoke on Trent
ST2 8LD
TEL: 01782 273510
FAX: 01782 213682

North Staffordshire Hospital Centre
  NHS Trust
City Gen Hospital
Newcastle Road
Stoke on Trent
ST4 6QG
TEL: 01782 715444
FAX: 01782 718671

North Tees Health NHS Trust
North Tees Gen Hospital
Hardwick Road
Stockton on Tees
TS19 8PE
TEL: 01642 617617
FAX: 01642 624089

North Tyneside Healthcare NHS
  Trust
Preston Hospital
North Shields
Tyne & Wear
NE29 0LR
TEL: 0191 259 6660
FAX: 0191 296 0281

Nuffield Orthopaedic NHS Trust
Windmill Road
Oxford
OX3 7LD
TEL: 01865 741155
FAX: 01865 742348

North Wales Ambulance NHS Trust
Preswylfa
Hendy Road
Mold, Clwyd
Wales
CH17 1PZ
TEL: 01745 585106
FAX: 01745 584101

North West Anglia Healthcare NHS
  Trust
53 Thorpe Road
Peterborough
PE3 6AN
TEL: 01733 363100
FAX: 01733 318139

North Warwickshire NHS Trust
139 Earls Road
Nuneaton
Warwickshire
CV11 5HS
TEL: 01203 642200
FAX: 01203 351434

North & West Belfast HSS Trust
Glendinning House
Murray Street
Belfast
TEL: 01232 327156
FAX: 01232 249109

North West London Mental Health
  NHS Trust
Ikea Tower
255 North Circular Road
Brent Park
London
MW10 0JQ
TEL: 0181 830 0033
FAX: 0181 830 1373

North Yorkshire Ambulance Service
  NHS Trust
Fairfields
Shipton Road
York
YO3 6XW
TEL: 01904 628085
FAX: 01904 627049

Oldham NHS Trust
Westhulme Avenue
Oldham
OL1 2PN
TEL: 0161 624 0420
FAX: 0161 627 3130

Optimum NHS Trust
Elizabeth Blackwell House
Wardells Grove
Avonley Road
London
SE14 5ER
TEL: 0171 635 5555
FAX: 0171 635 1188

Oxfordshire Ambulance NHS Trust
Churchill Drive
Old Road
Headington, Oxford
OX3 7LH
TEL: 01865 740100
FAX: 01865 741974

Oxfordshire Community NHS Trust
Bourton House
18 Thorney Leys Parks
Witney, Oxford
OX8 7GE
TEL: 01993 700311
FAX: 01993 707610

Oxford Learning Disability NHS
   Trust
Slade Hospital Resource Centre
Headington
Oxford
OX3 7JH
TEL: 01865 747455
FAX: 01865 228182

Oxfordshire Mental Health NHS
   Trust
Littlemore Hospital
33 Sandford Road
Oxford
OX4 4XN
TEL: 01865 778911
FAX: 01865 223061

Oxford Radcliife Hospital NHS
   Trust
Headley Way
Headington
Oxford
OX3 9DU
TEL: 01865 741166
FAX: 01865 741408

Papworth Hospital NHS Trust
Papworth Everard
Cambridge
CB3 8RE
TEL: 01480 830541
FAX: 01480 830067

Parkside Health NHS Trust
Paddington Community
   Hospital
Woodfield Road
London
W9 2BB
TEL: 0181 451 8000
FAX: 0181 451 8221

Pathfinder NHS Trust
Springfield Hospital
61 Glenburnie Road
London
SW17 7DJ
TEL: 0181 672 9911
FAX: 0181 767 7608

Pembrokeshire NHS Trust
Withybush General Hospital
Fishguard Road
Haverfordwest
Pembrokeshire
SA61 2PZ
TEL: 01437 764545
FAX: 01437 773353

Perth & Kinross NHS Trust
Perth Royal Infirmary
Perth
Scotland
PH1 1NX
TEL: 01738 623311
FAX: 01738 473206

Peterborough Hospitals
   Trust
Edith Cavell Hospital
Bretton Gate
Peterborough
PE3 9GZ
TEL: 01733 874000
FAX: 01733 874001

Phoenix NHS Trust
Stoke Park Hospital
Bristol
BS16 1QS
TEL: 0117 958 5000
FAX: 0117 975 6686

Pilgrim Health NHS Trust
Pilgrim Hospital
Sibsey Road
Boston
Lincolshire
PE21 9QS
TEL: 01205 364801
FAX: 01205 354395

Pinderfield Hospital NHS Trust
Rowan House
Aberford Road
Wakefield
WF1 4EE
TEL: 01924 201688
FAX: 01924 814929

Plymouth Community Services NHS
    Trust
Mount Gould Hospital
Mount Gould Road
Plymouth
PL4 7QD
TEL: 01752 268011
FAX: 01752 272371

Plymouth Hospitals NHS Trust
General Office, Level 7
Derrisford Hospital
Crownhill
Plymouth
PL6 8DH
TEL: 01752 777111
FAX: 01752 768976

Pontefract Hospitals NHS Trust
Friarwood Lane
Pontefract
WF8 1PL
TEL: 01977 600600
FAX: 01977 606852

Poole Hospital NHS Trust
Longfleet Road
Poole
BH15 2JB
TEL: 01202 665511
FAX: 01202 442462

Portsmouth Healthcare Trust
St James Hospital
Locksway Road
Milton, Portsmouth
PO4 8LD
TEL: 01705 822444
FAX: 01705 293437

Portsmouth Hospitals NHS Trust
St Marys Hospital
Milton Road
Portsmouth
PO3 6AD
TEL: 01705 822331
FAX: 01705 866413

Powys Healthcare NHS Trust
Bronllys Hospital
Bronllys
Brecon, Powys
LD3 0LS
TEL: 01874 711661
FAX: 01874 711601

Premier Health NHS Trust
Imex Shobnall Road
Burton on Trent
Staffordshire
DE14 2AU
TEL: 01283 515616
FAX: 01283 530630

Preston Acute Hospitals Trust
Royal Preston Hospital
Sharoe Green Lane North
Fulwood
Preston
PR2 4HX
TEL: 01772 716565
FAX: 01772 710194

Princess Alexandra Hospital NHS
    Trust
Parndon Hall
Hamstel Road
Harlow
CM20 1QX
TEL: 01279 444455
FAX: 01279 429371

Princess Royal Hospital Trust
Apley Castle
Telford
Shropshire
TF6 6TF
TEL: 01952 641222
FAX: 01952 243405

Queen Margaret Hospital Trust
Whitefield Road
Dunfermline
Fife
Scotland
KY12 0SU
TEL: 01383 623623
FAX: 01383 624156

Queen Mars Sidcup NHS Trust
Frognall Avenue
Sidcup
Kent
DA14 6LT
TEL: 0181 302 2678
FAX: 0181 308 3052

Queens Medical Centre
Nottingham University Hospital
    NHS Trust
Nottingham
NG7 2UH
TEL: 0115 924 9924
FAX: 0115 970 9196

Queen Victoria Hospital Trust
Holtye Road
East Grinstead
West Sussex
RH19 3DZ
TEL: 01342 410210
FAX: 01342 317907

Radcliffe Infirmary NHS Trust ✓
Woodstock Road
Oxford
OX2 6HE
TEL: 01865 311188
FAX: 01865 224566

Raigmore Hospital NHS Trust
Raigmore Hospital
Perth Road
Inverness
Scotland
IV2 3UJ
TEL: 01463 704000
FAX: 01463 711322

Royal Alexandra Hospital Trust
Corsebar Road
Paisley
Scotland
PA2 9PN
TEL: 0141 887 9111
FAX: 0141 887 6702

Ravensbourne NHS Trust
Basset House
Broadwater Gardens
Farnborough
Kent
BR5 7UA

Royal Berkshire Ambulance Service
    NHS Trust
41 Barkham Road
Wokingham
Berkshire
RG11 2RE
TEL: 01734 771200
FAX: 01734 773923

Royal Berkshire & Battle Hospitals
    NHS Trust
London Road
Reading
Berkshire
RG1 5AN
TEL: 01734 875111
FAX: 01734 878041

Royal Bournemouth & CC Hospitals
    NHS Trust
Castle Lane East
Bournemouth
BH7 7DW
TEL: 01202 303626
FAX: 01202 704077

Royal Brompton Hospital Trust
Sydney Street
London
SW3 6NP
TEL: 0171 352 8121
FAX: 0171 351 8473

Royal Cornwall Hospitals NHS Trust
Royal Cornwall Hospital
Treliske
Truro
TR1 3LJ
TEL: 01872 74242
FAX: 01872 40574

Royal Devon & Exeter Healthcare
    NHS Trust
Barrack Road
Exeter
Devon
EX2 5DW
TEL: 01392 411611
FAX: 01392 402067

Redbridge Healthcare NHS Trust
King George Hospital
Eastern Avenue
Ilford
Essex
IG2 7RL
TEL: 0181 983 8000
FAX: 0181 970 8001

Renfrewshire NHS Trust
Dykebar Hospital
Grahamston Road
Paisley
Scotland
PA2 7DE
TEL: 0141 884 5122
FAX: 0141 884 5425

Royal Free Hampstead NHS Trust
Royal Free Hospital
Pond Street
London
NW3 2PN
TEL: 0171 794 0500
FAX: 0171 435 5342

Royal Group of Hospitals Trust
Grosvenor Road
Belfast
BT12 6BA
TEL: 01232 240503
FAX: 01232 240899

Rhondda Healthcare NHS Trust
Llwynpia Hospital
Llwynpia
Rhondda, Wales
CF40 2LX
Wales
FAX: 01443 440440
FAX: 01443 431611

Royal Hull Hospitals NHS Trust
Hull Royal Infirmary
Anlaby Road
Hull
HU3 2JZ
TEL: 01482 328541
FAX: 01482 674857

Richmond, T & R Healthcare NHS
    Trust
Queen Marys University
Roehampton Lane
London, SW15 5PN
TEL: 0181 789 6611
FAX: 0181 780 1089

Royal Infirmary of Edinburgh NHS
    Trust
Royal Infirmary of Edinburgh
1 Lauriston Place
Edinburgh
EH3 9YW
TEL: 0131 536 1000
FAX: 0131 536 3001

Riverside Community Healthcare
    NHS Trust
Dabons Green Centre
5–7 Parsons Green
London
SW6 4UL
TEL: 0181 848 6767
FAX: 0181 846 7654

Riverside Mental Health Trust
3rd Floor, Commonwealth House
2–4 Chalkhill Road
London
W6 8DW
TEL: 0181 746 8954
FAX: 0181 746 8978

Royal Liverpool Childrens Hospital
   NHS Trust
1 Myrtle Street
Liverpool
L7 7DE
TEL: 0151 228 4811
FAX: 0151 228 0328

Koyal Liverpool University
   Hospital NHS Trust
Prescot Street
Liverpool
L7 8XP
TEL: 0151 706 2000
FAX: 0151 706 5824

Royal London Homoeopathic
   Hospital NHS Trust
Great Ormond Street
London
WC1N 3HR
TEL: 0171 837 8833
FAX: 0171 833 7229

Royal Marsden London NHS
   Trust
Fulham Road
London
SW3 6JJ
TEL: 0171 352 8171
FAX: 0171 376 4809

Royal Nat Hospital Orthopaedic
   NHS Trust
Brockley Hill
Stanmore
Middlesex
HA7 4LP
TEL: 0181 954 2300
FAX: 0181 954 7249

Royal National Hospital for
   Rheumatic Diseases NHS Trust
Upper Borough Walls
Bath
BA1 1RL
TEL: 01225 465941
FAX: 01225 421202

Royal National Throat, Nose & Ear
   Hospital NHS Trust
Grays Inn Road
London
WC1X 8DA
TEL: 0171 915 1300
FAX: 0171 833 5518

Robert Jones & Agnes Hunt
   District & Orthopaedic Hospital
   Trust
Oswestry
Shropshire
SY10 7AG
TEL: 01691 655311
FAX: 01691 652613

Rochdale Healthcare NHS Trust
Birch Hill Hospital
Rochdale
OL12 9QB
TEL: 01706 377777
FAX: 01706 755130

Rockingham Forest NHS Trust
St Marys Hospital
77 London Road
Kettering
Northants
NN15 7PW
TEL: 01536 410141
FAX: 01536 493244

Royal Orthopaedic Hospital
   Birmingham
Woodlands
Northfield, Birmingham
B31 2AP
TEL: 0121 627 8624
FAX: 0121 627 8211

Rotherham Gen Hospitals Trust
Moorgate Road
Oakwood
Rotherham
S60 2UD
TEL: 01709 820000
FAX: 01709 824000

Rotherham Priority Health Services
    NHS Trust
Rivelin House
Moorgate Road
Rotherham
S60 3AJ
TEL: 01709 820000
FAX: 01709 824890

Royal Hospitals NHS Trust
5th floor, Alexandra House
Whitechapel
London
E1 1BB
TEL: 0171 377 7000
FAX: 0171 377 7413

Royal Shewsbury Hospitals NHS Trust
Mytton Park Road
Shrewsbury
Shropshire
SW3 8XQ
TEL: 01743 261000
FAX: 01743 261006

Royal Surrey & St Lukes Hospital
    NHS Trust
Royal Surrey County Hospital
Egerton Road
Guildford
GU2 5XX
TEL: 01483 571122
FAX: 01483 37747

Rugby NHS Trust
24 Warwick Street
Rugby
CV21 3DN
TEL: 01788 572831
FAX: 01788 545151

Royal United Hospital
Bath NHS Trust
Combe Park
Bath
BA1 3NG
TEL: 01225 428331
FAX: 01225 824395

RVI & Hexham NHS Trust
Royal Victoria Infirmary
Newcastle upon Tyne
NE1 4LP
TEL: 0191 232 5131
FAX: 0191 201 0155

Royal Wolverhampton Hospitals
    NHS Trust
New Cross Hospital
Wolverhampton
WV10 0QP
TEL: 01902 307999
FAX: 01902 643173

Royal West Sussex Healthcare
    NHS Trust
St Richards Hospital
Spitalfield Lane
Chichester, West Sussex
PO19 4SE
TEL: 01243 788122
FAX: 01243 531269

Salford Community Healthcare
    NHS Trust
Joule House
49 The Crescent
Salford
M5 4NY
TEL: 0161 743 0466
FAX: 0161 743 0452

Salford Royal NHS Trust
Hope Hospital
Eccles Old Road
Salford
M6 8HD
TEL: 0161 789 7373
FAX: 0161 787 5974

Salford Mental Health NHS Trust
Prestwich Hospital
Bury New Road
Prestwich
Manchester
M25 3BL
TEL: 0161 773 9121
FAX: 0161 773 8186

✓ Salisbury Healthcare NHS Trust
Salisbury District Hospital
Salisbury
Wiltshire
SP2 8BJ
TEL: 01722 336262
FAX: 01722 330221

Sandwell Healthcare NHS Trust
Management Offices
Lyndon
West Bromwich
West Midlands
B71 4HG
TEL: 0121 553 1831
FAX: 0121 607 3117

South Ayrshire Hospitals Trust
Dalmellington Road
Ayr, Scotland
KA6 6DX
TEL: 01292 610555
FAX: 01292 288952

South Bedfordshire Community
    Healthcare NHS Trust
1 Union Street
Luton
LU1 3AN
TEL: 01582 485888
FAX: 01582 485667

South Birmingham Community NHS
    Trust
West Heath Hospital
Rednall Road
Birmingham
B38 8HR
TEL: 0121 627 1627
FAX: 0121 627 8228

South Birmingham Mental Health
    NHS Trust
Vincent Drive
Edgbaston, Birmingham
B15 2TZ
TEL: 0121 472 2294
FAX: 0121 471 1866

South Buckinghamshire NHS Trust
Oakengrove
Shrubbery Road
High Wycombe
Buckinghamshire
HP13 6PS
TEL: 01494 526161
FAX: 01494 426114

Scarborough & North East Yorkshire
    Healthcare NHS Trust
Scarborough Hospital
Scalby Road
Scarborough
YD12 6QL
TEL: 01723 368111
FAX: 01723 377223

Scottish Ambulance Service National
    HQ
Tipperlinn Road
Edinburgh
ED10 5UU
TEL: 0131 447 7711
FAX: 0131 447 4789

South Cumbria Community &
    Mental Health NHS Trust
2 Fairfield Lane
Barrow in Furness, Cumbria
LA13 9AH
TEL: 01229 820552
FAX: 01229 823224

Scunthorpe & Goole Hospitals
    NHS Trust
Cliff Gardens
Scunthorpe
DN15 7BH
TEL: 01724 282282
FAX: 01724 282427

Scunthorpe Community Healthcare
  NHS Trust
Brumby Hospital
East Common Lane
Scunthorpe
DN16 3TL
TEL: 01724 282282
FAX: 01724 271016

Southern Derbyshire Mental Health
  NHS Trust
Thorndale
Kingsway Hospital
Derby
DE3 3LZ
TEL: 01332 362221
FAX: 01332 331254

South Derbyshire Community
  NHS Trust
Meadow Suite, Babington Hospital
Derby Road
Belper
DE56 1WH
TEL: 01773 525099
FAX: 01773 820318

South Devon Healthcare Trust
Torbay Hospital
Lawes Bridge
Torquay
TQ2 7AA
TEL: 01803 614567
FAX: 01803 616334

South Downes Health NHS Trust
Elm Grove
Brighton, East Sussex
BN2 3EW
TEL: 01273 696011
FAX: 01723 698312

South Durham Healthcare Trust
Upper Thorpe
90 Woodland Road
Darlington
DL3 7PZ
TEL: 01388 605811
FAX: 01388 602548

South & East Belfast NHS Trust
Purdysburn Hospital
Saintfield Road
Belfast
BT8 8BH
TEL: 01232 790673
FAX: 01232 796632

South East London Mental Health
  NHS Trust
Leegate House
Burnt Ash Road
London
SE12 8RG
TEL: 0181 297 0707
FAX: 0181 297 0377

Severn NHS Trust
Rikenal
Montpelier
Gloucester
GL1 1LY
TEL: 01452 529421
FAX: 01452 308074

South & East Wales Ambulance NHS
  Trust
Ty Bronna
St Fagans Road
Fairwater
Cardiff
TEL: 01222 552011
FAX: 01222 554553

Sheffield Childrens Hospital NHS
  Trust
Western Bank
Sheffield
S10 2TH
TEL: 0114 271 7000
FAX: 0114 272 3418

Sheffield Community NHS Trust
Fulwood House
Old Fulwood Road
Sheffield
S10 3TH
TEL: 0114 271 6700
FAX: 0114 271 6712

Shropshire Community NHS Trust
Brayford House
Cross Houses
Shrewsbury
Shropshire
SY5 6JN
TEL: 01743 76142
FAX: 01743 761601

Shropshire Mental Health NHS Trust
Royal Shrewsbury Hospital
Bicton Heath
Shrewsbury
SY3 8DN
TEL: 01743 261000
FAX: 01743 261279

South Kent Community NHS Trust
Ash-Eton
Radnor Park West
Folkestone
Kent
CT19 5HL
TEL: 01303 222333
FAX: 01303 222334

South Kent Hospitals NHS Trust
William Harvey Hospital
Kennington Road
Willesborough
Ashford
Kent
TN24 0LZ
TEL: 01233 633331
FAX: 01233 616089

South Lincolnshire Community
    & Mental Health Services Trust
Rauceby Hospital
Sleaford
Lincolnshire
NG34 8PP
TEL: 01529 416000
FAX: 01529 416092

South Manchester University
    Hospitals NHS Trust
Wythenshawe Hospital
Southmoor Road

Manchester
M23 9LT
TEL: 0161 998 7070
FAX: 0161 946 2603

Solihull Healthcare NHS
    Trust
Berwicks Lane
Marston Green
Birmingham
B37 7XR
TEL: 0121 779 6035
FAX: 0121 779 5926

Southampton Community NHS
    Trust
Central Health Clinic
East Park Terrace
Southampton
SO9 4WN
TEL: 01703 634321
FAX: 01703 634375

Southampton University Hospitals
    NHS Trust
Southampton Gen Hospital
Tremona Road
Southampton
SO9 4XY
TEL: 01703 777222
FAX: 01703 794153

Southend Community NHS Trust
Union Lane
Rochford
Essex
SS4 1RB
TEL: 01702 546354
FAX: 01702 546383

Southend Healthcare NHS Trust
Southend Hospital
Prittlewell Chase
Westcliff on Sea
Essex
SS0 0RY
TEL: 01702 221100
FAX: 01702 221109

Southern Gen Hospital Trust
Southern Gen Hospital
1345 Govan Road
Glasgow, Scotland
G51 4TF
TEL: 0141 201 1100
FAX: 0141 201 2999

Southmead Health Services NHS
　Trust
Southmead Hospital
Westbury on Trym
Bristol, BS10 5NS
TEL: 0117 950 5050
FAX: 0117 959 0902

Southport & Formby Community
　NHS Trust
The Hesketh Centre
51–55 Albert Road
Southport
PR9 0LT
TEL: 01704 547471
FAX: 01704 530714

Southport & Formby NHS Trust
Southport Gen Hospital
Town Lane
Southport
PR8 6NJ
TEL: 01704 547471
FAX: 01704 548229

Staffordshire Ambulance Service
　NHS Trust
70 Stone Road
Stafford
ST16 2RS
TEL: 01785 53521
FAX: 01785 46238

St Albans & Hemel Hempstead
　Healthcare NHS Trust
St Albans City Hospital
Normandy Road
St Albans
AL3 5PN
TEL: 01442 213141
FAX: 01442 279201

South Tees Acute Hospitals NHS Trust
Middlesborough Gen Hospital
Ayersome Green Lane
Middlesborough
TS7 0NJ
TEL: 01642 850850
FAX: 01642 854136

South Tees Community & Mental
　Health NHS Trust
Acklam Road
Middlesborough
TS5 4EE
TEL: 01642 850850
FAX: 01642 821810

St George's Healthcare Trust
St George's Hospital
Blackshaw Road
London
SW17 0QT
TEL: 0181 672 1255

St Helens & Knowsley Hospital NHS
　Trust
Whiston Hospital
Prescot
L35 5DR
TEL: 0151 426 1600
FAX: 0151 430 8278

St Helens & Knowsley Community
　NHS Trust
Cowley Hill Lane
St Helens
Merseyside
WA10 2AP
TEL: 01744 733722
FAX: 01744 453615

St Helier NHS Trust
St Helier & Sutton Hospitals
Wrythe Lane
Carshalton
Surrey
SM5 1AA
TEL: 0181 644 4343
FAX: 0181 641 4717

Stirling NHS Trust
Stirling Royal Infirmary
Livilands
Stirling, Scotland
FK8 2AU
TEL: 01786 434000
FAX: 01786 450588

St James University Hospital NHS
    Trust
Beckett Street
Leeds
LS9 7TF
TEL: 0113 243 3144
FAX: 0113 242 6496

St Marys NHS Trust
St Marys Hospital
Praed Street
London
W2 1NY
TEL: 0171 725 6666
FAX: 0171 725 6200

St Marys Hospital NHS Trust
Parkhurst Road
Newport
Isle of Wight
PO30 5TG
TEL: 01983 524081
FAX: 01983 822569

Stobhill Hospital NHS Trust
133 Balornock Road
Glasgow
Scotland
G21 3UW
TEL: 0141 201 3000
FAX: 0141 558 2970

Stockport Acute Services Trust
Oak House
Stepping Hill Hospital
Stockport
SK2 7JG
TEL: 0161 483 1010
FAX: 0161 419 5033

Stockport Healthcare NHS Trust
Oak House
Stepping Hill Hospital
Hazel Grove
Stockport
SK2 7JE
TEL: 0161 483 1010
FAX: 0161 419 5169

Stoke Mandeville Hospital NHS
    Trust
Mandeville Road
Aylesbury, Buckinghamshire
HP21 8AL
TEL: 01296 315000
FAX: 01296 316604

St Peters Hospital NHS Trust
St Peters Hospital
Guildford Road
Chertsey, Surrey
KT16 0PZ
TEL: 01932 872000
FAX: 01932 874757

South Tyneside Healthcare NHS
    Trust
South Tyneside District Hospital
South Shields, Tyne & Wear
NE34 0PL
TEL: 0191 454 8888
FAX: 0191 427 9908

Surrey Ambulance NHS Trust
The Horseshoe
Bolters Lane
Banstead, Surrey
SM7 2AS
TEL: 01737 353333
FAX: 01737 370868

Surrey Heartlands NHS Trust
St Ebba's
Hook Road
Epsom, Surrey
KT19 8QJ
TEL: 01372 722212
FAX: 01372 725068

Sussex Ambulance NHS Trust
Ambulance HQ
30–42 Friars Walk
Lewes
East Sussex
BN7 2LW
TEL: 01273 489444
FAX: 01273 489445

Swansea NHS Trust
Singleton Hospital
Sketty
Swansea
SA2 0FB
TEL: 01792 205666
FAX: 01792 208647

South Warwickshire Gen NHS Trust
Lakin Road
Warwick
CV34 5BW
TEL: 01926 495321
FAX: 01926 403715

South Warwickshire Healthcare NHS
Trust
Alcester Road
Stratford upon Avon
CV37 6PW
TEL: 01789 269264
FAX: 01789 267799

South Warwickshire Mental Health
Services NHS Trust
Central Hospital
Hatton
Warwick
CV35 7EE
TEL: 01926 496241
FAX: 01926 401690

South West Durham Mental Health
NHS Trust
Winterton Hospital
Sedgefield
Cleveland
TW21 3EJ
TEL: 01740 623777
FAX: 01740 622646

Swindon & Marlborough Hospital
NHS Trust
Princess Margaret Hospital
Okus Road
Swindon
SN1 4JU
TEL: 01793 536231
FAX: 01793 480817

South Worcestershire Community
NHS Trust
Isaac Maddox House
Shrub Hill Road
Worcester, WR4 9RW
TEL: 01905 763333
FAX: 01905 610292

South Yorkshire Ambulance
& Paramedic Service NHS Trust
Fairfield
Moorgate, Rotherham
S60 2BX
TEL: 01709 820520
FAX: 01709 827839

Tameside & Glossop Acute Services
NHS Trust
Tameside General Hospital
Fountain Street
Ashton under Lyne, OL6 9RW
TEL: 0161 331 6000
FAX: 0161 331 6026

Tameside & Glossop Community
Services NHS Trust
Tameside Gen Hospital
Fountain Street
Ashton under Lyne
OL6 9RW
TEL: 0161 331 5151
FAX: 0161 3311 5007

Taunton & Somerset NHS Trust
Taunton & Somerset Hospital
Musgrove Park Branch
Taunton, Somerset
TA1 1DA
TEL: 01823 333444
FAX: 01823 336877

Tavistock & Portman NHS Trust
120 Belsize Park
London
NW3 5BA
TEL: 0171 435 7111
FAX: 0171 431 8855

Teddington Memorial Hospital
Hampton Road
Teddington
Middlesex
TW11 0JL
TEL: 0181 977 2212
FAX: 0181 977 1914

Thameside Community Healthcare
    NHS Trust
Thurrock Community Hospital
Long Lane
Grays
Essex
RM16 2PX
TEL: 01375 390044
FAX: 01375 364400

Thameslink Healthcare Trust
Archery House
Bow Arrow Lane
Dartford
TEL: 01322 227211
FAX: 01322 223492

Thanet Healthcare NHS Trust
Thanet General Hospital
St Peters Road
Margate
Kent
CT9 4AN
TEL: 01843 225544
FAX: 01843 220048

Tower Hamlets Healthcare NHS
    Trust
Mile End Hospital
Bancroft Road
London
E1 1BB
TEL: 0171 377 7926

Trafford Healthcare NHS Trust
Trafford General Hospital
Moorside Road
Davyhulme, Urmston
Manchester
M31 3SL
TEL: 0161 748 4022
FAX: 0161 746 7214

Two Shires Ambulance NHS Trust
The Hunters
Buckingham Road
Deanshanger, Milton Keynes
MK19 6HL
TEL: 01908 262422
FAX: 01908 265014

Ulster North Down & Ards NHS
    Trust
Ulster Hospital
700 Newtownards Road
Dundonald
BT16 0RH
TEL: 01232 484511
FAX: 01232 481753

University College London
    Hospitals NHS Trust
Gower Street
London
WC1E 6DB
TEL: 0171 380 9962
FAX: 0171 380 9536

University Dental Hospital Trust
Dental Hospital
Heath Park
Cardiff, CF4 4XY
TEL: 01222 747747
FAX: 01222 742421

University Hospital Birmingham
    NHS Trust
Selly Oak Hospital
Oak Tree Lane
Birmingham
B29 6JF
TEL: 0121 432 3232
FAX: 0121 627 8201

University Hospital of Wales
Heath Park
Cardiff
CF4 4XW
TEL: 01222 747747
FAX: 01222 743838

United Bristol Healthcare Trust
10 Marlborough Street
Bristol
BS1 3NP
TEL: 01272 290666
FAX: 01272 256588

United Leeds Teaching Hospital
  NHS Trust
Great George Street
Leeds
LS1 3EX
TEL: 0113 243 2799
FAX: 0113 292 6336

Velindre NHS Trust
Velindre Hospital
Velindre Road
Whitchurch, Cardiff
Wales
CF4 7XL
TEL: 01222 615888
FAX: 01222 522694

Victoria Infirmary NHS Trust
Queens Park House
Langside Road
Glasgow
Scotland
G42 9TY
TEL: 0141 201 6000
FAX: 0141 201 5825

Wakefield & Pontefract Community
  Health NHS Trust
3–5 St Johns North
Fernbank
Wakefield
WF1 3QD
TEL: 01924 814814
FAX: 01924 814 987

Walsall Community NHS Trust
Lichfield House
Walsall
WS1 1TE
TEL: 01922 720255FAX: 01922
  656040

Walsall Hospitals NHS Trust
Manor Hospital
Moat Road
Walsall, West Midlands
WS2 9PS
TEL: 01922 721172
FAX: 01922 656621

Walsgrave Hospitals NHS Trust
Walsgrave Hospital
Clifford Bridge Road
Walsgrave, Coventry
CV2 2DX
TEL: 01203 602020
FAX: 01203 622197

Walton Centre for Neurology &
  Neurosurgery NHS Trust
Walton Hospital
Rice Lane
Liverpool
L9 1AE
TEL: 0151 525 3611
FAX: 0151 529 4638

Wandsworth Community NHS Trust
Clare House
St Georges Hospital
Blackshaw Road
London
SW17 0QT
TEL: 0181 672 1255
FAX: 0181 725 2916

Warwickshire Ambulance Service
  NHS Trust
50 Holly Walk
Leamington Spa
CV32 4HY
TEL: 01926 881331
FAX: 01926 451162

Warrington Community Healthcare ✓
   Trust
Winwick Hospital
Winwick, Warrington
WA2 8RR
TEL: 01925 55221
FAX: 01925 235089

Warrington Hospital NHS Trust
Lovely Lane
Warrington, Cheshire
WA5 1QG
TEL: 01925 635911FAX: 01925
   662521

West Berkshire Priority Care
   Services NHS Trust
Prospect Park Hospital
Honey End Lane
Reading
RG3 4EJ
TEL: 01734 586161
FAX: 01734 591135

West Cheshire Priority Trust
Countess of Chester Hospital
Liverpool Road
Chester
CH2 1BA
TEL: 01244 365000
FAX: 01244 364227

Westcountry Ambulance NHS
   Trust
Morlaix Drive
Plymouth
PL6 5AB
TEL: 01752 767839
FAX: 01752 778747

West Cumbria Healthcare Trust
West Cumberland Hospital
Hensingham
Whitehaven
Cumbria
CA28 8JG
TEL: 01946 693181
FAX: 01946 523513

West Dorset Hospitals Trust
Dorset County Hospital
Princes Street
Dorcester
DT1 1TS
TEL: 01305 251150
FAX: 01305 254185

Weald of Kent Community Trust
Blackhurst
Halls Hole Road
Tunbridge Wells
Kent
TN2 4RG
TEL: 01892 539144
FAX: 01892 535522

Wearside Priority Health NHS Trust
Cherry Knowle Hospital
Ryhope
Sunderland
SR2 0NB
TEL: 0191 656 6256
FAX: 0191 569 9438

Wellhouse NHS Trust
Edgware Gen Hospital
Burnt Oak Broadway
Middlesex
HA8 0AD
TEL: 0181 952 2381
FAX: 0181 732 6807

Western Gen Hospital NHS
   Trust
Crewe Road
Edinburgh
Scotland
EH4 2XU
TEL: 0131 537 1000
FAX: 0131 537 1001

Westmorland Hospitals Trust
Burton Road
Kendal
Cumbria
LA9 7RG
TEL: 01539 732288
FAX: 01539 740852

Weston Area Health NHS Trust
Weston Gen Hospital
Grange Road
Weston Super Mare
BS23 4TQ
TEL: 01934 636363
FAX: 01934 647029

Weston Park Hospitals NHS Trust
Whitham Park
Sheffield
S10 2SJ
TEL: 0114 267 0222
FAX: 0114 268 4193

West Glasgow Hospital Trust
Western Infirmary
Dumbarton Road
Glasgow
Scotland
G11 6NT
TEL: 0141 211 2000
FAX: 0141 211 1920

West Hertfordshire Community
   NHS Trust
99 Waverley Road
St Albans
AL3 5TZ
TEL: 01727 811888
FAX: 01727 857900

Whittington Hospital NHS Trust
Highgate Hill
London
N19 5NF
TEL: 0171 272 3070
FAX: 0171 288 5550

Wigan & Leigh Health Services
   NHS Trust
Whelley Hospital
Bradshaw Street
Wigan
WN1 3XD
TEL: 01942 44000
FAX: 01942 822670

Wiltshire Ambulance NHS Trust
Malmesbury Road
Chippenham
Wiltshire
SN15 5LN
TEL: 01249 443939
FAX: 01249 443217

Wiltshire Healthcare NHS Trust
St Johns Hospital
Bradley Road
Trowbridge, Wiltshire
BA14 0QU
TEL: 01225 753610
FAX: 01225 777697

Winchester & Eastleigh Healthcare
   NHS Trust
Royal Hampshire County Hospital
Winchester
SO22 5DG
TEL: 01962 863535
FAX: 01962 825190

Wirral Community Healthcare NHS
   Trust
Victoria Central Hospital
Mill Lane
Wallasey
L44 5UF
TEL: 0151 678 7272
FAX: 0151 639 2478

Wirral Hospital NHS Trust
Arrowe Park Hospital
Arrowe Park Road
Upton, Merseyside
L49 5PE
TEL: 0151 678 5111
FAX: 0151 604 7148

West Lambeth Community Care
   NHS Trust
Tooting Bec Hospital
London
SW17 8BL
TEL: 0171 326 5400
FAX: 0171 761 1132

West Lancashire NHS Trust
Ormskirk & District Gen
  Hospital
Wigan Road
Ormskirk
Lancashire
L39 2AZ
TEL: 01695 577111
FAX: 01695 583028

West Lindsey NHS Trust
Natwest Bank Chambers
2a Market Street
Gainsborough
DN21 2BA
TEL: 01427 811851
FAX: 01427 811640

West London Healthcare Trust
Ealing Hospital
Uxbridge Road
Southall
Middlesex
UB1 3EU
TEL: 0181 574 2444
FAX: 0181 967 5002

West Lothian NHS Trust
St Johns Hospital
Livingston
West Lothian
Scotland
EH54 6PP
TEL: 01506 419666
FAX: 01506 461280

West Middlesex University
  Hospital NHS Trust
Twickenham Road
Isleworth
Middlesex
TW7 6AF
TEL: 0181 560 2121
FAX: 0181 560 2395

West Midlands Ambulance Service
  NHS Trust
4th floor, Falcon House
6 The Minnery

Dudley
DY2 8PN
TEL: 01384 455644
FAX: 01384 458884

Woverhampton Healthcare
10–12 Tetterhall Road
Wolverhampton
West Midlands
WV1 4SA
TEL: 01902 310641
FAX: 01902 716834

Worcester Royal Infirmary NHS
  Trust
Newton Branch
Newton Road
Worcester
WR5 1JG
TEL: 01905 763333
FAX: 01905 763467

Worthing Priority Care Trust
Swandean Hospital
Arundel Road
Worthing
West Sussex
BN13 3EP
TEL: 01903 264121
FAX: 01903 691179

Worthing & Southlands Hospital
  NHS Trust
Worthing Hospital
Park Avenue
Worthing
West Sussex
BN11 2DH
TEL: 01903 205111
FAX: 01903 823721

Wrexham Maelor Hospital Trust
Croesnewydd Road
Wrexham
Clwyd
LL13 7TD
TEL: 01978 291100
FAX: 01978 290951

Wrightington Hospital Trust
Nr Wigan
Lancashire
WN6 9EP
TEL: 01257 252211
FAX: 01257 253809

West Suffolk Hospitals Trust
Hardwick Lane
Bury St Edmunds
Suffolk
IP33 2QZ
TEL: 01284 713000
FAX: 01284 701993

West Wales Ambulance Trust
21 Orchard Street
Swansea
Wales
SA1 5BETEL: 01792 562900
FAX: 01792 281184

West Yorkshire Ambulance Service
 NHS Trust
Threelands
Bradford Road
Birkenshaw, Bradford
BD11 2AH
TEL: 01274 651410
FAX: 01274 651117

Yorkhill NHS Trust
Royal Hospital for Sick Children
Yorkhill
Glasgow, Scotland
G3 8SJ
TEL: 0141 201 0000
FAX: 0141 201 0836

York Health Services NHS Trust
Bootham Park Hospital
York
YO3 7BY
TEL: 01904 610700
FAX: 01904 454439

Appendix IV
Health Authorities, Family Health Service Authorities and Health Commissions

Anglia & Oxford RHA
6–12 Capital Drive
Linford Wood
Milton Keynes
Buckinghamshire
MK14 6OP
TEL: 01908 844400
FAX: 01908 844444

Argyll & Clyde Health Board
Ross House
Hawkshead Road
Paisley
Renfrewshire
PA2 7BN
TEL: 0141 842 7200
FAX: 0141 848 1414

Avon HC
10 Dighton Street
Bristol
BS2 8EE
TEL: 0117 976 6600
FAX: 0117 996 6601

Ayrshire & Arran Health Board
PO Box 13
Seafield House

12 Doonfoot Road
Ayr
KA7 4DW
TEL: 01292 611040
FAX: 01292 286762

Barking & Havering FHSA
St Georges Hospital
Suttons Lane
Hornchurch
Essex
RM12 6SD
TEL: 01708 472011
FAX: 01708 437183

Barking & Havering DHA
The Grange
Gubbins Lane
Harold Wood
Romford
RM3 0DD
TEL: 01708 349511
FAX: 01708 381368

Barnet Health Agency
Colindale Hospital
Colindale Avenue
London

NW9 5HG
TEL: 0181 205 1777
FAX: 0181 200 0998

Barnsley DHA
Hillder House
49–51 Gawber Road
Barnsley
S75 2PW
TEL: 01226 779922
FAX: 01226 730054

Barnsley FHSA
49–51 Gawber Road
Barnsley
S75 2PS
TEL: 01226 779922
FAX: 01226 298719

Bedfordshire HC
Charter House
Alma Street
Luton
Bedforshire
LU1 2PZ
TEL: 01234 327427
FAX: 01234 342028

Berkshire Health Commission
Pendragon House
59 Bath Road
Reading
Berkshire
RG3 2BA
TEL: 01734 503094
FAX: 01734 594620

Bexley & Greenwich HC
221 Erith Road
Bexleyheath
Kent
DA7 6HZ
TEL: 0181 301 2333
FAX: 0181 308 3205

Birmingham FHSA
Aston Cross
50 Rocky Lane
Brimingham

B6 5RQ
TEL: 0121 333 4444
FAX: 0121 333 4181

Bolton FHSA
43 Churchgate
Bolton
BL1 1JF
TEL: 01204 390014
FAX: 01204 390016

Borders Health Board
Newstead
Melrose
Roxburghshire
TD6 9DB
TEL: 01896 822265
FAX: 01896 823401

Bradford HC
New Mill, Victoria Road
Saltaire
Shipley
West Yorkshire
BD18 3LD
TEL: 01274 366007
FAX: 01274 366060

Brent & Harrow DHA
Grace Road
Harrovian Business Village
Bessborough Road
Harrow
HA1 3EX
TEL: 0181 422 6644
FAX: 0181 423 7314

Brent & Harrow FHSA
1st floor, 21 Building
21 Pinner Road
Harrow
Middlesex
HA1 4BB
TEL: 0181 427 7888
FAX: 0181 861 3126

Bristol & District DHA
10 Dighton Street
Bristol

BS2 8EE
TEL: 0117 976 6600
FAX: 0117 976 6601

Bromley HC
Global House
10 Station Road
Hayes
Kent
BR2 7EH
TEL: 0181 462 2211
FAX: 0181 462 6767

Buckinghamshire DHA
Ardenham Lane
Aylesbury
Buckinghamshire
HP19 3DX
TEL: 01296 394022
FAX: 01296 437075

Buckinghamshire FHSA
Merlin Centre
Gatehouse Close
Aylesbury
Buckinghamshire
HP19 3DP
TEL: 01296 310000
FAX: 01296 25392

Bury & Rochdale HC
Starring Office
Birchill Hospital
Rochdale
OL12 9QR
TEL: 0161 762 3100
FAX: 0161 764 5042

Calderdale FHSA
Royal Halifax Infirmary
Free School Lane
Halifax
HX1 2YP
TEL: 01422 385505
FAX: 01422 341840

Cambridge & Huntingdon HC
Hillview Office
Fulbourn Hospital

Cambridge
CB1 5EF
TEL: 01223 218829
FAX: 01223 218744

Camden & Islington HC
110 Hampstead Road
London
NW1 2LJ
TEL: 0171 383 4888
FAX: 0171 380 9733

Cheshire FHSA
1829 Building
Countess of Chester Hospital
Liverpool Road
Chester
CH2 1BQ
TEL: 01244 382111
FAX: 01244 366001

City & East London FHSA
St Leonards
Nuttal Street
London
N1 5LZ
TEL: 0171 739 6566
FAX: 0171 601 7901

Clwyd DHA
Preswylfa
Hendy Road
Mold
Clwyd
CH7 1PZ
TEL: 01352 700227
FAX: 01352 754649

Clwyd FHSA
Trinity House
Trinity Street
Wrexham
LL1 2NW
TEL: 01978 265515
FAX: 01978 361595

Cornwall & Isles of Scilly HC
John Keay House
Tregonissey Road

St Austell
Cornwall
PL25 4NQ
TEL: 01726 77777
FAX: 01726 71777

County Durham HC
Appleton House
Lanchester Road
Durham
DH1 5XZ
TEL: 0191 386 4911
FAX: 0191 384 9444

Coventry HC
Christchurch House
Greyfriars Lane
Coventry
CV1 2GQ
TEL: 01203 552225
FAX: 01203 226280

Croydon DHA
Knollys House
17 Addiscombe Road
Croydon
CR9 6HE
TEL: 0181 401 3900
FAX: 0181 680 2418

Croydon FHSA
100 London Road
Croydon
London
CR9 2RH
TEL: 0181 401 3900
FAX: 0181 680 2418

Dental Estimates Board
Eastbourne
East Sussex
BN20 8AD
TEL: 0323 417000
FAX: 0323 433517

Devon FHSA
Cecil Boyall House
Southernhay East
Exeter

EX1 1RB
TEL: 01392 75242
FAX: 01392 50861

Doncaster HC
White Rose House
Ten Pound Walk
Doncaster
DN4 5DJ
TEL: 01302 320111
FAX: 01302 730362

Dorset HC
Victoria House
Princes Road
Ferndown
Dorset
BH22 9JR
TEL: 01202 893000
FAX: 01202 861125

Dudley DHA
12 Bull Street
Dudley
West Midlands
DY1 2DD
TEL: 01384 239376
FAX: 01384 455068

Dudley FHSA
12 Bull Street
Dudley
West Midlands
DY1 2DD
TEL: 01384 239376
FAX: 01384 455068

Dumfries & Galloway Health Board
Nithbank
Dumfries
DG1 2SD
TEL: 01387 46246
FAX: 01387 252375

Dyfed DHA
Starling Park House
Johnstown
Carmarthen
Dyfed

SA31 3HL
TEL: 01267 234501
FAX: 01267 238520

Dyfed FHSA
Francis Well
Carmarthen
SA31 2AB
TEL: 01267 232691
FAX: 01267 234251

Ealing, Hammersmith & Hounslow HC
1 Armstrong Way
Southall
Middlesex
UB2 4SA
TEL: 0181 893 0303
FAX: 0181 893 0398

Eastern HSSB
12–22 Linenhall Street
Belfast
BT2 8BS
TEL: 01232 321313
FAX: 01232 233020

East Kent HA
7–9 Cambridge Terrace
Dover
CT16 1JT
TEL: 01304 227227
FAX: 01304 225775

East Lancashire Health Consortium
31 Kenyon Road
Lameshaye Industrial Estate
Nelson
BB9 5SJ
TEL: 01282 619909
FAX: 01282 610223

East London & the City DHA
Tredegar House
97–99 Bow Road
Bow
London
E3 2AN
TEL: 0181 983 2900
FAX: 0181 983 4122

East Riding DHA
Grange Park Lane
Willerby
Hull
HU10 6DT
TEL: 01482 658822
FAX: 01482 672099

East Surrey HC
West Park Road
Horton Lane
Epsom, Surrey
KT 19 8PH
TEL: 01372 727811
FAX: 01372 729841

East Sussex DHA
Westlords
250 Willingdon Road
Eastbourne
BN20 9BG
TEL: 01323 520000
FAX: 01323 524612

Enfield & Haringey FHSA
Holbrook House
Cockfosters Road
Barnet
Hertfordshire
EN4 0DR
TEL: 0181 440 9384
FAX: 0181 449 5945

Essex FHSA
Carnarvon House
Carnarvon Road
Clacton on Sea
Essex
CO15 6QD
TEL: 01255 221222
FAX: 01255 221765

East Sussex FHSA
8 North Street
Lewes
Sussex
BN7 2PB
TEL: 01273 485300
FAX: 01273 485400

Exeter & North Devon DHA
Dean Clarke House
Southernhay East
Exeter
EX1 1PQ
TEL: 01392 406135
FAX: 01392 70910

FHS Appeals SHA
Queen Building
Park Parade
Harrogate
HG1 5AH
TEL: 01423 530280

Fife Health Board
Springfield House
Cupar
Fife
KY15 5UP
TEL: 01334 656200
FAX: 01334 652210

Forth Valley Health Board
33 Spittal Street
Stirling
Stirlingshire
FK8 1DX
TEL: 0178 646 3031
FAX: 0178 645 1474

Greater Glasgow Health Board
112 Ingram Street
Glasgow
G1 1ET
TEL: 0141 201 4444
FAX: 0141 201 4401

Gloucestershire HC
Victoria Warehouse
The Docks
Gloucester
GL1 2EL
TEL: 01452 300222
FAX: 01452 318800

Grampian Health Board
Summerfield House
2 Eday Road

Aberdeen
AB9 1RE
TEL: 01224 663456
FAX: 01224 404014

States of Guernsey Health
    Board
Dept of Health
John Henry House,
Le Vauguedor
St Martins
Guernsey
GY4 6UU
TEL: 01481 725241
FAX: 01481 35341

Gwent HC
Mamhilad House
Mamhilad Park Estate
Pontypool
Gwent
NP4 0YP
TEL: 01495 765065
FAX: 01495 762086

Gwynedd FHSA
Eryldon
Campbell
Caernarvon Road
Caernarvon
LL55 1HU
TEL: 01286 672451
FAX: 01286 673209

Hampshire FHSA
Friarsgate
Winchester
Hants
SO23 8EE
TEL: 01962 853361
FAX: 01962 840773

Health Education Authority
Hamilton House
Mabledon Place
London
W1H 9TX
TEL: 0171 383 3833
FAX: 0171 387 0550

Health Promotion for Wales
Ffynnon-Las
Ty Glas Avenue
Llanishen
Cardiff
CF4 5DZ
TEL: 0222 752222
FAX: 0222 756000

Hereford & Worcester FHSA
99 High Street
Worcester
WR1 2HP
TEL: 01905 25881
FAX: 01905 611963

Herefordshire DHA
Victoria House
Eign Street
Hereford
HR4 0AN
TEL: 01432 272012
FAX: 01432 341958

Herts Health Agency
Charter House
Parkway
Welwyn Garden City
Hertfordshire
AL8 6JL
TEL: 01707 390855
FAX: 01707 390864

Highland Health Board
Reay House
17 Old Edinburgh Road
Inverness
IV2 3HG
TEL: 01463 239851
FAX: 01463 235189

Hillingdon Health Agency
Kirk House
97–109 High Street
Yiewsley
West Drayton, Middlesex
UB7 7HJ
TEL: 01895 452000
FAX: 01895 452108

Humberside FHSA
Grange Park Lane
Willerby
Kingston Upon Hull
HU10 6DT
TEL: 01482 650700
FAX: 01482 672157

Isle of Man Health Service Division
Markwell House
Market Street
Douglas
Isle of Man
IM1 2RZ
TEL: 01624 685138
FAX: 01624 685160

Isle of Wight HC
Whitecroft
Sandy Lane
Newport
Isle of Wight
PO30 3ED
TEL: 01983 526011
FAX: 01983 822142

States of Jersey Dept of Health
2nd floor, Kensington Chambers
46–50 Kensington Place
St Helier
Jersey
JE2 3PA
TEL: 01534 59000
FAX: 01534 37768

Kensington, Chelsea & Westminster
    HC
50 Eastbourne Terrace
London
W2 6LX
TEL: 0171 725 3333
FAX: 0171 725 3398

Kent FHSA
11 Station Road
Maidstone, Kent
ME14 1QH
TEL: 01622 655000
FAX: 01622 655001

Kingston & Richmond DHA
17 Upper Brighton Road
Surbiton
Surrey
KT6 6LH
TEL: 0181 390 1111
FAX: 0181 390 5028

Kingston & Richmond
Cooper House
40 Surbiton Road
Kingston
Surrey
KT1 2HX
TEL: 0181 547 0011
TEL: 0181 547 0441

Kirklees FHSA
Mill Hill Hospital
Dalton Green Lane
Huddersfield
HD5 9TT
TEL: 01484 466000
FAX: 01484 420147

Lambeth, Southwark & Lewisham
   HC
1 Lower Marsh
London
SE1 7RJ
TEL: 0171 716 7000
TEL: 0171 716 7039

Lanarkshire Health Board
14 Beckford Street
Hamilton
ML3 0TA
TEL: 01698 281313
FAX: 01698 423134

Lancashire FHSA
Caxton Road
Fulwood
Preston
PR2 4ZZ
TEL: 01772 704141
FAX: 01772 791100

Leeds DHA
St Mary House
St Marys Road
Leeds
LS7 3JX
TEL: 0113 2781341
FAX: 0113 2620246

Leeds FHSA
AEU House
Bridge Street
Leeds
LS2 7RJ
TEL: 0113 2450271
FAX: 0113 2425073

Leicestershire HC
Gwendolen Road
Leicester
LE5 4QU
TEL: 0116 273 1173
FAX: 0116 258 8577

Lincolnshire HC
Cross O Cliff Court
Bracebridge Heath
Lincoln
LN4 2HL
TEL: 01522 513355
FAX: 01522 540706

Liverpool DHA
1st floor
8 Matthew Street
Liverpool
L2 6RE
TEL: 0151 236 4747
FAX: 0151 258 1442

Liverpool FHSA
1st floor
8 Matthew Street
Liverpool
L2 6RE
TEL: 0151 236 4747
FAX: 0151 258 1442

Lothian Health Board
11 Drumsheugh Gardens
Edinburgh
EH3 7QQ
TEL: 0131 668 3940
FAX: 0131 536 9011

Manchester HC
Gateway House
Piccadilly South
Manchester
M60 7LP
TEL: 0161 237 2000
FAX: 0161 237 2001

Merton, Sutton & Wandsworth HC
Wilson Hospital
Cranmer Road
Mitcham
Surrey
CR4 4TP
TEL: 0181 648 3021
FAX: 0181 646 6240

Mid Glamorgan DHA
District HQ
Albert Road
Pontypridd
CF37 1LA
TEL: 01443 485122
FAX: 01443 485068

Mid Glamorgan FHSA
5th floor, Churchill House
Churchill Way
Cardiff
CF1 4TW
TEL: 01222 226216
FAX: 01222 222307

Morecambe Bay DHA
Tenterfield
Brigsteer Road
Kendal
Cumbria
LA9 5EA
TEL: 01539 735565
FAX: 01539 726687

National Blood Authority
Oak House
Reeds Crescent
Watford, Hertfordshire
WD1 1QH
TEL: 0923 212121
FAX: 0923 211031

North Birmingham DHA
1 Vernon Road
Edgbaston
Birmingham
B15 9SA
TEL: 0121 456 5566
FAX: 0121 454 7483

North Cheshire DHA
Lister Road
Astmoor West Estate
Runcorn, Cheshire
WA7 1SW
TEL: 01928 593000
FAX: 01928 569532

North Cumbria DHA & FHSA
The Lakeland Business Park
Lamplugh Road
Cockermouth
Cumbria
CA13 0QT
TEL: 01900 822155
FAX: 01900 826380

North Derbyshire Health
Scarsdale Hospital
Newbold Road
Chesterfield
S41 7PF
TEL: 01246 231255
FAX: 01246 206672

North Essex DHA
Collingwood Road
Witham
Essex
CM8 2TT
TEL: 01376 516515
FAX: 01376 514046

Newcastle & N Tyneside HC
Benfield Road
Newcastle upon Tyne
NE6 4PF
TEL: 0190 224 4040
FAX: 0190 224 3866

New River DHA
85 Tanners End Lane
Edmonton
London
N18 1SB
TEL: 0181 361 7272
FAX: 0181 361 6126

NHS Supplies Authority
Apex Plaza
Forbury Road
Reading
RG1 1AX
TEL: 0734 595085
FAX: 0734 567667

North & Mid Hants HC
Harness House
Aldermaston
Basingstoke
RG24 9NB
TEL: 01256 332288
FAX: 01256 312299

North Notts HC
Ransom House
Rainworth
Mansfield
NH21 0ER
TEL: 01623 22515
FAX: 01623 653527

Norfolk Health
St Andrews House
St Andrews Park
Thorpe St Andrews
Norwich
NR7 0SS
TEL: 01603 300600
FAX: 01603 300066

Northampton DHA
District HQ
Cliftonville Road
Northampton
NN1 5DN
TEL: 01604 615000
FAX: 01604 615010

Northamptonshire FHSA
Highfield
Cliftonville Road
Northampton
NN1 5DN
TEL: 01604 615000
FAX: 01604 615333

Northern HSSB
County Hall
182 Galgorm Road
Ballymena
County Antrim
BT42 1QB
TEL: 01266 653333
FAX: 01266 43094

North Thames RHA
40 Eastbourne Terrace
London
W2 3QR
TEL: 0171 725 5300
FAX: 0171 258 0530

Northumberland Health
East Cottingwood
Morpeth, Northumberland
NE61 2PD
TEL: 01670 514331
FAX: 01670 518873

North West RHA
930 Birchwood Boulevard
Millenium Park, Birchwood
Warrington
Cheshire
WA3 7QN
TEL: 01925 704000
FAX: 01925 704100

Nottingham DHA
Forest House
Berkeley Avenue
Nottingham
NG3 5AF
TEL: 0115 9691691
FAX: 0115 9627802

North Worcestershire DHA
The Croft
Sutton Park
Kidderminster
DY11 6LJ
TEL: 01562 824711
FAX: 01562 822695

Nottinghamshire FHSA
Ransom Hall
Southwall Road West
Rainworth
Nottinghamshire
NG21 0ER
TEL: 0115 969 1691
FAX: 0115 962 7802

North Yorkshire Health Project
Sovereign House
Kettlestring Lane
Clifton Moor
York
YO3 4XF
TEL: 01904 693322
FAX: 01904 691769

North Staffordshire DHA
PO Box 652, District Offices
Princes Road
Stoke on Trent
ST4 7JN
TEL: 01782 715444
FAX: 01782 49959

Oldham FHSA
Lindley House
1 John Street
Oldham
OL8 1DF
TEL: 0161 626 4615
FAX: 0161 652 0182

Northern & Yorkshire RHA
Benfield Road
Newcastle upon Tyne
Tyne & Wear
NE6 4PY
TEL: 0191 224 6222
FAX: 0191 224 1483

Orkney Health Board
Health Centre
New Scapa Road
Kirkwall, Orkney
KW15 1BQ
TEL: 01856 872763
FAX: 01856 874568

North West Anglia HC
St Johns
Thorpe Road
Peterborough
PE3 6JG
TEL: 01733 882288
FAX: 01733 882299

Oxfordshire HC
Manor House
Headley Way
Headington, Oxford
OX3 9DZ
TEL: 01865 741741
FAX: 01865 222777

North West Lancashire DHA
Wesham Park Hospital
Derby Road
Nr Kirkham
PR4 3AL
TEL: 01253 306305
FAX: 01253 306306

Portsmouth & SE Hants HC
Finchdean House
Milton Road
Portsmouth
PO3 6DP
TEL: 01705 838340
FAX: 01705 733292

Powys DHA
Mansion House
Bronllys
Brecon
LD3 0LS
TEL: 01874 711661
FAX: 01874 711618

Powys FHSA
Bronllys Hospital
Bronllys
Brecon
Powys
LD3 0LS
TEL: 01874 711677
FAX: 01874 711830

Prescription Pricing Authority
Bridge House
152 Pilgrim Street
Newcastle upon Tyne
NE1 6SN
TEL: 091 232 5371
FAX: 091 232 2480

Public Health Laboratory Servs
61 Colindale Avenue
London
NW9 5DF
TEL: 0181 200 1295
FAX: 0181 200 8130

Redbridge & Waltham Forest DHA
King Georges Hospital, West Wing
Eastern Avenue
Newbury Park
Ilford
Essex
IG2 7SH
TEL: 0181 518 2299
FAX: 0181 554 3752

Redbridge & Waltham Forest FHS
Ilford Lane Chambers
Ilford
Essex
IG1 2QU
TEL: 0181 478 5151
FAX: 0181 553 2954

Rotherham HC
220 Badsley Moor Lane
Rotherham
South Yorkshire
S65 2QH
TEL: 01709 382647
FAX: 01709 835049

Salford FHSA
Peel House
Albert Street
Eccles, Manchester
M30 0NJ
TEL: 0161 931 2000
FAX: 0161 737 0237

Salford & Trafford DHA
Peel House
Albert Street
Eccles, Manchester
M30 0NJ
TEL: 0161 789 7373
FAX: 0161 787 7436

Sandwell DHA
PO Box 1953
Sandwell District Gen Hospital
Lyndon
West Bromwich
B71 4NA
TEL: 0121 553 6151
FAX: 0121 607 3287

Sandwell FHSA
Kingston House
438 High Street
West Bromwich
West Midlands
B70 9LD
TEL: 0121 553 1774
FAX: 0121 525 4131

South Birmingham DHA
27 Highfield Road
Edgbaston
Birmingham
B15 3DP
TEL: 0121 456 5600
FAX: 0121 627 8475

South Cheshire DHA
324 Chester Road
Hartford, Northwich
CW8 2AH
TEL: 01244 364501
FAX: 01244 364430

South Derbyshire DHA
Derwent Court
Stuart Street
Derby
DE1 2FZ
TEL: 01332 636300
FAX: 01332 626350

Sefton DHA
3rd floor, Burlington House
Crosby Road North
Waterloo
Liverpool
L22 0QB
TEL: 0151 920 5056
FAX: 0151 920 1035

Sefton FHSA
3rd floor, Burlington House
Crosby Road North
Waterloo
Liverpool
L22 0QB
TEL: 0151 920 5056
FAX: 0151 949 0646

South Essex DHA
Charles House
Norsey Road
Billericay
Essex
CM11 1AG
TEL: 01277 633006
FAX: 01277 632127

South Glamorgan DHA
Temple of Peace & Health
Cathays Park
Cardiff
CF1 3NW
TEL: 01222 231021
FAX: 01222 238606

South Glamorgan FHSA
Churchill House
6th floor, East Wing
Churchill Way
Cardiff
CF1 4TT
TEL: 01222 374731
FAX: 01222 237282

Sheffield HC
Westbrook House
Sharrow Vale Road
Sheffield
S11
TEL: 0114 267 0333
TEL: 0114 266 0498

Shetland Health Board
Brevik House
South Road
Lerwick
Shetland
ZE1 0RB
TEL: 01595 696767
FAX: -1595 696727

Shropshire HC
William Farr House
Mytton Oak Road
Shrewsbury
SY3 8XL
TEL: 01743 261300
FAX: 01743 261303

South Lancashire DHA
Chorley District Hospital
Preston Road
Chorley
PR7 1PP
TEL: 01257 452222
FAX: 01257 450466

Solihull HC
21 Poplar Road
Solihull
B91 3AH
TEL: 0121 704 2555
FAX: 0121 711 3149

Somerset DHA
Wellsprings Road
Taunton
TA2 7PQ
TEL: 01823 333491
FAX: 01823 272710

Somerset FHSA
Osborne House
Trull Road
Taunton
Somerset
TA1 4PX
TEL: 01823 321 381
FAX: 01823 321 368

Southampton & South West Hants HC
The Western Hospital
Oakley
Millbrook
Southampton
SO9 4WQ
TEL: 01703 725 400
FAX: 01703 725 457

Southern HSSB
20 Seagoe Industrial Estate
Portadown
Craigavon
Co Armagh
BT63 5QD
TEL: 01762 336611
FAX: 01762 350071

South Thames RHA
40 Eastbourne Terrace
London
W2 3QR
TEL: 0171 725 2500
FAX: 0171 258 3908

South of Tyne HC
Horsley Hill Road
South Shields
Tyne & Wear
NE33 3BN
TEL: 0191 427 5444
FAX: 0191 455 3403

South & West RHA
Westnord House
Lime Kiln Close
Stoke Gifford
Bristol
BS12 6SF
TEL: 0117 984 1750
FAX: 0117 874 1861

Special Hospitals Services
Charles House
375 Kensington High Street
London
W14
TEL: 0171 605 9700
FAX: 0171 605 9728

South Staffordshire DHA
Corporation Street
Stafford
ST16 3SR
TEL: 01785 52233
FAX: 01785 52249

Staffordshire FHSA
Britannia House
6–7 Eastgate Street
Stafford
ST16 2NJ
TEL: 01785 56341
FAX: 01765 57114

St Helens & Knowsley HC
Cowley Hill Lane
St Helens
Merseyside
WA10 2AP
TEL: 01785 56341
FAX: 01785 57114

St Helens & Knowsley HC
Cowley Hill Lane
St Helens
Merseyside
WA10 2AP
TEL: 01744 733722
FAX: 01744 453085

Stockport HC
Springwood House
Poplar Grove
Hazel Grove
Stockport
SK7 5BY
TEL: 0161 419 4600
FAX: 0161 419 4699

Suffolk HC
PO Box 55
St Clements Hospital
Foxhall Road
Ipswich
IP3 8NN
TEL: 01473 712272
FAX: 01473 271438

Sunderland HC
Durham Road
Sunderland
SR3 4AF
TEL: 0191 565 6256
FAX: 0191 528 3455

Surrey FHSA
187 Ewell Road
Surbiton, Surrey
KT6 6AU
TEL: 0181 399 5133
FAX: 0181 390 8820

Plymouth & Torbay DHA
Derriford Business Park
Brest Road
Derriford
Plymouth
PL6 5XN
TEL: 01752 793793
FAX: 01752 770647

Tameside FHSA
Selbourne House
Union Street
Hyde
Cheshire
SK14 1NG
TEL: 0161 368 4464
FAX: 0161 367 8837

Tayside Health Board
Box No 75
Vernonholm Riverside Drive
Dundee
DD1 9NL
TEL: 01382 645151
FAX: 01382 665843

Tees Health
Poole Hospital
Nunthorpe
Middlesborough
TS7 0NJ
TEL: 01642 320000
FAX: 01642 324176

Trafford FHSA
Peel House
Albert Street
Eccles, Manchester
M30 0NJ
TEL: 0161 931 2000
FAX: 0161 787 0294

Trent RHA
Fulwood House
Old Fulwood Road
Sheffield
S10 3TH
TEL: 0114 263 0300
FAX: 0114 230 6956

UK Transport Support Services
Foxden Road
Stoke Gifford
Bristol
BS12 6RR
TEL: 0272 757575
FAX: 0272 757577

United Health
Grimsby & Scunthorpe DHA
The Health Place
Wrawby Road
Brigg
Humberside
DN20 8GS
TEL: 01652 659659
FAX: 01652 601160

Wakefield HC
White Rose House
West Parade
Wakefield
WF1 1LT
TEL: 01924 814400
FAX: 01924 814401

Walsall HC
Lichfield House
27–31 Lichfield Street
Walsall
WS1 1TE
TEL: 01922 720255
FAX: 01922 656000

Warwickshire DHA/FHSA
Westgate House
Market Street
Warwick
CV34 4DE
TEL: 01926 493491
FAX: 01926 410925

Welsh H Services
Heron House
35–43 Newport Road
Cardiff
CF2 1SB
TEL: 01222 500500
FAX: 01222 502502

Western HSSB
15 Gransha Park
Clooney Road
Londonderry
BT47 1TG
TEL: 01504 860086
FAX: 01504 860311

Western Isles Health Board
37 South Beach Street
Stornoway
Isle of Lewis
PA87 2BN
TEL: 01851 702997
FAX: 01851 704405

West Midlands RHA
Arthur Thomson House
146–150 Hagley Road
Birmingham
B16 9PA
TEL: 0121 456 1444
FAX: 0121 454 4406

West Glamorgan DHA
36 Orchard Street
Swansea
SA1 5AQ
TEL: 01792 458066
FAX: 01792 655364

West Glamorgan FHSA
41 High Street
Swansea
SA1 1LT
TEL: 01792 458066
FAX: 01792 655364

Wigan FHSA
Bryan House
61 Standishgate
Wigan
WN1 1AH
TEL: 01942 822724
TEL: 01942 496567

Wigan & Bolton DHA
43 Churchgate
Bolton, Lancashire
BL1 1JF
TEL: 01204 390064
FAX: 01204 390177

Wiltshire FHSA
Red Gables
Hilperton Road
Trowbridge
BA14 7JF
TEL: 01380 728899
FAX: 01380 722443

Wiltshire & Bath HC
Southgate House
Pans Lane
Devizes, Wiltshire

SN10 5EQ
TEL: 01380 728899
FAX: 01380 722443

Wirral HC
Clocktower St Catherines Hosp
Church Road
Tranmere
Wirral
L42 0LQ
TEL: 0151 651 0011
FAX: 0151 652 2668

West Kent DHA
Maidstone Hall Hospital
Maidstone
Kent
ME20 7NJ
TEL: 01622 710161
FAX: 01622 719802

Wolverhampton DHA
New Cross Hospital
Wolverhampton
WV10 0QP
TEL: 01902 20202
FAX: 01902 310161

Wolverhampton FHSA
St Johns House
St Johns Square
10–12 Terrenhall Road
Wolverhampton
WV2 4BP
TEL: 01902 20202
FAX: 01902 310161

Worcester & District DHA
Isaac Maddox House
Shrub Hill Road
Worcester
WR4 9EL
TEL: 01905 763333
FAX: 01905 617051

West Pennine DHA
Westhulme Avenue
Oldham
OL1 2PL
TEL: 0161 455 5700
FAX: 0161 455 5709

West Surrey DHA
The Ridgewood Centre
Old Bisley Road
Camberley
Surrey
GU16 5QE
TEL: 01276 671718
FAX: 01276 21760

West Sussex DHA
Courtlands
Parklands Avenue
Goring by Sea
West Sussex
BN12 4NQ
TEL: 01903 241515
FAX: 01903 504962

West Sussex FHSA
175 Broyle Road
Chichester
West Sussex
PO19 4AD
TEL: 01243 78144
FAX: 01243 786494

West Yorkshire DHA
St Lukes House
Blackmoorfoot Road
Huddersfield
HD4 5RH
TEL: 01484 654777
FAX: 01484 65477 x 3243

Appendix V
Useful Addresses

Association of Independent
   Multifunds
Unit of General Practice
National Heart & Lung Institute
1 Elm Road
Kingston-upon-Thames
Surrey KT2 6HR
TEL: 0181 974 9046
FAX: 0181 549 6616

A T Kearney Limited
Lansdowne House
Berkeley Square
London W1X 5DH
TEL: 0171 468 8000
FAX: 0171 468 8001

British Standards Institution
Information Centre
389 Chiswick High Road
London W4 4AL
TEL: 0171 629 9000
FAX: 0171 629 0506

Callum Watson
Re-engineering Programme
   Manager
The Leicester Royal Infirmary NHS
   Trust
Infirmary Square
Leicester LE1 5WW
TEL: 0116 258 6904
FAX: 0116 258 6448

CASPE Research
22 Palace Court
Bayswater
London W2 4HU
TEL: 0171 229 8739
FAX: 0171 221 9892

Health and Safety Executive
2 Park Street
Broad Lane
Sheffield S3 7HQ
TEL: 0114 289 2345
FAX: 0114 289 2333

Kings's Fund Organisational Audit
2 Palace Court
London W2 4HS
TEL: 0171 727 0581
FAX: 0171 229 3273

NHS Benchmarking Reference
   Centre
Croesnewydd Hall
Wrexham Technology Park
Wrexham
Clwyd LL13 7YP

NHS Estates
1 Trevelyan Square
Boar Lane
Leeds LS1 6AE
TEL: 0113 254 7000
FAX: 0113 254 7299

Safecode Support Group
CSA Building Division
Clifton House
Clifton Place
Glasgow G3 7YY
TEL: 0141 353 3814
FAX: 0141 353 3782

Southampton East Multifund
28 Cobden Avenue
Bitterne Park
Southampton SO18 1DW
TEL: 01703 678040

UK Clearing House for the
    Assessment of Health Outcomes
Nuffield Institute for Health
University of Leeds
71–5 Clarendon Road
Leeds LS2 9PL
TEL: 0113 233 6633
FAX: 0113 246 0899

Index

absence management, 140–44
access
   badge identification and, 217–19
   controls on, 219
Access to Medical Records Act
   1991, 65
appeals against redundancy, 131
Apple Macintosh computers, 186
Association of Independent
      Multifunds (AIM), 95
audit
   clinical, 79–87, 173
   of discharge planning, 12–14
   of health and safety, 56–7, 77
   of medical records, 65
Audit Commission, 22
automation, of pathology services,
   22, 24–7

badge identification, 217–19
Balmoral Test Centre, 32
Barbour Index, 78
benchmarking, 44, 111, 208
Biomedical Scientists, 22
block contracts, 99, 101
Bottomley, Virginia, 223
British Association of Medical
      Managers (BAMM), 233
British Standards Institution (BSI), 78
   BS5750, 67, 207
   BS7750, 207–8
BTEC, 165
buildings *see* estate management

bureaucracy, management of, 5–6
business managers, for multifunds,
   92
business planning in NHS, 106–11
business process re-engineering, 28–
   37, 127–8

capital investment, appraisal of,
   196–7
cardiotacograph (CTG) traces, 62, 64
Care Sector Consortium, 157
casemix system
   experience to date of, 172–5
   future of, 175–8
   history of, 171–2
catering services, 208–9
Central Council for Education and
      Training in Social Work
      (CCETSW), 149
change
   management of, 5, 26–7
   organisational, 83–5, 130–33
clerical staff, 34
clinic(s)
   clerical staff in, 34
   single visit, 28–31
clinical audit, 79–87, 173
Clinical Negligence Scheme for
      Trusts (CNST), 62
clinical risk management, medical
      records and, 61–6
Clinical Scientists, 23
clinical staff *see* doctors

315

Index of Advertisers